NEWTON D. BAKER

A BIOGRAPHY

C. H. CRAMER

Newton D. Baker

A BIOGRAPHY

THE WORLD PUBLISHING COMPANY

CLEVELAND AND NEW YORK

PUBLISHED BY The World Publishing Company
2231 WEST 110TH STREET, CLEVELAND 2, OHIO

PUBLISHED SIMULTANEOUSLY IN CANADA BY
NELSON, FOSTER & SCOTT LTD.

Library of Congress Catalog Card Number: 61-5805

FIRST EDITION

CONTENTS

FOREWORD   7

I.   Martinsburg to Cleveland   13

II.   Tom Johnson   34

III. Mayor   46

IV.   Orator   64

V.   Secretary of War   76

VI.   Secretary of A War—Men   93

VII. Secretary of A War—Administration   122

VIII. Secretary of A War—Supplies   139

IX.   Secretary of War—Demobilization   155

X.   Lawyer   171

XI.   *Pro Bono Publico*   187

XII. Treaty of Versailles and the League of Nations   209

CONTENTS

XIII. Reluctant Candidate 235

XIV. Unhappy Democrat 259

XV. Sentimental Stoic 272

NOTE ON MANUSCRIPT COLLECTIONS 281

NOTES BY CHAPTERS 283

INDEX 305

ILLUSTRATIONS

(The following photographs will be found in sequence after page 126.)

Newton Baker as a boy.

Newton Baker as a young lawyer in Martinsburg, West Virginia.

Peter Witt, Tom Johnson, and Newton Baker, December 31, 1909.

Mayor Baker, 1913.

Secretary Baker drawing the first numbers in the second draft.

Baker on his way to be sworn in as Secretary of War.

President Wilson and Secretary Baker review the National Guard.

The President and the Secretary of War on the reviewing stand at Fort Myer, Virginia, 1916.

The Council of National Defense.

ILLUSTRATIONS

The Cabinet, June, 1916.

Secretary Baker with General Pershing somewhere in France,
1918.

General March, Newton Baker, King Albert of Belgium, and
General Pershing, 1919.

Baker nominating James Cox at the 1924 Democratic National
Convention.

Baker with Franklin Roosevelt at the start of the 1932 presidential campaign.

CARTOONS

"Bakerized Streets"   57
The fight against the unit rule   69
"The Show-Down"   148
"When Uncle Sam Laughs!"   149
"Here is the man the Nation needs"   237
Baker beats the drum for the League   241

FOREWORD

THIS IS THE FIRST full-length biography of Newton Diehl Baker—American politician, orator, lawyer, and educator. It is based largely on the voluminous collection of manuscripts recently made available at the Library of Congress.

Under the liberal influence of Tom Johnson and the Progressive Movement, Mr. Baker was Law Director (1901–11) and Mayor of Cleveland (1912–16). As Secretary of War under President Wilson from 1916 to 1921 he prepared the punitive expedition into Mexico—and in a period of eighteen months raised an army of almost four million men, transported half of them to France, administered the draft law, selected General Pershing, and supervised the rapid expenditure of fifteen billion dollars with a minimum of scandal.

A Wilsonian idealist, after World War I he fought American isolationism as an advocate of the League of Nations. Often mentioned as a Democratic nominee for the Presidency, he had strong support as a dark horse candidate in 1932. As a humanitarian he gave unstintingly of his time

7

and energy in active support of dozens of reform and charitable societies. In the profession of law he was appointed to the Hague Tribunal in 1928 and was especially prominent in cases concerning freedom of the press, water diversion by Chicago, and the TVA. He showed his abiding interest in education as a trustee of several colleges, and as a staunch supporter of adult education. Diminutive in size but large in heart, he enjoyed a wide circle of friends—both in this country and abroad.

In international affairs he was a steadfast advocate of a low tariff, and of American participation in the League of Nations and the World Court. On the domestic front he was on the left wing in local affairs, and right of center on national issues. In Cleveland Baker was a gradualist who achieved a reputation as a "reliable radical and a prudent progressive." Later he was to question the augmentation of national authority under the New Deal, and in his last years was to be characterized as a genial conservative with an open mind.

The author is indebted to a number of specialists for invaluable assistance in the preparation of this biography. At the Library of Congress grateful acknowledgment is given to the staff of the Manuscript Division. At Western Reserve University's Freiberger and Law School libraries, Lyon Richardson and Helen Garee were unfailingly helpful. At the library of the Western Reserve Historical Society I have learned over the years to rely on Mrs. Alene Lowe White. For the use of the libraries and reference sections of the *Cleveland Press* and the *Cleveland Plain Dealer,* my special thanks go to Editors Louis Seltzer and Wright Bryan for their co-operation. At Cleveland's City Hall, Librarian Lee Wachtel has been of assistance in many ways, and the same generosity has been manifested by James F. Hudson and Roland J. Hinz of *Phi Gamma Delta.*

I am obligated to the following for their contribution of additional manuscript material: to Curtis Lee Smith for the

Munson Havens correspondence, to Roger Brown for the letters between his father (Percy Brown) and Baker, and to Alfred A. Benesch for the loan of his personal correspondence with Baker.

In the preparation of the chapter on Baker as lawyer the author had the advantage of case files provided by, and consultation with, colleagues of Mr. Baker in the law firm of Baker, Hostetler and Patterson—particularly William H. Bemis, Howard F. Burns, Joseph R. Fawcett, Benjamin F. Fiery, Raymond T. Jackson, and R. T. Sawyer. They were generous with their time, gracious in their comments, and patient with the author's lack of familiarity with legal procedure and the complex details involved in extended litigation. Obviously, any errors in fact or interpretation that may be found, in the chapter on Baker as lawyer, are the sole responsibility of the author.

Four men have been good enough to read and comment critically on the biography in its entirety. One is Dean Carl F. Wittke of the Graduate School at Western Reserve University, who has been my mentor for three decades. The second is William H. Bemis, a law colleague of Baker, who has been more than kind and helpful in many ways. Ben D. Zevin and David N. Keightley, my publisher and editor at The World Publishing Company, have been both understanding and acute in their observations.

I am particularly grateful to the American Philosophical Society for a financial grant from the Penrose Fund, which made possible the research required for this biography.

C. H. CRAMER

Cleveland, Ohio
July 1960

NEWTON D. BAKER

A BIOGRAPHY

I. Martinsburg to Cleveland

NEWTON DIEHL BAKER II was born on December 3, 1871, in Martinsburg, West Virginia, the child of Confederate parents still living in the shadow of the Civil War. It was during the trying years of Reconstruction when friends and neighbors went about in gray military trousers because there was nothing else to wear. Born within five miles of the Potomac River he recollected that he swam in it as a boy, fished it as a youth, and romanced over it as a young man until the stream held Biblical connotations for him as "The river Kishon, that ancient river, the river Kishon." As a child he also played in the hills near Harper's Ferry, and remembered a cave where it was claimed that John Brown had set up a forge and had manufactured thirty thousand spearheads for the slave insurrection that never came off. When Baker moved to northern Ohio in 1899, he was to say that he "was a carpetbagger in reverse, although I was never made to feel so. . . ."

Martinsburg is located at the northern entrance of the

famous Shenandoah Valley, and is now the largest town in the Eastern Panhandle of West Virginia. During the Civil War both sides fought frequently in and around the village, because of its strategic location and the presence of the east-west line of the Baltimore and Ohio Railroad. Possession of the town itself alternated between North and South in per-plexing succession; sometimes the occupying forces changed several times in the same day. Stonewall Jackson occasionally made Martinsburg his headquarters, once taking a number of locomotives from the Baltimore and Ohio Railroad and transporting them over the unpaved highway to Winchester. West Virginia was admitted to the Union in 1863 but Martins-burg's County, Berkeley, did not become a part of the new State until 1865, and Virginia was to make unsuccessful efforts to reclaim it after the War was over.

In this no man's land between the rival military lines not only was county arrayed against county, but families fre-quently were split by differing loyalties. Grandfather Elias Baker was devoted to the Union, received an appointment from President Lincoln as postmaster at near-by Shepherds-town, and retained the Federal office throughout the War. Newton Baker's mother was an unreconstructed rebel who once boarded in the same house with John Wilkes Booth, ran the blockade, smuggled quinine and other necessaries to Confederate prisoners in Fort McHenry, and until her death in 1922 never saw a good-looking Negro girl without a desire to buy her. Baker's father was a member of the First Virginia Cavalry commanded by Jeb Stuart, fought at Gettys-burg, was captured, and exchanged to fight again at Rich-mond. But the elder Baker had a tolerant attitude that was one of his strongest qualities. He felt that the War ended with Lee's surrender and he was willing to accept the North-ern victory. In later days the son would express his father's reconstructed Confederate viewpoint in a story about the wise old custodian at Hampton Institute. Some Northern visitors asked the Negro guide whether he thought the late War was necessary. The old fellow scratched his head reflectively and said: "Well, sir, they did not have 'telligence enough to fix it, so they fit it."[1]

Family trees are never solid to the core, and Newton D. Baker harbored no illusions about the soft spots in his own. He was sure that persistent probing into ancestral records would always lead to a scandal. He had discovered a great-aunt on his mother's side, a "fierce old lady" who gave her family no peace except for one pleasant period when she broke her leg in a fall from a stepladder and was out of action for quite a spell. He could take no pride in great-great-grandfather Elias Baker, an Englishman who settled about 1760 in Maryland near the later site of the battle of Antietam. There Elias married, started a family, and then deserted it. Newton Baker was never able to discover just what streak of meanness there was in him.

There was nothing ignoble about Elias's great-grandson, Newton Diehl Baker I, who sired four sons including the namesake who is the subject of this biography. He was a cultured and unselfish country doctor who became Secretary of the State Board of Health of West Virginia. The younger Newton practically lived in his father's office and often accompanied him by horse and buggy on tireless ministrations to the sick in and about Martinsburg. The son admired the efforts made by his father to keep abreast of his profession through the purchase and careful reading of medical books and periodicals.

Baker inherited his father's name in full. Both Christian names came into the family by adoption. A great-aunt had married Newton Lemon, and Baker's father was named out of respect for the uncle by marriage. The son had another version; he liked to think that his relatives were scientifically disposed and had named their children after Sir Isaac. The

name Diehl had been adopted in affectionate compliment to
a minister with that surname who lived in the village where
Baker's father was born. The family was English-Irish on the
paternal side; his mother's forebears were German and Irish.
Baker showed little interest in these national derivations. He
once observed that although one of his great-grandparents
came from Tipperary, whatever Irish blood he had was not
green—it was red, white, and blue![2]

On the paternal side his forebears were all Lutheran, some
of them distinguished clergymen. His mother was an ardent,
high-church Episcopalian and Newton followed her religious
preference, although he admitted that his own sectarian practice never reached above the bottom step in the low-church
section of the ecclesiastical ladder. Late in life he acknowledged that from "the days of my first break away from the
orthodoxies" he was unable to overcome a shyness about
religious discussion, with the consequence that he never spoke
publicly on the subject. Once he taught a Sunday school
class and regarded the year's experience as the most complete
and distinguished failure in his career. In this assignment
Baker admitted that he had never approached a religious
subject at any time, but enjoyed talking with the boys about
poetry, art, history, and athletics. He evinced little interest
in what he called "ecclesiastical millinery," but some features
of the Episcopal service always impressed him, particularly
the solemn dignity of the Elizabethan English. This Biblical
language never failed to "summon" him, and all revised ver-
sions of either Old or New Testaments "left him cold." In
his judgment there were but one or two vital and fundamental facts about the life spiritual, and upon these everyone based his assumptions and conduct; beyond this it
mattered little to which religious body a person was attached, or indeed whether he was formally attached to any.
The important considerations were just relations with one's

fellow men and constant fidelity to the truth as one saw it. In complimenting Walter Lippmann on his *Preface to Morals,* Baker stated his assumption that nothing great in this world had ever been done without faith, and added:

> Man seems to me incapable of greatness except when conditioned by beliefs which he has attained so passionately that he subordinates all other considerations to the service of his faith. Of course, the faith does not have to be formally religious, and whether or not if religious it be anthropomorphic, seems to me to make little difference. . . . But I find it very hard to imagine a stable social order or a helpful metaphysical order which does not have some stakes at which men are willing to be burned, and I think there are some stakes of that sort. . . .
>
> It is, therefore, the task of the humanist to disclose these stakes and to group around them the evidences of their validity. . . . In the accomplishment of this task, I think Shakespeare much more important than Darwin, and perhaps that comparison tells the whole story of the makeup of my mind.

In later days varied political charges were made that Baker was Roman Catholic or Jewish. He recalled the observation of Matthew Arnold, who had reached a position in his own religious life where he could worship God equally well in a Roman Catholic cathedral or in an open-field Methodist camp meeting. Baker went a step beyond Arnold. He said that he had been deeply moved in a Quaker meeting and had found himself filled with reverence at services in an Orthodox Hebrew synagogue. He did not doubt there were members of the Catholic Church who wished to introduce an intolerant culture into the United States, but the same could be said of almost any other denomination. He would not trust even the mildest religious sect with power, but preferred to accord them freedom in matters of faith, separating that domain rigidly from intellectual and political affairs.

During his anti-Semitic crusade Henry Ford published a circular alleging that Baker's name was actually Newman

Becker and that he was a Russian Jew. Baker related that
Ford sent two young men to West Virginia to examine bap-
tismal records and to take photographs of moldering grave-
stones in two family cemeteries, where his long-dead ancestors
had their first experience with modern photography. This
extraordinary research revealed only that the family name
was Baker and that both sides of the family were Protestant.
Actually, both of Baker's parents were slightly anti-Semitic,
but the son ascribed this attitude not to religious prejudice
but to suspicion against strangers in a rural Protestant community. In 1930 he was to be the first recipient of the American Hebrew Medal for promotion of better understanding
between Christians and Jews. Baker was appreciative but
doubted that he had done anything to merit the award; early
in life he had derived great satisfaction in ridding his mind
of the most irrational of prejudices, those which generalize
on "races and religions and take no account of individual
variations and qualities."[3]

As a boy Baker was Puck with a book; he was the "angel
child" who did not play baseball and seldom visited the swim-
ming hole. In later life he was to be included in the list
of former newsboys who made good. Lawyer Baker denied
that he ever carried papers and observed that he had never
sold anything "except advice, such as it is." He was small,
dark-haired, and brown-eyed, with, in Brand Whitlock's phrase,
a sensitive face and the ideals of a poet. In manhood he
finally achieved a height of five feet six inches, wore a size
14 shirt and collar, and weighed 125 pounds. In college he
once accompanied a group of students who were seeking
assignments as supers in a Shakespearean production. The
stage manager took one look and shoved Baker aside with the
devastating comment, "There are no Cupids in this show."
As a budding politician in Cleveland the initial reaction of
his first audience was to laugh at the boy orator. It was in-

evitable that he would be compared with the Little Corsican; by 1905 he was being introduced as "the Napoleon of Democratic eloquence, our Little Corporal, Newton D. Baker." As Secretary of War, often maligned by the opposition as "Newtie Cootie," he would sit in his chair with one leg tucked under him, leaving the other one swinging free but barely reaching the floor. During World War I Baker once entered a restaurant in a railroad station and ate at the lunch counter. The waiter shouted an incongruous inquiry to the unidentified customer who was a member of Wilson's Cabinet. His question was: "Want cream in your coffee, kid?" In later years, when his name was proposed for high national office, a cynic would observe that he was a few inches short of being President.

There was nothing small about Baker's head in either quantity or quality. He had the pate of a George Bernard Shaw and the physique of a small undergraduate; the disparity gave him the appearance of top-heaviness. His friends were to claim that he wore a small shoe and a large hat. They averred that he did not arrive in the world, as did Theodore Roosevelt, with a chip on his shoulder and a pirate sword in his teeth; instead Baker was born with a book under his arm. When the Civil War ended his father began to read the entire *Encyclopaedia Britannica* in an attempt to compensate for the college education that had been interrupted by four years with Stuart's cavalry. The country doctor found his practice too preoccupying and lost himself in darkest Africa while working on the *A*'s. Newton was told that an award of Hulme's *History of England* would be given if he read the whole of the *Britannica;* he accepted the challenge and earned the prize. As he grew older Baker was certain that his father, through stimulating conversation and suggestions for reading, had much the greatest influence on his early education. The parental training was so adult and mature that the son became impatient with what he regarded as the childish learning at the public schools in Martinsburg. There were some disadvantages because he neglected a few basic things; in later life Baker confessed that he had always known how to spell complicated words and been uncertain about simple ones, was fairly fluent with trigonometry and conic sections but "amazingly stupid" about addition and subtraction.

Baker was an ardent bibliophile throughout life. He read so many books that it is not surprising that he wore glasses from the age of eight, nor is it incongruous that his one invention, on which he took out a patent, was a vacuum attachment for cleaning the volumes in his library. As a youth he went through his father's medical books and was a regular client at the Martinsburg Library. From childhood he recalled that the morning *Baltimore Sun* was the intellectual breakfast food of his family and remembered the seriousness with which that newspaper took its editorial task in those days. In the last year of his life he was asked what three books he enjoyed most before he was ten. The recollection was dim but he thought the probable answer was: *Scottish Chiefs, The Days of Bruce,* and *Thaddeus of Warsaw.* He was certain that the volume that influenced him most in early youth was John W. Draper's *History of the Intellectual Development of Europe.* By contrast, he had scant regard for his school textbooks. The grammar by Harvey employed an exasperating geometrical technique in which sentences were dissected and the words were placed in complicated diagrams which were supposed to indicate relationships. From Mitchell's geography he learned nothing except the erroneous notion that the various countries were "yellow, pink, green or red splotches on a piebald globe." The highly sentimental and moral McGuffey's *Readers* did make quite an impression; they contributed to a "mood of persistent melancholy" which Baker did not outgrow until he was twenty.[4]

At college he came to the conclusion that Edmund Burke was the greatest political philosopher since Plato, a feeling that became a conviction when he found how much confidence Woodrow Wilson placed in Burke's speculations. An active interest in the social studies continued throughout his life. While he was a busy City Solicitor of Cleveland he was reading the Italian historian Guglielmo Ferrero on *The Greatness and Decline of Rome,* with the result that his earlier judgments on Roman civilization changed measurably. In later years he corresponded regularly with many historians, among them William E. Dodd, George Fort Milton, Claude Bowers, Alfred Jay Nock, and James Truslow Adams. In 1935 he was writing Douglas Southall Freeman, the distinguished authority on Lee and Washington, that the most needed biography in the entire history of the United States was one on Thomas Jefferson, "the supreme political philosopher of our history."

In literature he did not believe in starting with the remote past and reading into the present; he began with Tennyson and finished with *Beowulf* and Caedmon. As a child his favorite was Wordsworth, in adolescence it was Browning. To his dying day he had high regard for Browning's *The Ring and the Book;* he believed that it was "in all literature the best exposition of the fact, which lawyers can never forget, that there are many sides to every proposition and many points of view from which each human breakdown can be viewed." In 1913 he advised a graduating class at the Cleveland Law School to substitute Thackeray, Hugo, and Eliot in the place of dime novels—and jolted the fledgling lawyers, who were about to receive their diplomas, with the observation that the person who had not read and pondered Shakespeare's great plays should not be allowed to practice law. During World War I Baker asked novelist Brand Whitlock, then Ambassador to Belgium, to send a list of Russian books.

Whitlock suggested fifteen to twenty titles (by Tolstoy, Tur-
genev, Gogol, Gorky, and Dostoevski), intimating that the
list might keep the Secretary of War busy for some time. In
the later years of his life Baker speculated on the four or
five indispensable plays and novels; his list included Balzac's
Le Père Goriot, Shakespeare's *King Lear,* Dickens's *Bleak
House,* and George Eliot's *The Mill on the Floss.* There was
lighter reading. Shortly before his death Baker finished *Gone
With the Wind,* and as an ex-parte argument against the
North thought it one of the greatest legal briefs he had ever
read. In this respect he found it too effective; he was astonished to discover the vehemence with which Northerners, who
had read the novel uncritically, spoke against General Sherman. As a "carpetbagger in reverse" he found himself in the
anomalous position of defending Sherman, because he believed that the tragedy of the South was not caused as much
by the cruelty of Northern soldiers as it was by the incredible
brutality of Northern politicians, particularly Thaddeus
Stevens. So far as the story of *Gone With the Wind* was concerned he believed it to be one of the most repellent books
he had ever read. He thought he was fairly familiar with
literary and historical female monsters from Jezebel through
Shakespeare's Goneril to a few contemporaries, but in his
judgment Scarlett O'Hara was the "most abandoned baggage
of the lot."[5]

Baker attended the village schools in Martinsburg through
the second year of high school, finishing his preparatory training at Episcopal High School near Alexandria, Virginia. This
private institution trained young men primarily for the University of Virginia; Baker found its standards high, and its
atmosphere appealing in both manners and morals. But Dr.
Baker had selected a college for his son when the boy was
five. In 1876 his father had gone to Baltimore to hear Thomas
Henry Huxley, the well-known British biologist, at the open-

ing of Johns Hopkins University. He was so impressed that on his return to Martinsburg he had taken the youngster on his knee and had said that he wanted to send him there as a college student.

Baker entered Johns Hopkins in the fall of 1889, graduated with the degree of Bachelor of Arts with the Class of 1892, and stayed on for one postgraduate year of study in jurisprudence and Roman law. At Johns Hopkins these were the days of its first great president, Daniel Coit Gilman; of historian Herbert Baxter Adams, who introduced his famous seminar based on methods learned at Heidelberg; of economist Richard T. Ely, one of the great teachers of his time and a founder of the American Economic Association. Baker knew them well and benefited from their instruction. He also met Professor Woodrow Wilson of Princeton, who found time each spring to deliver twenty-five lectures on political economy at Johns Hopkins. Baker was interested in history and government, and took Professor Wilson's course. More important, he lived at the same boardinghouse with Wilson, sat at the same table, and had the benefit of table talks during two years.

The curriculum laid heavy stress on the humanities and languages. Baker had taken Greek and Latin at Episcopal High School and continued study in these subjects at Johns Hopkins, but was the first to deny stories in the 1920s and 1930s that he still read the classics in the original languages. German was his best language, and he read most of the Teutonic classics probably because of the influence of Professor Adams. As late as World War I while Secretary of War he was to surprise his aides by explaining the intricacies of the draft law in German to a delegation of Hutterian Brethren, an offshoot of the Mennonites. French he never knew well. In the last decade of his life he claimed that his speaking knowledge of French was limited to the two forms of the definite article, and he said that "by dint of long examination" he had finally fathomed the meaning of R.S.V.P., although he thought P.A. (Please Answer) was to be preferred.

Education at Johns Hopkins in the early 1890s was a serious business. There was little to distract students from the great adventure on which they were embarked, except an occasional dance at the gymnasium or an evening in one of the comfortable beer saloons around the University. Sunday was the one day when Baker and his colleagues felt they had a right to take liberties with time; on the Sabbath they slept late or took long tramps in the country. Baker was enough of a gregarious, all-round man that President Gilman made him head of the graduate students' association in his last year. His scholastic rating was sufficient to win election to Phi Beta Kappa, but it was a close squeak. There was no chapter of the honorary scholastic fraternity at Johns Hopkins when Baker was there; later, when a chapter was established, the ten highest men in each early graduating class were elected retroactively to membership. Baker was tied for tenth place in his class; the deadlock was broken by the generous election of eleven men from the Class of 1892. Baker's wry comment was that he won this intellectual distinction by so narrow a margin that he had always had a sense of humility about the inclusion of his name in the lists of the society.[6]

With four years at Johns Hopkins behind him Baker finished in nine months the normal two-year course in the School of Law at Washington and Lee University, graduating as a Bachelor of Laws in June 1894. The short course was dictated by economic necessity. Money was not plentiful in a country doctor's house, and there were three other children to be educated. The one-year program proved successful but it represented quite a gamble. In the previous year only four students had attempted the accelerated course. But one

had made it, and he had been reading law for some time.
Baker was fascinated by his new environment at Lexington,
Virginia. The area was a focal point of a sturdy Calvinism
that had taken root in the Shenandoah Valley before the
American Revolution. The University was denominational
in all but name; all members of the board of trustees save
two and all faculty members but one were Presbyterians.
Baker remembered that the Calvinist dominie was a more
absolute potentate in Lexington than the Pope ever was in
Rome, and that nobody "would have dared to have dissented
from his opinion except by candlelight after midnight in the
cellar." The town presented a curious combination of for-
mality and folksiness. On the one hand, all seniors in the
University were expected to wear the Oxford cap and gown,
habiliments which Baker thought exceedingly uncomfortable.
The townspeople represented a kind of ante-bellum ennui,
so marked that Baker felt as if he had suddenly been trans-
planted to China. They did not appear to realize that a new
era had begun in 1865; the favorite indoor sport was climbing
about on the family tree. The old men were all "gentlemen,"
the women were "queens," prefacing their conversation with
the dual queries, "Who was your grandfather?" and "Where
did he live?" (meaning in what *county* of Virginia). Baker
noted that he was a curiosity because he had temporarily forgotten his paternal grandfather's first name and was under
the delusion that he might not have come from any county
in Virginia! The puzzled queens merely exclaimed in be-
wilderment, "Where else could he have come from? Whoever
heard of a man not coming from some county?" In later years
Baker's fraternity brothers remembered him as the law student who chewed tobacco and smoked strong pipes. Baker's
classical rejoinder was:

> Alas! *noscitur in sociis!* I am forced to content my longings
> for fame and ambition to be widely known in the fraternity,

with a reputation won on my worst faults, and either to be
forgotten or to ingloriously survive in the recollection of my
talents as a tobacco chewer.[7]

In the summer of 1894 the young solicitor, now twenty-
three years of age, hung out his shingle in Martinsburg and
waited for clients. Many years later Baker was to explain
to a class of law students why there was no carpet on the
stairs leading to his first office. The first reason was that he
could not afford it; the second was that he wanted to hear
his first client as he climbed the stairs:

> I used to sit up there and listen by the hour. And when he
> did finally come you cannot imagine how much I enjoyed just
> sitting there and counting his steps. He used to drop around
> every day or so, to see what progress I was making, and I
> learned to know his footsteps almost as well as his voice. The
> sound of those footfalls was the best music I ever heard.

In 1896 he received a brief and puzzling telegram re-
questing a visit to Washington. It was from William L.
Wilson, a prominent low-tariff Democrat from West Virginia
who had become Postmaster General in President Cleveland's
second administration, and was later to assume the presidency of Washington and Lee where Baker had studied
law. Baker had seen him only once but his father, a lifelong
tariff-reform Democrat, knew Wilson well as a former Confederate cavalryman. Wilson's academic interests were identi-
cal with those of Baker. He was known as the "scholar in
politics"; years before when preparing his baggage for Confederate war service he had packed a trunkful of books including Greek and Latin texts.

Several years earlier Baker had asked Wilson by letter for
a position as instructor of history at the University of West
Virginia. There had been no reply. At the later conference
in Washington Wilson stunned the nascent lawyer with a

salutation followed by a series of perplexing questions. The
opening gambit was: "Hello, Newt! Are you a stenographer?"
Baker's dignified reply was that the skill was unknown to
him. Wilson went on: "Well, perhaps it doesn't make any
difference. What I (wanted) was to see whether you would
. . . be my private secretary." Baker shifted uneasily but finally
mustered enough courage to say that he was a lawyer and
had never considered giving up his profession. Wilson was
ready with the next embarrassing query: "Have you much to
give up?" Baker was forced to admit that he would sacrifice
"large hopes chiefly." Wilson then advised the young man
that in his opinion a year in Washington would represent no
loss to his professional progress, indeed it would present a
splendid opportunity to meet prominent people. After consultation with friends Baker was compelled to agree, and
as he wrote later:

> I took down my little sign, distributed among the lawyers
> (who looked less pleased than I thought they ought to, perhaps
> knowing the debtors better than I did) the few difficult if hope-
> less cases which had been entrusted to me, and a week later I
> appeared in Washington to begin an experience as delightful
> as any young man ever had or is likely to have.

On his first workday in the nation's capital Baker practiced the promptness he had learned in bucolic Martinsburg
by arriving at the Post Office Department at eight o'clock in
the morning. As he recalled the incident charwomen were
still at work and a watchman admitted him with suspicious
reluctance. He was told that the Department did not open
till nine. After a long walk he again seated himself in the
anteroom, where he was confronted by a tall and finely appointed young man who removed a beautiful muffler and
an impressive overcoat. After these precious habiliments had
been stowed away Baker was asked if he was the new secretary. The reply was in the affirmative. The new arrival then
remarked: "I am your page." Baker said he would not have

been more astonished if the man had said he was the Cardinal Archbishop of Prague.

Baker's job was to save the Postmaster General's time by answering the voluminous mail that was erroneously marked "Personal," and by satisfying callers who came either to pay their respects or to discuss matters of no consequence. He made some mistakes. Once an old gentleman called to see Mr. Wilson and Baker decided that he was unimportant. He spent an hour, using all the resources of his college education and the politeness of his family training in a vain attempt to sidetrack the ancient fellow. Later Wilson remarked: "Newt, my father-in-law . . . tells me he had a delightful conversation with you this morning, but the dickens of a time getting in to see me."

It *was* a pleasant experience. Baker pedaled around Washington on his bicycle, performed his duties as secretary, and began to form opinions on prominent politicians. In 1895 President Cleveland's unusual extension of the Monroe Doctrine (to a boundary dispute between British Guiana and Venezuela) threatened to provoke a war between the United States and Great Britain. Baker said his "timid soul" shrank from Cleveland's brashness but he preferred the President to the saber rattling of Theodore Roosevelt. "Cleveland was all character without brilliance," he wrote, "and Roosevelt seems to have been all brilliance without character." Between Baker and Roosevelt it was the first of many differences of opinion, which were to continue until the Rough Rider's death. In the Presidential campaign year of 1896 Western debtors gained control of the Democratic Party and nominated the "Boy Orator of the Platte," William Jennings Bryan, on a platform designed to bring inflation through the free coinage of silver. Conservative Eastern Democrats, including Cleveland and Postmaster General Wilson, favored the status quo through the prevailing gold policy and refused to support Bryan. In this campaign, which to many drew a clear line between Plenty and Poverty, Baker stood with the gold Democrats; as for the Westerners he was certain that the free silver mania had "stolen away their brains like Michael Cassio's whiskey." It was a paradoxical position for the Baker who was soon to join Tom Johnson and to call himself a radical, but this early conservative stand was matched by his staunch support of right-wing Democrats during the New Deal in the 1930s.[8]

Baker's first political appointment came to an abrupt conclusion in March 1897, with the change of Presidents and the inauguration of Republican William McKinley. In the following summer he made his first trip to Europe, a journey made possible with funds saved from another first—his salary in Washington. He traveled on what he called the "London, Paris, Switzerland, Rhine tourist survey," but also spent three weeks in Heidelberg brushing up his German, in which he had a competent reading knowledge. On his return to Martinsburg Baker resumed the practice of law, this time in the firm of Flick, Westenhaver, and Baker. The senior partners were to influence his later career in Cleveland. Before moving to West Virginia, W. H. H. Flick, who was born in Cuyahoga County on Lake Erie, had attended Hiram College and the Cleveland Law School. As a native West Virginian David C. Westenhaver was honored with the presidency of the State Bar Association in 1898 and followed Baker to Cleveland in 1903, becoming a Federal judge in the Northern District of Ohio in 1917. For more than three decades Westenhaver was Baker's intimate friend and mentor. A fortuitous incident also had a direct bearing on Baker's move to Cleveland. On the return voyage from Europe he sat at the same dining table with an English barrister and Martin Foran, an Irish lawyer from Cleveland. Baker did his best to serve as impartial arbiter in a violent controversy over Irish Home Rule that developed between the two men. The issue proved insoluble, and Foran finally brought it to a conclusion by asking the umpire if he knew the game of chess. Baker did, and the two played the silent game for the rest of the voyage. Foran did not forget his young friend from West Virginia.

Baker found legal practice little better on his second professional attempt in Martinsburg. He began to look elsewhere for opportunities and in 1897 made exploratory trips to Cleveland and Pittsburgh. His luck was bad in Cleveland. The prominent industrialist and politician, Tom L. Johnson, to whom he had a letter of introduction, was out of town. The city had not recovered from the Panic of 1893 and few jobs, legal or otherwise, were available. Baker was appalled by the "frightful grime and dust" of both Cleveland and Pittsburgh, and was inclined to believe that the discomfort of life in both places was in decided contrast to their exceptional opportunities. He was certain that both cities were better places to "get a start" than conservative towns "down east." He was also impressed with the public spirit of Cleveland; everyone seemed to be aware of the importance of good government and public improvement, and the young men appeared to be cultivated and sophisticated. He imagined Cleveland would be an "inspiring atmosphere to live in—but for the smoke of innumerable black-belching iron furnaces, which overhang the city like a hurricane cloud."[9]

Two years later Martin Foran asked Frederick C. Howe, a Cleveland lawyer and Baker's former classmate at Johns Hopkins, if he knew a capable and available young lawyer who might come into his law office. Howe replied that the ablest young lawyer he knew was Newton D. Baker of Martinsburg, West Virginia. Foran remembered the man as his chess companion on shipboard and hired him. By this chance Baker began his thirty-eight years in Cleveland. He set up housekeeping again with Howe—in college they had roomed together as fraternity brothers. It was an interesting ménage because both were absent-minded bachelors, indifferent to domestic comfort. Baker always retained a warm regard for Martinsburg and his many friends there but never regretted departure from the limited outlook of the small town to the broader vistas—intellectual and professional—of the metropolitan community.

The experience with Foran, which lasted two years, was both pleasant and rewarding. The Irishman had been a farmer, a barrelmaker and President of the Cooper's International Union, a soldier in the Army of the Potomac during the Civil War, and twice a member of Congress. On Baker's first day he was greeted warmly, shown to an office which was to be his own, told that his name would be placed on the firm's stationery, and informed about his share of the earnings—which Baker thought unusually generous and far beyond his own estimate of his worth. He soon found that he would earn every penny because Foran immediately presented a complicated case of several thousand pages and said tersely: "Get ready to argue this in the Circuit Court. You will have about four weeks." From that time Baker appeared constantly in court with Foran. The relationship was one of two men, disparate in age, who were friends as well as law partners.[10]

In the summer of 1902, when Baker was thirty years old, his bachelor days came to an end with his marriage to Elizabeth Leopold, the daughter of an old Dutch Presbyterian family from Pottstown, Pennsylvania. The bride was intelligent, charming, and well-educated; a graduate and member of the faculty of Wilson College at Chambersburg, she was an accomplished soprano. When she sang at one of Cleveland's "pop" concerts in 1911 Baker was proud to report that she performed well, wore a new dress with "as large a hat as anybody, which is something in this day and generation," and that the Baker children applauded their mother "with vigorous partiality." The music critic of the *Cleveland Press* was also charmed, and commented favorably on her brilliant voice and artistic intelligence. From time to time when her husband was scheduled for an address, Mrs. Baker would sing a few numbers during the introductory portion of the program.

During the early years of the marriage Mrs. Baker suffered from a goitrous ailment known as Basidow's disease, with accompanying high blood pressure and rapid pulse, which caused her to be bedridden for considerable periods of time. The indisposition was so serious that shortly after the marriage several doctors, including Baker's conservative father, told him that she could not live a year. Fortunately the illness was overcome, in due course three children (Newton III, Elizabeth, and Margaret) were born, and the family settled into a happy existence. Soon after the return from Washington in the early 1920s Baker built a large and comfortable residence, with pillars reminiscent of the South from which he had sprung, on Cleveland's fashionable South Woodland Avenue.

At home Baker was a collector of books, pewter, pipes, and razors (he used a different one for every day of the week); he believed that people needed no exercise and after his early attempts at tennis participated in no games except chess. Although the Baker residence on South Woodland Avenue adjoined the Shaker Heights Country Club, he never played golf. His relationship with golf balls was limited to returning errant hooks and slices that strayed into the garden —according to Mrs. Baker, "he throws his at the men, I save mine for the women." Mrs. Baker was an avid gardener; in newspaper stories she was said to wield a "mean mattock" and to push a wheelbarrow with vigor. During World War I she cultivated a "Victory garden" assiduously; at that time and later her efforts were productive of great quantities of flowers and vegetables for the family and its neighbors. When

Baker was being mentioned as a Presidential candidate he joked that his election would be embarrassing because he would have to appoint Mrs. Baker as Secretary of Agriculture (daughter Peggy—who was attractive, unattached, and twenty —wanted to be Commandant at West Point!). He helped occasionally with the garden but from long observation Mrs. Baker found that he liked the "gross crops," and that he preferred to hill cucumbers and hoe corn. Ralph Hayes (Baker's close friend who was his secretary during the First World War) recalled his own labors in the Baker garden, particularly the hoeing of "serried rows" of Irish potatoes "stretching toward the horizon as far as my weary eye could see." He also professed to see political implications in the production of so many "murphies" and once wrote a mock denial of any national bias in the selection of flora at the Baker homestead:

> Mr. Baker . . . authorizes me to say that about a year ago he realized that the Poles, Czechs, Hungarians, Slovaks, Germans and Americans might regard with suspicion the extent to which his garden was devoted to the production of potatoes, and immediately took steps to have the space diminished so gradually that the Irish would not notice it, and the space thus rescued given over to the cultivation of the national flowers of the various nations above referred to so far as careful horticulture would cause them to grow in this climate.[11]

II. Tom Johnson

B AKER'S LAW PRACTICE in Martinsburg from 1894 to 1899,
such as it was, had been interrupted by an interlude
of government service. He began his legal career in Cleveland
in 1899, and called that city home until his death in 1937.
Again there was a long interval of public service, this one
lasting twenty years from 1901 to 1921. During these two
decades Baker was engaged as Solicitor and Mayor of Cleveland, and as Secretary of War. By contrast his private legal
practice during his thirty-eight-year residence in Cleveland
lasted eighteen years—from 1899 to 1901, for two months in
1916, and from 1921 until his death in 1937.

In his later years Baker pondered the role played by sheer
accident in the life of every person and concluded that
chance acquaintance with four very great men had directed
his own destiny. The first had been William L. Wilson. The
second was Tom Loftin Johnson.

The turn of the century inaugurated the Progressive Move-

34

ment, a development in American politics that placed emphasis on greater popular controls over voting procedure, an awareness of the danger of plutocracy, and a desire to expand the functions of government. Representative of the reform movement in national politics were Theodore Roosevelt and Woodrow Wilson in the White House, Robert La Follette and George Norris in Congress. On the local scene the period produced an unusual array of reform mayors: Hazen Pingree in Detroit, Joseph Folk in St. Louis, Samuel Jones and Brand Whitlock in Toledo, Tom Johnson and Newton Baker in Cleveland.

As Mayor of Toledo from 1897 to 1905, Samuel ("Golden Rule") Jones was the first prominent municipal leader identified with the Progressive Movement. A successful producer of oil-pumping machinery, he came to the conclusion that most manufacturers kept for themselves eight out of ten dollars earned by their employees, and added "because I keep only about seven . . . they call me 'Golden Rule' Jones." Because of the nature of his opposition, Jones was proud to announce that he had been elected in Toledo in spite of six hundred saloons, the streetcar company, and the devil. A man of wide reading and broad culture, he would quote from memory Browning, Emerson, Epictetus, Lowell, Burns, Ruskin—but most often from Walt Whitman and Jesus. His work in Toledo required remarkable vitality, and Jones had it. Baker met him only once. He entered the great hall of Tom Johnson's residence on Euclid Avenue one evening, and saw the family and guests gazing intently into a dark corner of the spacious room. There he saw a gray-haired man standing on his head. Shortly the elderly gymnast reversed his position with a nimble jump, and Baker was introduced to the Mayor of Toledo. Jones was paying Johnson a visit, the talk had turned to the question of physical vitality, and Jones demonstrated his own by standing on his head for two minutes, while one of the guests timed him with a watch.[1]

The crusading editor and author Lincoln Steffens once called Tom Johnson, who was chief magistrate of Cleveland from 1901 to 1909, the "best mayor in the best-governed city in America." In his early days Johnson was a typical robber baron in attitude, and had been highly successful in the operation of street railways and steel plants. Quite an inventor, his inquiring mind set in motion a series of experiments for improved fare boxes, better rails, and faster-running railways; in the late years of his life he was busy in his basement on a magnetic railway with no wheels! Johnson would have gone on being a robber baron if he had not been an avid reader of books, a habit which can bring both satisfaction and disquietude. He read scientific works, studied French during the busiest part of his mayoralty in Cleveland, knew Gibbon well, and in his last hours was entertained by friends who read Plutarch aloud to him. But the volume that had the most profound influence was *Progress and Poverty* by single-taxer Henry George, which hit Johnson like Paul's vision on the road to Damascus. Johnson took the book to his lawyer and said: "Unless you can prove this book wrong, I'll have to go out of business." The attorney was unable to complete the assignment, and ultimately Johnson forsook business for politics. He had gotten an idea—the idea that poverty, unemployment, slums, disease, crime—could be eliminated.

To accomplish his objectives Johnson got himself elected to Congress where he fought for a low tariff in spite of his own profits based on protection for steel. But Johnson never cared for the national capital because of its detachment from the populace. Government was efficient, he believed, only when it was close to the people; like Jefferson he thought that power should be taken from the Federal government and given to the States. He went one step further; he would take it from the States too, and give power to the cities, endowing them with full home rule. To secure this decentralized government, Johnson believed in direct primaries, the short ballot, and the initiative and referendum. Only in this way did he feel that real progress could be made in the fight against monopolies in transportation and industry, supported as they were by special franchises, tax privileges, tariffs, and patents. Relations with former colleagues at the aristocratic Union Club of Cleveland became somewhat strained when Johnson was quoted as saying: "I would rather have the ingratitude of the crowd than the applause of the Union Club, for with the ingratitude of the crowd I would have at least one chance in two of being right, while with the applause of the Union Club I am sure to be wrong!"

Like all Progressives in his day Johnson believed in greater popular control of governmental processes, and decided to take issues directly to the people of Cleveland. He hoped to cleanse the disgraceful city government by developing an informed and interested electorate. Moreover he did it, and Cleveland got a "million dollar mayor . . . for five thousand dollars." By taking every issue directly to the voters, he was elected mayor of Cleveland four times. He had no radio but he did have a vast tent that seated 5,000 people, a public forum in the fullest sense of the term, which he moved from one part of the city to another during campaigns. Johnson had discovered the device by accident when no hall was available and he had rented a small tent pitched on a vacant lot by a traveling showman. He found it most advantageous; everyone liked the informal atmosphere of the tent meeting, while only partisans would go to halls.

Johnson was successful in spite of powerful economic and political interests that opposed him. On his first election as mayor in 1901, Cleveland and Cuyahoga County had a Democratic majority but the rest of the State went to the opposition. The Republican majority in the Ohio Legislature was

so worried about Johnson that it decided all local bills for
Cleveland must first be approved by two prominent Republican businessmen of the city—banker Myron T. Herrick, and
lawyer Homer H. Johnson. It was obvious that the Republicans were not convinced that the Democratic legislators from
Cleveland really represented the city. In 1903 Mark Hanna,
the prominent Cleveland capitalist who was United States
Senator, characterized Kentucky-born Johnson as a "carpet
bagger followed by a train of all the howling vagrants from
Ohio, with a crazy quilt ticket and pretending to stand upon
a pessimistic, socialistic and anarchistic platform." In 1907
the popular Republican Congressman Theodore Burton was
persuaded that it was his civic duty to run against Johnson,
who won the election with ease although Burton had received
the blessing of President Theodore Roosevelt and William
Howard Taft. Johnson also overcame the lampoons of the
famous cartoonist, Homer Davenport, who was imported from
New York by the *Cleveland Leader* in an effort to laugh the
Mayor out of town.[2]

Johnson carried out his policies with the aid of a cabinet
of unusual talent, bound to him by close ties of affection
and loyalty. A superb executive, he selected able subordinates
and then gave them responsibility and power; he was wise
enough not to expect infallibility, and generous in sharing
criticism of their inevitable errors. One political opponent
observed that the Johnson cabinet was like an opera troupe
in its appeal to all members of the electoral audience. There
was Peter Witt to stir up the rabble, Reverend Harris R.
Cooley for the uplifters, Baker and Dr. Edward W. Bemis to
impress the intelligentsia, "Billy" Stage for the young college
crowd, and Charles P. Salen to keep the politicians in line.
Salen was a veteran war horse of the Democratic Party who
became Director of Public Works. Stage was a brilliant young
lawyer who had been the greatest athlete in the history of

Adelbert College of Western Reserve University; he had captained the football team and once held the national record of 9 4/5 seconds for the 100-yard dash. Dr. Cooley, who became Director of the Department of Charities and Corrections, was a single-tax preacher who had spent twenty-one years at the Cedar Avenue Disciple Church. Sociologist, as well as pastor, he was responsible for the tuberculosis sanitarium, a model home for the aged, and the attractive Cooley Farm which he substituted for the old workhouse. Professor Bemis received his Ph.D. from Johns Hopkins and had been eased out of the faculty at the University of Chicago because of alleged radicalism. He was an expert in municipal government; Johnson made him Superintendent of the Waterworks and "unofficial" statistician and civil service expert for the city.

It was an unusual group of men. Most reform movements would have rallied bank presidents, heads of civic organizations, eminent ministers, and distinguished professional men. Instead Johnson anticipated the idea of the "brain trust" by surrounding himself with young college men whose reputations were not yet made but whose social consciences had been kindled by the Progressive Movement. All of them later became prominent in various capacities—with the pen, in the law, on the bench, and in legislative halls. They would become Secretary of War Baker and the well-known writer Fred Howe from Johns Hopkins; prominent lawyer "Billy" Stage and Judge Carl Friebolin from Western Reserve University; Senator Robert J. Bulkley and lawyer-educator Alfred A. Benesch from Harvard; Congressman Robert Crosser from Kenyon. In addition, Johnson had selected a black-listed iron molder with a public reputation of being an anarchist (Witt), a preacher from a little congregation on a back street (Cooley), and a professor who was no longer *persona grata* in the academic groves (Bemis). Baker was the first to admit that his own appointment represented a great gamble; he had been

a country lawyer who had lived in Cleveland for only two
years and had spent most of his time trying cases for in-
digent people. In Baker's judgment a great movement was
never started with more humble beginnings, but Johnson was
shrewd. Every one of the men so chosen was forced to justify
his selection by constant pressure from the dynamic mayor.

The most colorful personality in Johnson's entourage was
Peter Witt, director of the short-lived citizen's "tax school"
and clerk of the city council. Witt was an *enfant terrible* who
had been a labor organizer, had been black-listed for organizing a strike, had turned to the street corner to expound
his opinions. A century earlier as one of the Incorruptibles
of the French Revolution he might have cut off heads and
lost his own. Witt tangled with tax boards, corporations,
courts, "grafting" Democrats or Republicans—or any one who
got in his way. It was Witt, as a twentieth-century sans-culotte,
who conducted the forensic "tannery" on the hides of the
opposition; it was Witt who referred to the Union Club, of
which Mayor Johnson was a member of qualified but dubious
standing, as the "Onion Club." Baker recognized Witt's effectiveness as a public speaker but disapproved of the violence
with which he "skinned the skunks"—crudity which Baker
could condone only "by the defects in his early education
and the bitterness of his early life, when frequently his wife
and children almost starved because he could not find employment for his hands without agreeing to silence his tongue,
a bargain which he was never willing to make." In some ways
a tragic figure, Witt was to conclude that his reward, for what
he considered to be passionate devotion to the common
good, had been "the blacklist of the criminal rich and the
distrust of the ignorant poor."[3]

In this unusual cast of dramatis personae Baker played a
distinguished and anomalous role. As "Johnson's Joseph" he
was the youngest member of the troupe; the Mayor called

him the "little mental giant" who was really "head of the cabinet and principal adviser to us all." He was aware that Baker as City Solicitor had been pitted against the most prominent lawyers in the State. In Johnson's judgment no other person could have done the job so well. He ranked Baker with the highest-paid corporation lawyers in ability, in spite of the fact that the latter were paid five times as much for their work. Baker was closer to the Mayor than any other person outside his family; from 1901 until 1911 Baker said they were "together daily and almost without intermission." In Johnson's last days it was Baker who was always admitted to the sick chamber, and it was Baker with whom the Mayor confided on the final settlement of his affairs.

In return Baker was to say throughout his life that his debt to Johnson was immeasurable for whatever wisdom and breadth of spirit he had, and he believed that the Deity must have created a special heaven for such men. He occupied a position in the cabinet, however, that was completely unlike the role of the frenetic Witt, the evangelistic Cooley, or the partisan Salen. Baker was basically an aristocrat who had little in common with Witt's savage attacks, ruthless sarcasm, and lack of refinement. The two worked together for years, but it was an unstable alliance. On the question of means and ends, Baker believed sincerely in the ultimate objectives of the Progressive Movement but often disagreed with his colleagues on the most suitable means to achieve them. With Johnson he agreed in the soundness of the anti-privilege position taken by Henry George; unlike Johnson he never believed there could be a wholesale application of single-tax principles to the old and established society in which he lived. There was a lot of Southern tradition in Baker, and it sometimes seemed contradictory that this lawyer and scholar should espouse the cause of the people and take an abiding interest in modern sociology and politics. But he had a warm heart along with his cool head, and the heart

was moved by Tom Johnson just as it was to be excited later
by Woodrow Wilson.[4]

Baker's first appointment from Johnson was as legal adviser to the City Board of Equalization in May 1901; the
following fall he became Assistant Law Director, and in
November 1902 was appointed Law Director. A new municipal code, which became effective in 1903, provided for an
elected city solicitor, as the former law director was now
designated. Baker was elected to the new position and was
returned to the office regularly until 1912 when he became
mayor. His major work as city solicitor was in the "Seven
Years' War" to establish a three-cent fare on municipally
controlled street railways. It was a battle between Johnson
and "Little David" Baker on the one hand and private-
interest Goliaths—including "Dollar Mark" Hanna—on the
other. During the encounter, Hanna employed restrictive
court orders, so many that it was claimed injunctions were
distributed with streetcar tickets, and Baker was to be known
popularly as the man of fifty-five law suits. On his annual salary of $5,000 he was pitted against handsomely paid corpora-
tion lawyers who, in Baker's judgment, were "case-hardened
and class-conscious plutocrats, with splendid abilities, but
with human sympathy reduced to a minimum." On one
occasion when he appeared before a committee of the Ohio
Legislature he noticed that Dr. John N. Stockwell, who
had established quite a reputation as a mathematician and
astronomer, was unable to restrain his mirth during the
solemn pleading. Baker could not understand the basis for
all the amusement until he heard Stockwell's explanation.
"The irresistibly funny part of your appearance before the
Legislature," Stockwell stated, "is that you are the only man
who comes here and argues things just because they are right.
You seem to think that the Legislature will act on reason
and sound argument and to be entirely unaware of the fact

that their actions are governed by entirely different motives."

The fight for low streetcar fares was going on at the same time in other American cities. In Toledo, where "Golden Rule" Jones and Brand Whitlock fought the battle, the traction men hired a physician to testify that low fares were bad for public health because they discouraged walking! In Cleveland one company controlled the majority of the lines on the East Side and was known as the Big Consolidated, or Big Con. Another company controlled all the West Side lines and was called the Little Consolidated, or Little Con. Ultimately the two companies were merged, to be known popularly as the Con-Con. The Con-Con insisted on a five-cent fare and was soon in competition with low-fare companies allied with Johnson which were popularly known as the "three-fer" lines. The struggle between private and public control was a bitter civil war during which citizens occasionally wakened in the morning to find that street-railway tracks had been laid through the small hours of the night in front of their houses. Baker carried the legal burden deftly; Whitlock was to testify that "he did it all with skill and ability and withal with such grace and courtesy and good nature that he never offended his opponents, who were the leading corporation lawyers of the city."

By 1908 Johnson and Baker appeared to have won the war. The private companies agreed to a low evaluation of their properties which were leased to a municipal operating corporation of five men appointed by the mayor. The public corporation was to pay operating costs plus 6 per cent on the low evaluation of capital stock, with all excess earnings retained by the city. Tariffs were established on a sliding scale dependent on earnings, but were to begin at a low rate. The fight for the three-cent fare with universal transfers seemed to have been won, and April 28, 1908, was designated as a very special "Streetcar Day" with all comers riding free of charge.

It was a glorious victory with an inglorious end. The municipal corporation was plagued by an unfortunate strike, some sabotage, and falling revenues during the depression of 1907–8. In October 1908, the electorate, fatigued and disillusioned, voted to return the streetcar system to private ownership. Years later, in retrospect, Baker believed Johnson had moved too quickly, that the experiment in municipal operation had begun "when public opinion was just about 50.1% in favor of doing so." The result was that the "49.9% developed such an enormous hostility that every little fault, trifling as compared with the misconduct and incompetence of the private management, was magnified into almost criminal proportions and we lost our experiment in the test-tube stage." Whatever the reason, in 1909 Johnson was defeated for re-election; as a tolerant Democrat he was able to smile as he said to Brand Whitlock, "The people are probably right." Baker was surprised but philosophical about the reaction of the electorate to a city administration that had been both pure and honest. He decided that eight years of "even a good thing" had produced a weariness of spirit, and that "an excess of virtue is as tiresome, if not more so, than an occasional dip into vice." For that reason the defeat was no disappointing sign; it was merely the fulfillment of a social law. He hoped that the four-term mayor would make his comeback at the next election, but it was not to be. Two years later Johnson was dead. He had been an authentic Progressive, deserving of the inscription on his statue in Cleveland's Public Square:

> Beyond his party and beyond his class
> This man forsook the few to serve the mass.[5]

Baker was the only member of the cabinet, the "solitary survivor of an ancient regime," who remained after Johnson's defeat in 1909, continuing as City Solicitor from 1910 to 1912 in the Republican administration of Mayor Herman C. Baehr. As the only Democrat in the new government Baker's position was an uneasy one, and he was effectively isolated by the first action of the city council, which barred him from its meetings. In this anomalous situation Baker was "perplexed, embarrassed, and unhappy"; he had not wanted to run for re-election, had been persuaded by Johnson to do so, and now found himself in a trap with no Johnson to rescue him. Because the ex-mayor was in his last illness Baker took over leadership of the Cleveland Democracy, managed the local campaign for State and congressional offices in 1910, and spoke regularly against the controversial Payne-Aldrich protective tariff which he said had been written by men who "sat in marble halls in Washington, at great gilded tables, with gold pens in their hands." His reputation was Statewide but when he was proposed for Attorney General of Ohio Baker said he was not interested, and when the United States Senate was suggested as a possibility he said he could not live in Washington on the salary. On the local scene Mayor Baehr was a substantial citizen of German heritage whose administration was reasonably honest but dull; within two years the city was ready to be stimulated again by the progressivism of Tom Johnson. Because the "Great Leader" was dead the electorate turned to his first lieutenant, so enthusiastically that the *Cleveland Plain Dealer* was to say that success in all elections from 1903 through 1913 warranted the sobriquet of N. D. "Never Defeated" Baker. At thirty-nine he became one of Ohio's three "boy Mayors"—all inspired by Johnson—Henry T. Hunt in Cincinnati, Whitlock in Toledo, Baker in Cleveland.[6]

III. Mayor

IN HIS INITIAL mayoral campaign Baker fought for approval of a proposed two-million-dollar bond issue to expand the municipal light plant and provide a three-cent rate for electricity, which became the major subject for dispute in the contest. His Republican opponent was Frank G. Hogen, a businessman whose public experience had been limited to a term as Director of Safety in Mayor Baehr's administration. The issue between wealth and commonwealth was soon joined; Baker not only said there were too many millionaires around to suit him, but added that he believed every natural monopoly—streetcars, gas, water, and electric light—ought to be owned and operated by the people. The most exciting debate was with the vice-president of the privately owned Cleveland Electric Illuminating Company before an audience of a thousand businessmen in the city. Johnson had once said: "The public utility corporations are a bunch of thieves. I ought to know. I was one of them." Baker echoed these words with the statement that public service corpora-

tions had "consistently corrupted and depraved government"
for fifty years, and that municipal ownership was necessary
for the purification of city politics. His opponent charged in
turn that Baker was "more guilty of prostitution of public
office, to his own private advantage and political preferment,
than any one else." Baker concluded with a dramatic peroration to listeners seated in the auditorium of the Cleveland
Chamber of Commerce: "I am in the house of have. I appeal
on behalf of the house of want—for justice."

During the campaign the Republicans contended that
Baker was a curious machine politician with a gift for words.
His principle asset, they said, was beautiful language replete
with classical allusions, but in their judgment language
would not "build bridges or mend thoroughfares." They
claimed that Baker's election would bring to power an Irish
politician with the telltale name of Tim McDonough, who
was a member of the local Executive Committee of the Democratic Party as well as the proprietor of a saloon in downtown
Cleveland. This prospect horrified pastor William W. Bustard
of the Euclid Avenue Baptist Church, of which John D.
Rockefeller was a member. Bustard preached against the
Democratic ticket from his pulpit. Witt's rejoinder was that
Bustard was merely obeying the orders of his boss, John D.
Rockefeller; Baker simply observed that he regarded the Bap-
tist minister as a "Republican preacher."[1]

Baker's campaign methods were a copy of those employed
so successfully by Tom Johnson. He used the familiar tent,
as he wrote to a friend:

> Beginning October 9, our campaign will be on. You can
> picture us: a circus tent holding about three thousand people,
> three speakers, Dr. Cooley a former preacher and under Mr.
> Johnson the soul of our charities and corrections, Peter Witt
> an iron moulder, forceful, crude, direct, incorruptible,—and last
> me. The audience quiet but now and then asking questions

> which are always welcomed and answered so that sometimes the
> meetings are almost running debates. So it will run until Nov.
> 7 when the votes will be counted and really the result seems
> less important to all of us than the message.

There was one significant difference between teacher and
pupil: Baker used a rapier instead of the Johnsonian meat
ax. His campaign was on such an elevated plane that he was
able to quote Latin and get away with it.

How he brought it off was puzzling to skeptics who regarded
him as the "most intellectual mayor in captivity." Here was
a shy, diminutive scholar who was to order the director of
municipal music to change his programs from ragtime to
Wagner, Verdi, and Donizetti. Four years earlier the ponder-
ous Theodore Burton (who looked as though he should have
been the author of *The Anatomy of Melancholy*) was running
against Tom Johnson and had opened an address to an
audience of workingmen with the phrase *Jacta est alea*—the
die is cast. Johnson had feigned ignorance as to the meaning,
but told the Irish, who were convulsed with laughter, that
he thought it meant "Let 'er go Gallagher, we're off." Despite
this worrisome precedent Baker announced his political philosophy in 1911 in classical terms: *Lex citium tolerare vult
privatum damnum quam publicum malum.* When the C.E.I.
proposed a sweet-sounding compromise he used the original
of a common warning: *Timeo Danaos et dona ferentes.* The
same citizens, who had almost run Burton out of town, now
applauded Baker. The secret seems to have been the elevated
and sincere tone of Mr. Baker, which was at once convincing
and effective; he possessed a singular ability to participate in
Saturday night ward meetings and to deliver Sunday lectures
at the University without raising or lowering the plane of his
lectures.

The denouement was a rousing victory for Baker; his
plurality of 17,838 was the largest received by a candidate

for mayor up to that time. During the campaign the opposition had made fun of his small stature. Baker's prompt announcement was that he did not "expect to be a little mayor"; it was his intention to be the "biggest mayor I know how to be." In years to come he was to be known as the "Big Little Mayor" of Cleveland.[2]

In his four-year tenure from 1912 to 1916 Baker fostered Johnson's ideal of a Utopia of Civic Righteousness. He coined a new word to designate his policy; it was "civitism," once described as a combination of "Home Rule and the Golden Rule for Cleveland." Baker believed that the greatness of a city did not depend on its buildings, either public or private, but rather on the intensity with which its citizens loved the city as their home. Such a pervasive feeling would inevitably produce beautiful parks, cleaner streets, honest government, and widespread adherence to justice as the ideal of its social and economic life. It was his firm intention to make "civitism" mean the same thing for the city that patriotism signified for the nation.

Civitism obviously meant home rule, and Baker was largely responsible for its establishment during 1912–13, not only in Cleveland but in other cities as well. Previously municipal governments had been under the close control of the Ohio Legislature, which made all major decisions. Baker began working for home rule in 1910 when he was the first president of the Ohio Municipal League. His interest in local autonomy was so profound that he believed *self*-government more important than *good* government; under self-government people could educate themselves to support intelligently the institutions upon which the social order rested, whereas a government imposed from without was so little understood or appreciated that it produced neither satisfaction nor stability. With Brand Whitlock he wrote a new constitutional amend-

ment authorizing municipal home rule, worked diligently on
its precise language, and was to be disappointed in his handi-
work. The two men had

> worked over it with unlimited zeal, examined it, re-examined
> it, criticized it, and changed it. Finally when it was perfect the
> convention adopted it and the people . . . gave it their approval.
> I remember that in the course of our work Brand said, "Newton,
> let's write this with such definite and unmistakable clarity that
> no court will ever be called upon to interpret the meaning of
> any of its sentences." The vanity of that hope, however, appears
> from the fact that this amendment adopted in 1912, has been
> perhaps the most constant statute in Supreme Court litigation
> ever since. . . .

Baker concluded sadly that "most attempts to outwit the
ingenuity of the future are useless." None the less the per-
missive amendment was added to the State Constitution in
1912, under Baker's guidance the new home-rule charter was
adopted by the Cleveland electorate in 1913, and he was the
first mayor elected under this form of government. The new
city charter was a document in the Progressive mold; it called
for a centralized mayor-council system (rather than the commission form), eliminated partisan primary elections, and
provided for the recall of both the mayor and members of
the council.[3]

Baker was sometimes called the "three-cent" mayor because of his battle for three-cent streetcar fares, light, dances,
and fish. One of his local adversaries remarked, with what he
regarded as facetious disdain, that his own future platform
might promise three-cent meals—which he hoped would bring
victory by out-Bakering Baker. In Washington, Cleveland's
Democratic Congressman Robert J. Bulkley introduced a bill
for three-cent coins which were potentially useful in the
metropolis on the south shore of Lake Erie. Baker believed
that the city should own all public utilities—street railways,
waterworks, electric plants, and telephones; on the national

level he favored the abolition of the tariff plus government ownership of railroads as the first necessary step toward the annihilation of trusts. There were not a few who thought his policies would make Cleveland a semisocialistic experiment station. One Republican opponent claimed that these radical policies would soon foment the ignorant element of Cleveland into such a frenzy that they would "arise in their wrath and burn the city." Baker's calm rejoinder was that he had alerted the fire department!

The slogan of "three-cent light" was adopted in the struggle against the six- to seven-cent average charged by the privately owned Cleveland Electric Illuminating Company. Baker wanted the municipal plant as a yardstick for the determination of rates. He argued that manufacturers could install their own electric facilities but that residential consumers were unable to do so; as a result C.E.I. charged manufacturers less and small consumers more, until the municipal competition was provided. The new municipal plant, the largest in the nation at the time, began operations in 1914; during the next eight years Baker estimated that it saved the people of Cleveland almost fourteen million dollars. Opponents charged that Baker's yardstick reached much too far; they claimed that the city even sold ice-cream cones in the public parks in competition with private vendors. Baker admitted the charge and said that "the people of Cleveland had decided to set up a little private yardstick of their own on ice-cream cones" because the private supply had become both expensive and poor in quality. He popularized the three-cent dance by opening two municipal dance halls in city parks where a five-minute dance cost three pennies, in competition with private dance halls charging five cents for a three-minute whirl. The music and crowds were both good, and the municipal venture was self-supporting. Three-cent fish accompanied the same low charges for electricity, streetcar rides, and dances. Because the price was too high the City Park Department equip-

ped a fishing tug which set its nets in Lake Erie. The catch
was retailed to the public at three cents per pound.

On trolley lines Baker and Peter Witt achieved the three-
cent fare and a little more; for a brief period they managed
to push rates as low as two tickets for five cents. This was
accomplished under the Tayler Grant of 1910 (after Federal
Judge Robert W. Tayler) which had brought to a conclusion
the long war between Mayor Johnson and private street-railway lines. Baker had played a major role in the writing of
the compromise; he claimed that Judge Tayler had decided
only four major points and that as city solicitor his office had
drafted the plan around these points. The Grant provided
for private ownership with municipal control through a publicly appointed traction commissioner; it made the private
company an agent of the city and guaranteed stockholders a
6 per cent return. Johnson had realized that the municipal
usefulness of the new arrangement would be good only as
long as there was someone in the position of traction commissioner who knew how to run the operation in the public
interest. The first appointee in the administration of Herman
Baehr had been ineffective although at $12,000 per year he
received $2,000 more than the mayor. Baker appointed Witt
to the post and thereby insured dedicated public control, in
spite of a reduction in the annual salary to $7,500. Witt filled
the position with distinction for three years. He not only
offered a fare of three cents or better but championed the
demands of car riders, extended lines, rerouted cars, improved
schedules, opened aristocratic Euclid Avenue for the first time
to streetcar traffic, and ordered "Sunday Stops" at all churches
(for which he was accused of angling for the church vote).
Witt was ingenious enough to design a center-exit car, known
as "Pete's Pet," from which he was to derive substantial
royalties although he waived them for the use of his invention
in Cleveland. His contribution drew national attention, and
after his term of service he was to become a transportation

consultant for other cities. Baker contended that Witt's stewardship saved patrons of street railways an annual sum of four million dollars, which went instead into market baskets, clothes, and savings accounts.[4]

There were other achievements. Baker supported the Municipal Symphony Orchestra (a precursor of the present Cleveland Symphony) with $10,000 from the city's budget, in spite of severe protests from conservatives who attacked both the general expenditure and the specific salary of $3,000 paid to the German director Christian Timmner. The Mayor's answer was that Cleveland was known for its culture as well as its municipal light plant, and he looked forward to the day when there would be a municipal theater and a municipal stock company as well, which would enable the public to see classical plays rather than the "degenerate catchpenny devices of to-day." The cultivated Baker had no sympathy with lurid drama or gambling sports, and as mayor he prohibited professional boxing and occasionally censored movies.

Baker shared Johnson's vision in downtown Cleveland of a beautiful Mall, a spacious development with buildings around trees and grass, originally designed by a commission that included Daniel H. Burnham, the prominent architect and city planner who had been responsible for the general plan of the promenade at the Columbian Exposition at Chicago in 1893. Baker contributed to the realization of the Mall concept through the construction of the City Hall, arrangements for the addition of a new Union Station beside it, and improvements to the waterfront. New municipal passenger boat docks at the foot of East Ninth Street took the place of their ancient and malodorous predecessors on the Cuyahoga River. The City Hall was all but completed before Baker left office, replacing an old structure that had been designated as one of the "most notorious architectural infamies in the U. S." The municipal building was constructed without scandal, graft, or extravagance—and cost less than half the amount expended on the similar and adjacent County Court House. The Union Depot Ordinance of 1915 was a monument to Baker's skill in negotiation, and appeared to close the long dispute between the city and the railroads about lake-shore real estate. Among other things, the railroads were to pay the city more than one million dollars for the depot site next to the City Hall, and the municipality was to use the sum in buying more land for the Mall. Unfortunately the main provisions of the ordinance were not followed, the Union Station was later built into the Terminal Tower on the Public Square, and the dispute over the lake front was to continue for years.

Women were to take pride in the encouragement which both Mayors Johnson and Baker gave to their increasing participation in civic affairs. It had been during Johnson's terms, when Baker was Law Director, that women in Cleveland had first occupied positions of public trust, particularly in the Department of Health under Mildred Chadsey. Baker was an early advocate of women's suffrage, persuaded the prominent Cleveland Democrats Mrs. Harris R. Cooley, Bernice S. Pyke, and Frances Bushea to run for the State Legislature, and was one of the men interested in the career of Florence E. Allen, who became a judge of the Supreme Court of Ohio and was the first woman to be appointed to a United States Circuit Court of Appeals. As Law Director and Mayor he organized the Woman's Department in the City Employment Bureau, took great interest in the Juvenile Court and the Humane Society (which was concerned with the placement of dependent children in foster homes and institutions), and appeared before the City Council as an advocate of the Woman's Police Bureau. Later as Secretary of War, Baker was to send almost 25,000 women overseas as nurses and social workers, and organized the Committee on Woman's Defense Work with the well-known suffragist Anna Howard Shaw as chair-

man. He was to say that if women stopped working during
the war, the United States would be forced to withdraw
from it.[5]

There were some worrisome issues, particularly in connection with the police department, the filter plant, and the
budget. The Civil Service Commission found it necessary to
remove Chief of Police Fred Kohler (who came back as Mayor
of Cleveland in 1921) on the charge of "gross immorality
. . . and conduct unbecoming to an officer and a gentleman."
In the Johnson days Kohler's "Golden Rule" policy had
elicited from Theodore Roosevelt the comment that he was
the "best chief of police in America." Prisoners had been
placed in custody only as a last resort; those charged with mis-
demeanors were released after signing the "Golden Rule"
book, unless the evidence indicated that the offense was committed with malice or injurious intent. In 1912, however,
Kohler became involved in an *affaire d'amour* which became
extremely embarrassing when a husband returned home unexpectedly to find his wife in what appeared to have been
close collaboration with the scantily clad Chief of Police. The
scandal became a public sensation as the Reverend William
Bustard, before a clamorous crowd of two thousand at the
Euclid Avenue Baptist Church, flayed Kohler directly and the
Baker administration collaterally. Kohler had to go, but Baker
did not turn his back on the achievements of the policeman.
His comment was that the "tragedy of his present separation
from the force ought not to blind us to the devotion and
zeal with which he has served the city."

The trouble over water supply concerned Baker's delay in
building a filter plant until sewage disposal facilities had first
been completed. The "diluted mud flavored with chlorine"
that came from the city's mains was so unpalatable that those
who worried about typhoid fever or undertaker's bills bought
distilled water, boiled the mixture that emerged from their

taps, or filled bottles and casks at the springs in city parks. The congestion at Wade and Rockefeller Parks was so great that it was necessary to post policemen at these sources for drinking water to preserve order. For too long Baker held stubbornly to the opinion that the trouble was in the minds rather than on the palates of the citizenry. He claimed that "the turbidity of the water was an aesthetic phenomenon, largely subjective and possible of elimination by the self-directed psychological reaction of changing one's taste." It required the threat of a referendum plus a mighty storm that roiled the waters of the lake to change his mind and to get work started, in 1914, on a new filter plant.

Baker practiced personal economies but there was a municipal deficit that contributed to the growing indebtedness of the city. He had a shoeshining outfit in his office, polished his own shoes, and liked to quote Lincoln's query, "If a man cannot shine his own shoes, whose shoes can he shine?" On the municipal budget, by contrast, an investigation by the Civic League indicated that Baker's financial administration was reasonably economical and effective but that Cleveland was at a disadvantage by comparison with other large cities in the rate of growth of its debt. This was in large part due to a practice common to Ohio municipalities: the evasion of sinking fund requirements and failure to liquidate debts as they came due. By 1915 Cleveland had general revenues of more than four million dollars annually but was paying a third of the sum for debt service. Baker was criticized for too heavy dependence on borrowing rather than unpopular taxation in order to balance his budget. In addition, his unwillingness to authorize an independent audit in order to ascertain the facts as objectively as possible was thought by some to have been partly responsible for Witt's defeat in the mayoral election of 1915.[6]

In spite of these difficulties there was general agreement

that Baker had given Cleveland both dignified and distinguished service, and 1913 saw him re-elected in the city's first nonpartisan election. His chief opponent was Harry L. Davis who had known poverty in his early days, had worked in the Newburgh steel rolling mills, and had become City Treasurer in 1910. Baker charged that Davis was a stooge for the Hannas and the C.E.I.; he was represented as an inexperienced "do-nothing" fellow with a pleasant smile. By contrast some of Baker's enthusiastic friends claimed that he had proved himself as effective in municipal affairs as was his namesake in the baseball world, the famous J. Franklin ("Home-run") Baker of the World Champion Philadelphia Athletics. The Davis supporters denied this allegation vehemently; another

"J-J-John, d-d-didn't you vote for B-B-Baker?"
"Heaven for-g-give me, I d-did--once!"

A cartoon from the Hanna-owned Cleveland Leader of November 1, 1913, opposing what it called "Bakerized streets."

term under Baker, they charged, would change Cleveland
from the "City on the Hill" into the "City in the Hole." They
ridiculed the intellectual language—the "Hot Air and English
Literature"—employed by Baker and insisted that the Mayor
should "rate well-kept streets above well-turned phrases in
political conventions." There was contempt for the "uplift
chorus" of Baker, Witt, and Cooley—a trio later subject to
the following lampoon in a City Club show: "When Newton
Baker makes a political speech he knows it is bunk, but the
crowd doesn't know; when Peter Witt makes a political speech
he knows it is bunk and so does the crowd; but when the
dear old doctor [Cooley] pours out his soul he doesn't know
it is bunk and neither does the crowd." By contrast with the
jovial Davis it was claimed that Baker had the temperament
of a refrigerator—"icy, indifferent, austere, aloof and superior
in his own estimation of himself." The specter of the Irish
Democratic machine was resurrected; Baker was said to be
a Janus with "one head toward Tim McDonough, the other
toward the people, saying 'I am your non-partisan candidate.' "

Baker was re-elected by 3,258 votes, a slim margin compared to the 17,000 by which he led his Republican rival in
1911. The anti-Baker *Cleveland Leader* grudgingly admitted
that the returns were a personal, rather than an organization,
success for the Mayor; he was saved from defeat by his popularity in districts that were conservative and Republican in
normal elections. Conservatives had been surprised and impressed by his nonpartisan honesty; among other things he had
returned a baseball pass to the Cleveland Baseball Club because, as he phrased it, "as a public officer I find myself freer
from every sort of embarrassment by not permitting myself
to accept kindnesses of this kind. . . ." It was also believed by
many that his insistence on merit, and his refusal to pass out
jobs "to the boys" during his first term, had been largely
responsible for the decisive nonpartisan support he received
from independent Republicans. In any case Baker was pleased

with the outcome but gave early notification that this was to
be his last quest for municipal office. A third term, he said,
might result in permanent separation from his métier; he
hoped some day to return to his profession and to practice
law. Two years later he was to support Peter Witt as his
successor, but the fiery traction commissioner was defeated
by Harry Davis in a close election, although in the preferential balloting Witt had more first-place votes than his successful rival.[7]

The position in City Hall was destined to be the last
elective office held by the "Big Little Mayor," but he was
prominent throughout his life in local and national Democratic circles. For a quarter of a century after the death of
Tom Johnson, the intellectual Baker was recognized as the
head of the Democratic Party in Cuyahoga County although
he relinquished most of the administrative responsibility in
1924 to W. Burr Gongwer who became chairman of the party's
executive committee. Gongwer had been a young political
writer on the *Cleveland Plain Dealer* when he changed his
allegiance from the Republican to the Democratic Party and
became secretary to Mayor Tom Johnson.

Judgments varied on the municipal effectiveness of the
Baker-Gongwer regime. In 1931 reporter Nat Howard (later
editor) of the *Cleveland News* designated Baker as the "only
head of an active city political organization in the history
of current times who has never been called a boss." Emphatic
disagreement with this opinion was heard from Jack Raper,
the waspish, wiry, and irrefragably independent columnist of
the *Cleveland Press*. He was the originator of the famous
"Raper Bull," a bovine facsimile inserted from time to time
in a particularly outlandish statement made by a public
figure. Gongwer had the dubious distinction of initiating the
device; the Raper animal first appeared in 1907, indented
into a campaign statement uttered by the Democratic leader.
In the 1920s Raper turned his attention to Baker, and said

flatly that he was the boss of a machine that was a menace to the city of Cleveland. When people countered that Gongwer rather than Baker was the boss, Raper refused to believe it. Such statements, he said, caused the little animal to roar loudly because "he can't be fooled by any kind of bull." Raper's major objection to Baker as the Democratic Elder Statesman was based on his complacency to the group he designated as the Big Crooks—the Van Sweringen brothers and the bankers who were largely responsible for the local debacle of the depression-ridden 1930s. Raper admitted that Baker was splendid in his operations against the little brigands—the gun-toting racketeers and the labor thugs—but that his voice was silent where the big plunderers of Cleveland were concerned.[8]

Baker had little use for nonpartisan programs, believed firmly in the theory of party responsibility, and thought the United States should have two major parties—one conservative and the other liberal. He was certain that coalitions of many parties, as in France, produced government by private barter rather than by public decision. He would not join the nonpartisan Citizens League of Cleveland because he felt that it undermined the authority of political parties, whereas he found himself "coming more and more to believe that true progress lies in strengthening political parties and building up their respectability and power, rather than by causing them to be distrusted and disregarded." He recognized Peter Witt's ability but deplored his hostility to party responsibility, his support of independent Bob La Follette in the Presidential election of 1924, his pride in being an individualist rather than a Democrat in politics. Baker felt that it was difficult, for Witt or anybody else, to be a good leader in politics without first serving as a good follower. When the *Cleveland Press* criticized the local Democratic organization in 1930 Baker (although his law firm represented the Scripps-Howard chain in which the *Press* was a link) counterattacked with an assault on the editorial policy of the newspaper. He said that the *Press,* as an independent journal, had preached political independence as a high civic virtue and had castigated party allegiance in municipal affairs as an absurd vice. This policy had discouraged association on political grounds and had replaced a natural, gregarious development with loyalties to racial, religious, and social groups. Baker thought the strategy had undesirable results: it had neither curbed the power of the "boss" nor produced a nonpartisan ticket of ability or responsibility. He was convinced that in the long run better results could be obtained by stimulating party pride and discipline than were possible through casual independent selection and subsequent irresponsibility of action.

Because of his faith in party responsibility Baker had little confidence in proportional representation or the city manager form of government, which Cleveland had from 1924 to 1932. When municipal administration got bad, some people succumbed to an understandable temptation to change the form of government. Baker was certain that it was personnel who were important, that good government came from good men rather than by experimentation in the forms of government. Cleveland had been the first large city to adopt the new system and was fortunate in having two capable city managers, but in due course Baker was convinced that a bad manager would come along and that public indignation would bring a return to the mayor-council plan. (He was wrong: it was the economic depression of the 1930s that gave the city manager system its *coup de grace* in Cleveland.) Basically he thought the city manager system was inferior to the mayor-council plan because the "business" manager was responsible to the council (which elected him) rather than to the people, and this device both divorced power from responsibility and encouraged "buck-passing." A mayor elected by the people was therefore the best assurance of successful and honest local administration.

For similar reasons he came to believe that proportional

IV. Orator

BAKER FIRST WON national attention at the Democratic National Convention of 1912 at Baltimore. He came to the assembly a relative stranger; he left it with a country-wide reputation as one of the key figures who won the nomination for Woodrow Wilson. Baker's eloquence at Baltimore opened the breech by making it possible for nineteen Ohio delegates to vote for the successful candidate. This tour de force turned out to be an important development in the chain of events leading to Wilson's nomination, and Baker's brilliance was not to be forgotten. Josephus Daniels, the North Carolinian who was later to be his colleague as Secretary of the Navy, said that Baker's effort was a prime example of oratory at its best; he had never seen a verdict won so completely by eloquence and logic. Years later the *Illinois State Register* commented that Baker's subsequent selection as Secretary of War was no surprise because "any man who could successfully lead a war upon political bosses in a national convention was qualified to lead in a world war!"

Before the National Convention, which was held in June 1912, Baker had not only pledged himself to Wilson but had fought and lost a titanic struggle in the Ohio Democratic Convention at Toledo. In March he announced for Wilson, with a "wealth of rhetoric and classical allusion," in a speech during which he called the tariff the mother of trusts, quoted Emerson, scored the courts for conservative decisions, and talked about "fattened privilege." In April he joined Wilson on a political speaking tour in Massachusetts, and came home filled with enthusiasm for his candidacy. In May it was claimed that he was interested in the second place on the national Democratic ticket, as vice-president to Wilson. By this time he was actively involved in the fight in Ohio between the Progressive Democrats supporting Wilson and their conservative brethren who were behind the presidential aspirations of Ohio's Democratic Governor Judson Harmon. Baker classified himself as "radical and progressive" by comparison with the Governor's ultraconservatism; he said that Harmon's "retrospective politics" were shaped like a ship's anchor that provided a cumbersome drag against the "voyage to better things." In the State primaries Democratic voters had been asked to elect to the National Convention district delegates who favored Harmon or Wilson; there was also a State preferential primary, in which the popular choice for President was to be binding only on the six delegates-at-large who were to be selected by the State convention itself. Before the voting took place the Progressive Democrats arranged a two-day swing through Ohio by William Jennings Bryan. To their satisfaction the "Great Commoner" flayed Harmon as the prince of reactionaries, the friend of Wall Street, and an anachronism from the Stone Age. In spite of these efforts Harmon won by a nose in the Ohio preferential primary—in round figures, 100,000 for Harmon, 89,000 for Wilson, 2,500 for Champ Clark (a leading candidate who was Speaker of the House of Representatives), and 2,500 for

Bryan. By his victory Harmon gained the six delegates-at-large. But Wilson won nineteen of the forty-two district delegates, and the total result was a disappointing and dubious plurality for Ohio's favorite son.

In Cuyahoga County where Baker was in control, the three Congressional districts had chosen six Wilson delegates including Baker himself. Subsequently at the Ohio Democratic Convention at Toledo Baker tried to break the traditional rule, which had been in effect for more than sixty years, requiring the State delegation to vote as a unit for Harmon because he had won a slight majority of all the delegates. Baker took the fight to the floor, asking the Ohio Convention if it wanted to send Roman delegates to Baltimore who were "chained to Harmon's chariot wheels." The Convention did, by an action which the *Cleveland Plain Dealer* called undemocratic and un-American. The Convention endorsed the unit rule in favor of Harmon by the decisive vote of 597 to 395. Baker took the defeat philosophically, commenting that the decision was similar to the ruling by a circuit court. The real fight would come before the "Supreme Court" at Baltimore.[1]

At the National Democratic Convention the controversy was resumed when the Committee on Rules decreed that the nineteen Wilson delegates from Ohio must vote for Harmon under the unit rule. The majority argued that traditional Democratic practice should not be altered, and stated that Baker was supported by a local machine as perfect as Tammany. The minority report against the unit rule was presented by Robert L. Henry of Texas, but Baker was its foremost champion. In an impassioned appeal on the convention floor Baker stated that the Ohio Convention could bind only the delegates-at-large; it had no authority or right to dictate to the district delegates of whom he was one:

When the legislature of the State of Ohio, at the insistent

demand of those in that State who believed then and believe now that the mission of Democracy is to restore to the people the powers of government, took away from State conventions the power to select and give authority to district delegates . . . then the reason for that old unit rule was gone, and of course it ought not to be applied after the reason for it ceased. . . .

I shall not mention the name of any candidate for President. I do not want to appeal to any prejudice here, either favorable or unfavorable. I want to argue this case to you as a lawyer and win it on my rights. In Ohio I ran for district delegate in the Twenty-first Congressional District. I live in a great city that is set like a gem on the southern shore of Lake Erie. I said to my people, "If I am elected a delegate I will vote in the National Convention for whatever presidential candidates you in this district shall prefer by your majority." They believed me. They knew I would do as I promised if I were permitted so to do, and my case here as a representative of those people is to ask you to allow me to fulfill my pledge, and to keep me from being prevented from fulfilling it. . . .

My point is this: I ran in a district where I received 7,000 votes. Later a convention was held in the State, that convention being attended by 900 people. My authority and my instructions are from the 7,000 and not from the 900. . . .

I gave my solemn promise to the people in my district that I would vote as they voted. . . . The pledge of a Democrat made when he is a candidate for office ought to be inviolate, and every Democrate ought to rally to the support of a man who wants to carry out his pledge. . . . Ohio as a sovereign state speaks through her statute book, and not by a scant majority of a convention called for another purpose.

Shortly after Baker's speech, impartial or not, wild demonstrations for Wilson erupted on the floor, led by delegates from New Jersey, Virginia, and Mississippi. A band struck up "The Star-Spangled Banner" and Virginia delegates from Wilson's home town of Staunton tried to scale the platform. One of them reached the press stand, tramped on telegraph keys and the heads of newspapermen, was finally seized by an offended reporter and thrown back into the crowd on the convention floor. A half-hour passed before the temporary chairman was able to restore order.

By this time the fight against the unit rule had been won through what James M. Cox, later a Democratic candidate for President, called one of the greatest efforts of Baker's career. Although at the moment Wilson did not have a majority, Baker's plea won over some anti-Wilson delegates who were moved more by their conception of broad democratic principles than by presidential preference. By a vote of 595½ to 492½ the Convention upheld the minority report, in spite of the opposition of a 148-vote bloc controlled by William Randolph Hearst and "Boss" Charles Francis Murphy from New York. This important victory not only checked the growing belief that Speaker of the House Champ Clark was certain to be nominated, it also added nineteen important votes for Wilson and gave a decided impetus to the drive toward his ultimate nomination. One of the interesting subsidiary features of this episode was that a few Clark men voted with Baker against the unit rule. At the time this seemed to be good strategy against Harmon, but it turned out the other way. Harmon was justifiably peeved; later when Clark had a majority (but not the required two-thirds for the nomination) and begged support from Harmon, the Ohio Governor, still miffed, refused it. Some commentators believed that this development, which was an indirect result of Baker's speech, clinched the nomination for Wilson.[2]

One result of Baker's *chef-d'oeuvre* at the National Convention was that a number of delegates, including William Jennings Bryan, tried to interest him in the vice-presidential nomination. Baker told them he was not available; he enjoyed being Mayor of Cleveland but said it would be impossible for him to spend four years in a job where "the propriety forbids one speaking his mind." During the fall campaign he played an active role not only in Ohio but in

Iowa and Wisconsin as well, where he made a number of
speeches for the Democratic National Committee. Of the two
Republican candidates in 1912 Baker was more indignant
about Bull-Mooser Theodore Roosevelt than the regular Republican William Howard Taft. Years before he had classified
Roosevelt's appropriation of the Panama Canal Zone as
"reckless immorality." In 1912 he stated that Socialist Eugene

Talking About Fly Swatters, What's the Matter With Newton D.?

The fight against the unit rule, from the Cleveland News *of
June 27, 1912. As Mayor, Baker also waged war on houseflies.*

Debs was to be preferred over the Rough Rider, and that on
election day he would have stayed at home or moved out
of the country had TR been the only candidate. When
Wilson was elected he considered Baker seriously for the post
of private secretary (which Joseph Tumulty was to fill), and
in 1913 offered him a Cabinet post as Secretary of the Interior.
Both men were scholars in politics, able lawyers, and brilliant
orators. Wilson had not forgotten the support at Baltimore
from the progressive Mayor of Cleveland, asked him to come
East for a conference, and offered the Cabinet position. Years
later Colonel Edward M. House, the close adviser of the
President, was to say in his *Intimate Papers* that Baker refused the offer with the statement that he had more important things to do: he was the only person who could save
the city of Cleveland from disaster. Baker had little affection
for House and observed privately that he had "long ago
reached the judgment that all keepers of diaries ought to
be locked up and all publishers of diaries hanged." The truth
was that he had declined the Cabinet appointment because
he had recently been elected mayor after a heated campaign
and was definitely charged with the responsibility of erecting
a municipal light plant.[3]

Baker first became a national figure in 1912 through his
forensic virtuosity at Baltimore; in time he was to achieve
such renown as an orator that his addresses were front-page
copy in major newspapers, were often quoted extensively in
The New York Times, and for weeks thereafter were dis-
cussed with appropriate solemnity on the editorial pages of
both newspapers and magazines. This talent for swaying the
multitudes by the spoken word was as much a political asset
as that of Mark Hanna—an early contemporary of Baker's in
Cleveland—who had arisen to prominence through business
rather than forensic ability. As mayor of Cleveland, Baker
had enjoyed ample opportunity for practice on the platform;

on leaving City Hall in 1916 he estimated that he had delivered something more than two thousand speeches (plus
the conduction of weddings and funerals in his official capacity) during his four-year tenure, and he was to observe
that the most significant aspect of the mayor's office was "its
preaching function." Political opponents recognized his effectiveness and claimed that Baker neglected more important
duties by spending too much time as municipal minister
before the local political parish. They charged that he was
booked for seven evening performances, and seven matinees,
every week.

Baker's rhetorical distinction was achieved in spite of the
paradox that he was neither a politician's nor an orator's
orator. He had little confidence in the effectiveness of political speeches, agreeing with John W. Davis (the Democratic presidential nominee in 1924) that they were a success
if *no* votes were lost. In technique he belonged to the new
school of speakers who avoided the sound, fury, and flap-
doodle of the traditional Boanerges with frock coat, long
hair, and black string tie. In reply to letters from budding
orators and professors of speech, who inquired about the se-
crets of his technique, Baker always answered that he had
none. Gestures were limited to the occasional use of an
uplifted forefinger or the unconscious removal of his spec-
tacles. His speech was delivered in conversational tone; there
was no attempt to make the welkin ring, and his voice was
never raised in protest or command.

The only book on oratory that ever impressed him was a
little one by John Peter Altgeld, the famous "Eagle Forgotten" of American politics who had been a progressive
Governor of Illinois during the 1890s. The brief volume
was so good that Baker recommended it as an indispensable
guide for both oratory and writing. Altgeld's emphasis on
simplicity, clarity, and candor insured the avoidance of either
fine writing or high-flown rhetoric, both of which stressed

fancy ornamentation at the expense of authentic feeling and sincerity. Baker's practice was to speak frankly and clearly about issues on which he had both conviction and belief; the only "secret" he had discovered was that very simple speech, if deeply felt, made at least as good an impression as formal oratory. He added but one rule to the basic regulations Altgeld had laid down—to stop speaking the instant "you have said all that is worth while to say."

Because of the importance of candor and conviction in public address Baker spoke extemporaneously, would not appear where admission was charged, and accepted no honoraria (except during the economic depression of the 1930s when he gave deficit-ridden Cleveland College fees from a few lectures). The absence of an economic motive gave him a sense of freedom about his public speaking that would have been difficult to achieve if he had been paid for his efforts. Baker did not write his speeches in advance because he found that such addresses never pleased anyone except himself (on two occasions newspapers insisted on an advance draft which was reluctantly given, but Baker purposely left his copy in the office lest he be encumbered by a set speech). Notes made him both unhappy and ineffective; for that reason he stipulated in advance that he would not speak if he was obliged to bring a manuscript. All he needed was one or two "robust" ideas which he would sometimes organize en route to the lecture hall or during the introduction. There was such fine co-operation between mind and tongue that the rest was reasonably easy, as Baker described it to a perplexed professor of speech at Heidelberg College:

> I always speak extemporaneously, without outlines or notes, have never even thought about gestures and I can not remember that I have ever deliberately decided how a speech should be concluded let alone write out and memorize a conclusion. So far as I am conscious of preparation, it consists in thinking to myself as consecutively as I can about the subject upon which

I am going to speak. Then when I get up I look the audience over and try to make them share my feeling that I am there for the purpose of discussing seriously a serious problem. Then I discuss it and stop.[4]

In the 1930s Baker became a director of the Radio Corporation of America, an ironical obligation because of his own dislike of speaking over the air waves. His aversion to radio was based on two factors: he could not see the audience, and the meticulous time schedule sometimes necessitated speeches written in advance. Younger men might have the imagination to construct a vast unseen audience, but Baker could not conjure the illusion and preferred the intimacy of looking an audience in the face. Every time he confronted a microphone he was reminded of the unhappy occasion when he spoke in complete darkness to a country audience and could not distinguish the dim outline of a single human form. Written speeches bored him beyond expression; the formal statement of his ideas in print transformed them into "old thoughts" lacking in the spontaneity and effervescence which they seemed to have when he spoke extemporaneously. But extemporaneous speeches, no matter how pleasing to the ear, were difficult to record and Baker frequently claimed misquotation, but found himself in the unenviable position of having no manuscript to prove exactly what he had said. Because of the "gattling-gun" rapidity of his delivery reporters usually caught some of the words on the fly but dropped a great many during the forensic game. Even when the addresses were transcribed verbatim it was difficult, as Secretary Ralph Hayes found to his sorrow, to persuade Baker to edit them for publication. It was only at the insistence of his close friend Justice John Hessin Clarke that he finally corrected the press account of the famous speech (which many thought the most dramatic he ever delivered) at the Democratic Convention in 1924; this procrastination Hayes found so sinful and exasperating that he hoped God would punish Baker appropriately for it. The point was that speaking was much easier for Baker than writing; by his own admission it was less bother to make half a dozen speeches than to write one magazine page for formal publication. In early life he had once decided to write a novel, selected two characters, and planned to have them under a tree saying wonderful things to each other. He admitted sadly that he got them as far as the tree and "then couldn't for the life of me make them say a word."

Because of the unstudied eloquence with which Baker moved most of his audience, there were those who referred to him as a "voice and a brain." Antagonists such as Jack Raper, the caustic columnist of the *Cleveland Press,* thought he soft-voiced himself into prominence by using all the stops on his vocal organ. Although Baker believed readiness in the choice of words was in part inherited, he knew that his artistry with language was largely due to extensive reading of the best writers of both prose and poetry. There was no necessity to resort to the "this-reminds-me" gambit, followed by a story about Pat and Mike. Baker's allusions were literary, spontaneous, and effective. As he recalled a trip to England:

> I went about the country feeling that there was the place where my language had been made; the hills and valleys and lakes and rivers were imbedded in the very speech I spoke. It seemed to me as dusk settled on the forests of England that Spenser's Faerie Queene and all her company were in those woods. At Stratford-on-Avon, I thought of the life and traditions that surround the man who had given my language so fixed a literary form that subsequent ages have not changed it. I thought of the contests between cavalier and roundhead, and being a lawyer, I sought out the court houses in which the great cases have been tried; the hall in which the impeachment of Warren Hastings took place; the place where the case of the Seven Bishops was tried; the place where Pym and Hampden stirred up England with their protest against "ship money,"

and set the example that later in Boston led to the breach between the American colonies and the mother country. All of it gave me a sense that the history of my race was floating to me in the breezes that blew over England; it was a thrilling experience.

In spite of the frequency of his speeches and the facility of his delivery, Baker suffered from the same fears and worries that plague less professional orators. He admitted that he never began a speech without a momentary feeling of stage fright, and during the introduction he always wondered how he could keep going for more than two or three minutes. He noted ruefully that he was always confident that he could speak for half an hour when a scheduled address was six months away, was disturbed over the idea of speaking more than fifteen minutes within three months of the address, and was extremely doubtful whether he could talk longer than one minute when he went on stage. He found these attacks of stage fright temporary in duration, and after they had passed, the flow of words was so abundant that the chief problem was the provision of terminal facilities.[5]

V. Secretary of War

O N NEW YEAR'S DAY, 1916, Baker left municipal service, in which he had been engaged for the past fifteen years, to resume the private practice of law. He formed the new firm of Baker, Hostetler and Sidlo, with which he was to be associated until his death. During the first five years of its existence, however, his services to the partnership were brief indeed; two months after its organization Baker was appointed Secretary of War, as successor to Lindley M. Garrison. In 1913 Garrison's appointment had been a curious one. The post had first been offered to A. Mitchell Palmer, who as Attorney General was to be associated with the famous "Red Scare" of 1920–21. Palmer was a Quaker, and declined the position. By this time three days remained before the inauguration, and Wilson asked his private secretary, Joseph Tumulty, to suggest somebody. Tumulty thumbed through the Lawyers' Directory and came across the name of Garrison, whom he knew casually as a resident of his home town and as a vice-chancellor of the State of New Jersey. Garrison was summoned to the White House and to his surprise, as Secretary of the Treasury William Gibbs McAdoo recalled the incident, "a place in the Cabinet descended upon him like manna from heaven. He walked in as Lindley M. Garrison, a little-known but worthy citizen, and he walked out as Secretary of War Garrison, with the bugles blowing and the flags waving, and the guns throbbing."

Garrison was sincere and able; he was also impatient, individualistic, and tactless. He once told Secretary of the Navy Josephus Daniels, his colleague in the Cabinet, "I am glad if anybody can convince me that I am wrong, but I am damn sure that nobody lives who can do it." This included Congress and the President of the United States, who disagreed with Garrison on the kind of army the country should develop as a neutral in the world war then going on. Garrison favored a large national army, while Congressman James Hay (Chairman of the House Military Affairs Committee) placed his reliance on the States and their National Guard. Garrison also endorsed compulsory military training, which had no support from Democrat Wilson but was being advocated up and down the country by Republicans Theodore Roosevelt and General Leonard Wood. It was just as inevitable that Garrison would ultimately part company with President Wilson as it was that Bryan would leave the Cabinet; the latter was too pacific, the former too belligerent. Garrison attempted to resign four times before Wilson accepted his retirement. The enemies of the President immediately proclaimed that the departing Secretary was a much-abused official, and girded themselves for the fight against his successor. Baker was to fall into a political hornet's nest.[1]

Garrison's resignation was submitted on February 10, 1916. On a Saturday evening in early March Baker and his wife were on the point of leaving their house for a party when the manager of Western Union rushed up and announced that he had an important message. As Baker told it:

> I was handed a wireless message . . . signed by President Wilson, "Will you come to Washington and accept the office of Secretary of War?" I had never played even with tin soldiers. I telegraphed him that I would come to Washington the next day and gave him what I regarded as conclusive reasons why I should not be Secretary of War. I came to Washington, went in to see the President, and gave him what it would seem to me were perfectly adequate reasons, and when I finished my explanation, to which he listened with great patience, he said, "Are you ready to be sworn in?" I then learned my first lesson in a soldier's duty and said I would do whatever I was bid to do.

To *The New York Times* the reasons for Baker's appointment seemed obvious. He had been a leading Wilson supporter in the Ohio Democratic Convention in 1912 and was now free from the civic responsibilities that had caused him to decline a Cabinet position in 1913. Furthermore an experienced lawyer was useful in the War Department because of the frequent legal questions arising from negotiation of contracts, and with a political campaign in the offing the Party would be strengthened by the selection of a prominent Democrat from the Midwest. (Secretary of Agriculture David Houston of Missouri was the only Cabinet representative from this region, and he had gone to Missouri late in life after a long career in the South.) At forty-four Baker was easily the youngest member of Wilson's Cabinet, but it was his intention to stay in Washington for one year only, until the end of Wilson's first term in March 1917. He told his friend Judge Clarke that associations in Cleveland meant more to him than national politics; he believed firmly that the "problems of democracy have to be worked out in experiment stations rather than by universal applications, so that I regard Cleveland and Ohio as a more hopeful place to do things than any national station anywhere." He was destined to stay in the national station for five years and to become involved in many universal applications.

It was assumed by all who were friendly to Garrison's belligerent policy, as well as those angered by Wilson's neutralism, that Baker had been appointed for political reasons. They were certain that Wilson was thinking less of the army than of the forthcoming campaign of 1916, in which he needed Baker both as a popular citizen of a large and doubtful State and as a pacifist who could flaunt the Wilsonian banner with its inscription, "He kept us out of war." Baker was therefore open to attack from a number of directions; in the beginning he was charged with puny unpreparedness, at the end of the war with mismanagement and extravagance on a colossal scale. His most abusive critic was George Brinton McClellan Harvey, editor of the *North American Review* and of *Harper's Weekly*, who had the worst case of Bakerphobia. Harvey had helped initially in putting Wilson on the political road but later broke with him. A decade later Wilson would confess he had "forgotten that God ever made so great a fool as Harvey," and would "doubt if even He could have made a greater." Harvey was to use his magazines as springboards for aggressive attacks on everybody and everything connected with Wilson's administrations, and was to close his political career as ambassador to Great Britain for Republican Warren Gamaliel Harding.[2]

The first attack was on Baker's physical appearance. Many thought subconsciously that the man in charge of the War Department should be of impressive stature, with a grizzled head and a fee-faw-fum voice—a cross between General Phil Sheridan and the gigantic boxer Jess Willard. Baker was to say later that if he had possessed Goliath's build, complete with whiskers and a gruff manner, his job would have been a lot easier. As it was he was always conscious of his inability to look the part, and he had to accustom himself to being mistaken for the office boy. He was the particular target of George Harvey, who derived pleasure in calling him the "nobby little Secretary of War."

The next assault was on Baker as a pacifist whose nearest approach to any kind of military experience had been his rejection as a volunteer, because of defective eyesight, in the Spanish-American War. Harvey hammered away at the "chattering ex-Pacifist" who as Secretary of War enunciated "piddling, pacifist piffle" and mouthed smug platitudes to the effect that everything was for the best in this best of all possible worlds. After the United States entered World War I, Harvey resorted to puns: he said we needed "a butcher, not a baker," and he observed that transposition of the letters in BAKER could result in BRAKE, which was what the "pacifist Secretary of War" had been from the beginning of the conflict. By March 1918, Harvey was commenting on a strange anomaly: "murder, rapine and sudden death, horror piled on horror, the world burnishing its armor, while a lamb-like little gentleman, serene in his certitude of the triumph of morality, sat like a monk in his cell, unvexed by gross passions, ruminating on the Golden Rule."

Prior to the outbreak of World War I Baker, as a so-called pacifist, had been in most respectable company. At the turn of the century Czar Nicholas II had called a conference to establish a court of international arbitration, and Alfred Nobel, the dynamite king, had established an annual peace prize of 150,000 kronor for the "person who shall have done most to promote the fraternity of nations and the abolition of standing armies and the formation . . . of peace congresses." In 1906 the belligerent Rough Rider, Theodore Roosevelt, actually won the Nobel award for his work in bringing the Russo-Japanese War to a close. In 1910 a brilliant Englishman, Norman Angell, attacked motivations for war in a prominent book titled *The Great Illusion,* arguing that the victor as well as the vanquished lost by armed conflict. In the same year the Endowment for International Peace was established by the former steel king, Andrew Carnegie. Peace societies flourished; on the eve of World War I pacifism in the United States was both respectable and triumphant. Young intellectuals seemed to be uncertain on one point only; i.e., how many years would go by before war became extinct.

In 1915 Mayor Baker joined the American social worker Jane Addams in the endorsement of an antiwar film *Lay Down Your Arms* which was being shown in Cleveland and other cities. It was an indictment of modern warfare (including the conflict then raging in Europe) and was based on a novel with the same title written by the Austrian Baroness Bertha von Suttner, one of the early winners of the Nobel peace prize. In the same year at Philadelphia's Independence Hall, Baker participated in the first meeting of the League to Enforce Peace, which elected the eminently respectable William Howard Taft as president and the dignified president of Harvard, A. Lawrence Lowell, as chairman of its resolutions committee. The philosophical left wing of the pacifist movement, which considered itself as the only legitimate branch of the peace operation, would have no part of the new organization because its very name contained a seeming paradox—it was for peace even if a fight was necessary to achieve it. As a voracious reader and a man of good will Baker had joined forces with Nicholas II, Nobel, Carnegie, and Taft; as a pragmatist he was no more a theoretical pacifist than they. He was frank enough to admit that he had been in sympathy with all peace societies, and that he had been a member of several of them. He was courageous in telling the Reserve Officers Association in 1916:

> I am a pacifist. I am a pacifist in my hope; I am a pacifist in my prayers; I am a pacifist in my belief that God made man for better things than that a civilization should always be under the blight of this increasingly deadly destruction which war leaves us.

But he never believed in nonresistance as an aid to peace, and he established his speculative beachhead on the very day he took office as Secretary of War: "I believe in peace and in the proper enforcement of the laws of peace—by force if necessary."

After our entry into World War I Baker, in spite of his reputation as the pacifist Secretary of War, was about as peaceful as Nobel or Carnegie probably would have been— or Woodrow Wilson was—under the prevailing circumstances. In the summer of 1916 Baker said that he was for peace at *almost* any price, but at the moment was not willing to make up his mind as to the meaning of "almost"; his decision would be determined by circumstances. "I do not think world peace will come," he said, "through passive resistance on the part of any one nation, but I think a really great nation can afford to wait a long while and give a great many benefits of doubts before going to war." When the United States entered the conflict he said that as much as he hated war and deplored the taking of human life, he had been sadly convinced that there was "nothing left to do . . . but provide men and means to kill Germans, just as the Germans were trying to kill us. . . . Of course, President Wilson's statement of 'force to the uttermost' embodied the same thought." In the 1930s he wrote to journalist Roy Howard that although he had always been a pacifist he had "nevertheless constantly felt the necessity of having a power rifle behind the kitchen door," and he could think of nothing "more fatuous than the kind of pacifism which thinks great objects attainable merely because they are desirable."[3]

At the very moment the pacific Baker became Secretary of War he was compelled to grasp the power rifle behind the kitchen door. He had just been sworn in and was receiving the congratulations of officers and staff members of the War Department when a newspaper reporter rushed in with the startling salutation, "Hell has broken loose in Mexico!" It developed that the bandit Francisco Villa had sacked Columbus, New Mexico, leaving behind seventeen slain Americans. Baker recalled later that he had a vague notion that Mexico was south of the Rio Grande River and remembered that the area had been yellow on the map in his school geography, but he had never visited the country and had no inkling as to the cause of the trouble in that direction. He soon learned that every town along the international border was panic-stricken and that Senator Fall of New Mexico, always the representative of oil interests, was demanding the complete occupation of Mexico by half a million American soldiers. Occupation never occurred but fifteen thousand cavalry under General John J. Pershing were sent across the Rio Grande in hot pursuit of Villa, with orders to capture him dead or alive. The unrepentant bandit was never found in his mountain refuge and the Mexican Government was most unhappy about the American invasion. As our entry into the First World War became imminent American forces were finally withdrawn from Mexico in February 1917.

In Baker's opinion, however, the Pershing expedition had several happy results. The presence of his force south of the border was a brilliant success in stopping additional raids across the Rio Grande. American troops had a quieting and reassuring effect in the Southwest; the American expedition hung like a pendulum into Mexico, ready to close behind any bandit making trouble to the north. Baker thought the American "pendulum" was the most effective regulator of border trouble that could have been devised, short of occupation of Mexico. In addition, the Mexican exercise provided valuable training for the National Guard, numbering 150,000, which was stationed in Texas during the crisis. This had the indirect effect of preparing it for overseas duty a year later—according to Baker "about the only preparation which I felt we could make without adopting a provocative attitude at a time when President Wilson's policy and hope was that we would be able to keep out of a European war." The result was that the National Guard, as a relatively large and trained force, was to become an important element in the dispatch of troops to Europe in 1917.[4]

Along with the Mexican affair Baker was also cast in an exasperating role during another campaign in 1916, the presidential contest which resulted in re-election for Woodrow Wilson. He was not a delegate to the Democratic National Convention at St. Louis, but he carried there a platform entrusted to his care by the President. With the Mexican imbroglio on his mind he denied that he had any role in the proceedings except for his service as messenger; in later years he could not recall that he did any "political thinking" at the time. His name was mentioned as a candidate for Vice-President and as chairman of the Democratic National Committee, but nothing came of the rumors.

In the fall of the year Baker made several speeches for Wilson, including one in Jersey City that created a Republican tornado of abuse against him and the Democratic Party. Baker always spoke extemporaneously, there were few stenographers who could cope with his rapid diction at 225 words a minute, and without a definitive manuscript misquotation was easy. At Jersey City Baker was defending the Wilson policy in Mexico, and according to the stenographic report of the arch-Republican *New York Tribune* compared the Mexican rebels with George Washington and his band of patriots:

Why are we impatient at the Mexicans? We say they do not respect the lives and property of our people. Perhaps they don't. We say they do not pay their honest debts. They don't. We say they are a ragamuffin lot. We say their money is not any good. That's true. . . . We say they do not respect church property. That, also, is true.

The amazing thing is that people never respect these things in a revolution. We had a revolution, and from the beginning to the end of that revolution the conditions in this country were so like Mexico that it is perfectly astounding to read.

Washington's soldiers on the march to Valley Forge stole everything they could lay their hands on. They stole the silver vessels from the churches and melted them up to buy things to drink. They drove ministers of the Gospel and preachers of churches out of their churches and out of the country. The money of the Confederation was so worthless that when they tried to make the merchants take it the latter hid their provisions in their cellars.

The President of the United States is in favor of letting the 14,000,000 people in Mexico, who have not had an opportunity to do so, fight out their independence the way we fought ours. Whenever you hear anybody say they cannot understand the President's Mexican policy, tell them to go and read the Declaration of Independence and the Golden Rule.

Republicans joined with patriots in characterizing Baker's alleged remarks as "preposterous," "grotesque," and "slanderous." The Daughters of the American Revolution demanded his resignation on the ground that a man so ignorant of history and so lacking in ideals was not fit to be Secretary of War. The Republican presidential candidate, Charles Evans Hughes, said, in what was described as a "hushed voice," that he had never supposed the day would come when a Cabinet member would say such things about the patriots who gave us our liberty. Theodore Roosevelt called it desecration to compare the men of Valley Forge with the "band of bloodthirsty bandits who ravaged Mexico and whom the President has been . . . supporting in their murders and outrages for the last three and a half years in Mexico." The *New York American* was indignant:

Washington and Carranza! Jefferson and Villa! Franklin and

Zapata! An American Secretary of War to link those names together! God save the mark!

Why, man, you are indecent. You insult the dead! And that
is the very nadir and abyss of indecency.

You should resign, Mr. Baker. The President should demand
your resignation, sir![5]

The Secretary of War did submit his resignation but Wilson refused to accept it. Baker answered his critics by stating
that he had been misquoted, both directly and out of context:

I said we complain of Mexico that property rights are not
always respected, and that among us to some extent that was
no doubt true, as the so-called loyalists who adhered to the
cause of King George, even the ministers of the churches, were
driven out and their property devoted to the revolution. I said
it is complained that in the present state of affairs Mexico cannot pay her debts, and said nor could we until after the establishment of a stable government. In 1789 we inaugurated a
proper financial system.

With these premises I urged that a people who had won
freedom through marvelous courage and steadfastness in the
face of every peril, difficulty and discouragement should have
sympathy with any other people struggling for freedom, and
should apply the Golden Rule to Mexico while she sought to
apply a principle of our own Declaration of Independence. . . .

I did not compare Washington's soldiers to Villa or to any
Mexican bandits whatever. I did not say that Washington's
soldiers stole anything or that they stole silver out of churches
to buy drink . . .

I did not refer to Washington's soldiers as "bad characters"
or compare them with Mexicans in any particular, but on the
contrary I referred to them as different in training, race, and
ideals from the Mexican people.

There is no reason to believe that Baker's speech at Jersey
City, in spite of the clamor it raised, had any influence on
the spirited election of 1916—a contest so close that it reminded Brand Whitlock of Democrat Tom Kidd in 1876

who celebrated Tilden's election in the orthodox democratic

manner of those antiprohibition days, coming to himself six
weeks later to learn that Hayes had been elected. He therefore
renewed his spree with other emotions emerging some weeks
after with an ailment that the doctors diagnosed as whisky
paralysis.

In 1916 Baker's embarrassment appears to have been regarded
by the public as nothing more than the usual political in-
fighting just before the voting took place. In mid-November
Wilson was accepting Baker's congratulations with the observation that he rejoiced in the opportunity for four more
years of association. A year later Baker was particularly grat-
ified about his election as an honorary member of the military
Order of the Cincinnati (although he had no hereditary
claim inasmuch as none of his ancestors had been officers in
the American Revolution) because of the excitement over the
speech at Jersey City. He thought this honor ought to "set at
rest any doubts there are on that subject." His judgment was
fortified by the fact that the only other honorary members
were President Wilson and the Marquis de Lafayette.[6]

"He kept us out of war" was the Democratic slogan in 1916,
and it contributed materially to Wilson's slight margin of
victory in November, coming as it did to a country which
was not yet convinced that we should enter the European
conflict. Five months later we were very much in the war.
It was alleged in later years (particularly in the legislative
investigating committee headed by Senator Gerald P. Nye in
the 1930s) that Wilson had been insincere in his campaign,
and had been unduly influenced not only by economic pressure from "merchant-of-death" bankers and munitions makers
but by the propaganda of pro-British diplomats abroad, particularly from the American Ambassador in London, Walter
Hines Page.

Throughout his life Baker was consistent in denying all
of these allegations. He insisted that the slogan "He kept us

out of war" got into the platform by accident; it was not found in the recommended document that Baker had taken to St. Louis on behalf of the President. Baker was never able to ascertain just which member of the Resolutions Committee inserted the slogan into the final draft of the platform, but he was sure that the President never liked the phrase even though it drew applause and made the Democratic Party popular with the electorate. It was known that Wilson had said to Secretary of the Navy Josephus Daniels:

> I can't keep the country out of war. They talk of me as if I were a god. Any little German lieutenant can put us into the war at any time by some calculated outrage.

As proof of Wilson's insincerity there was much discussion later about a famous "Sunrise Conference" in April 1916, between the President and certain Democratic leaders: Speaker Champ Clark, Majority Floor Leader Claude Kitchin, and Representative Harry Flood who was Chairman of the House Committee on Foreign Affairs. Months before Wilson ran for re-election on a pacific and isolationist slogan it was claimed that he had summoned these leaders at an early-morning hour in order to avoid newspapermen, and that "he had banged the table and demanded that we go to war with Germany at once." The shocked and indignant congressmen were reported to have told Wilson that they would block any war resolution. In subsequent months, during the presidential campaign, the country rang with the slogan "He kept us out of war"; it was said that the Kitchin-Clark-Flood triumvirate paraphrased the statement to read, "We kept *him* out of war."

Baker said the story was silly nonsense; in his judgment it rested on nothing more than vague gossip about three people, all of whom were dead by the time the story was widely circulated:

> This story is supposed to rest upon some observations in letters by Mrs. Champ Clark and some entries of conversations

in a diary by Claude Kitchin. Curiously enough, there is no
record of any letter or conversation by Hal Flood on the subject. He was the one perfectly balanced and rational person in
the whole group. But Champ Clark and Mrs. Clark were a bit
beside themselves and Kitchin was a passionate, misunderstanding kind of man. It just happens that I went to Washington to
be Secretary of War early in March 1916. If President Wilson
had been in any such state of mind at that time, he would have
told me to begin to get ready and both he and Lansing would
have told me that war with Germany was inescapable. On the
contrary, both of them told me that there was not going to be
any war so far as the United States was concerned. This the
President told me repeatedly beginning in April and running
throughout the year 1916. I think nothing is more demonstrable
than that the President did not give up his hope of bringing a
"Peace Without Victory" settlement of the World War until
January 1917. As a matter of fact, he was very busy about this
subject in January 1917. Bernstorff [the German Ambassador
in Washington] was cooperating with him and both the President and Bernstorff believed that he would have succeeded but
for the precipitate action of the German Government in renew-
ing unrestricted submarine warfare.[7]

Baker felt the same way about the charge that Walter
Hines Page had had a great, perhaps a predominant, influence on Wilson and his decision to go to war. It was
claimed that Page, as American Ambassador in London, was
so much an Anglophile that instead of representing the
United States in England he really represented the British
cause in Washington. In later years much publicity was given
to a cable from Page to Wilson, sent on March 5, 1917, a
bare month before the United States entered the war:

> The pressure of the approaching financial crisis has gone
> beyond the ability of the Morgan financial agency. . . . It is
> not improbable that the only way of maintaining our present
> trade position and averting a panic is by declaring war on
> Germany.

Many interpreted this cable to mean that Page was callous

enough to discount the casualties in the war in favor of a continuing economic boom; i.e., jobs for American munitions workers, farmers, and Democrats.

Baker said flatly that there was no truth in this charge. He admitted that Page, House, and, later, Lansing were pro-British and that House might have had some influence on Wilson. In his judgment Page had none. On the contrary, he agreed with Josephus Daniels that Wilson was

> so incensed at Page's partisanship with Great Britain that any recommendation of Page's irritated rather than convinced him. This irritation was all the greater because of his long friendship for Page and real affection for him. He felt, and had good grounds for thinking so, that Page . . . did not represent the United States in England but represented the British Government and took his cue from it.

Baker acknowledged that economic pressure in the United States created an atmosphere in favor of our participation in World War I, and he prophesied that economic tensions would have the same influence in future emergencies. He denied vehemently that any *particular* economic interest, such as that of bankers or munitions makers, had any influence on Wilson or his Cabinet. He claimed that if any one economic group worried the Government, it was probably the cotton farmers (who had lost their European markets) more than the munitions makers. He was certain that J. P. Morgan and the Bethlehem Steel Corporation had not the slightest influence on Wilson's thinking; as for the Cabinet he had heard no discussion about bankers, and if they had exercised pressure for entry into the war Baker concluded that his "Cabinet associates conspired to keep me in ignorance of the plan." In 1934 he wrote a letter of reminiscence to his former private secretary Ralph Hayes, and said that he

> was in and out of the White House for five years and do not recall that I ever saw a banker there or heard of one having been there, and I think you will bear me out that so far as the

War Department was concerned neither of us would have known where to borrow $500.00 during any of the five year period we were together in the War Department, which I think will show that neither international nor national bankers were on our calling list.

Historians are still debating the influence of economic factors as a cause for American entry into World War I, and the problem is not solved by Baker's adroit distinction between general economic pressure—which he admits was present —and particular economic interests—which he claims had no influence. His essential thesis was that we actually entered the war for idealistic rather than materialistic reasons. A group of "revisionist" historians disagreed with this interpretation and in the antiwar climate of the 1930s Baker's point of view was criticized severely. Historian Harry Elmer Barnes was quoted as saying that Wilson "lied like a gentleman" about his ignorance of the secret treaties among Allied nations, and that the President knew this country would intervene when he campaigned on the antiwar slogan in 1916. The *New Republic* commented disdainfully about Baker's naïveté in interpreting the economic argument in "anthropomorphic terms."

Baker disposed of Barnes by saying that the historian was basing an assumption on what was on the inside of Wilson's mind. On this issue, he added:

> I am in no better position to contradict than Mr. Barnes was to affirm. As a matter of fact, I do not know what was in Mr. Wilson's mind on either subject. I only know what he said, and nothing that he ever said bears out the statement of Mr. Barnes.

The interpretative divergence was particularly apparent in Baker's varying reactions to two books by journalist Walter Millis, for whose father, a colonel in the Corps of Engineers, he had the highest regard. When Millis's *The Martial Spirit* (1931) poked good-natured fun at the comic opera Spanish-American War, Baker thought it was a brilliant presentation of the thesis that propaganda (in Hearst and Pulitzer news-papers) and the weakness of President McKinley were more important than the idealistic reason (freedom for Cuba) for going to war in 1898. In 1935 Millis published his best-seller on World War I, the mildly isolationist *Road to War;* its emphasis was on British propaganda and economic motiva-tion rather than such moral issues as freedom of the seas and making the world safe for democracy. The second book made Baker very unhappy. He thought *The Road to War* was a bad book, that Millis could still be trusted on fact but on interpretation had now become a "man from Mars" because of his avoidance of humanitarian and ethical considerations. To him the evidence was clear that American idealism had taken us into the war, and his ultimate conclusion was that Millis had "discarded the obvious as unreasonable and em-braced the unreasonable because it was not obvious."[8]

VI. Secretary of A War—Men

THERE IS TROUBLE enough in the War Department in peacetime; in the midst of armed conflict pandemonium reigns. After the Spanish-American War, according to the irrepressible Mr. Dooley, Secretary of War Russell A. Alger said to Senator Chauncey Depew:

> But, oh, Chanse, don't iver aspire to my job. Be sicrety of war, if ye will; but niver be sicrety of A war!

Despite the pacific assurances heard in the 1916 presidential election the United States was at war with Germany on April 6, 1917. Baker was more than Secretary of War; he was now a full-fledged Secretary of a War. There were many who volunteered prescriptions for certain victory, including the amateur strategists who wanted to send fire engines to France for the allegedly simple operation of flooding the Germans out of the trenches! Actually Baker's efforts were concerned with three major problems: the development of a large army, the selection of a commanding general for the American Ex-

peditionary Forces, and the provision of supplies necessary
for the millions who were to serve in the armed forces.

In the beginning the American people did not dream of
sending a mighty force to Europe. Neither did the Allied
Powers. When General Joffre was in Washington with the
French Commission in May 1917, he spoke optimistically
about an American Army that might, some day, be as great
as 500,000 men. It was thought that Britain, France, and
Russia would furnish the soldiers; the United States would
provide supplies, money, and the protection of the Navy in
convoying materials to the Continent. During 1917 the Russian withdrawal from the war, the horrible British losses in
Flanders, and the open mutinies in the French army destroyed the American hallucination that its soldiers would
not be needed. It was apparent that the Allies not only had
an empty war chest but had reached the bottom of their
manpower barrel as well; in the very month the United States
entered the war General Henri Pétain, the French Commander in Chief, was saying, *"J'attends les Américains et les
tanks."* The idea of a token military force, symbolic of our
economic support, was replaced by the concept of a gigantic
American Expeditionary Force. Before the war was over its
Commanding General, John J. Pershing, was asking for one
hundred and ten divisions—five million men in France supported by three million replacements in the United States.
By the autumn of 1918 at Le Havre Brand Whitlock, the
former Mayor of Toledo who had seen Belgium fall while
American Ambassador in Brussels, was writing Baker as an
old friend:

> All summer long . . . we have watched our boys file by, an
> unending stream of khaki. . . . I have watched them with a
> lift of the heart, with a lump in my throat and with moisture
> in my eyes, and an almost personal affection for each one of
> them. . . . And as I have looked at this strange, everflowing
> stream, I have thought of your hand behind it all, and I have

wished that I might tell you what it meant to me. I had watched other soldiers so long, those Germans in field gray over on the other side of the line, with what sensations you may imagine, with feelings I should not always like to own, surgings of hatred and despair, but now, to see this altogether lovely spectacle— well, it is as though mine eyes had seen the glory of the coming of the Lord!

On the day of the Armistice the United States had more soldiers in France than did Great Britain; in another three months there would have been more Americans in France than there were French soldiers under arms in their own country; and by November 1919, American doughboys would have outnumbered the combined total of their British and French counterparts.[1]

When Baker was a boy his father acquired most of the important books that were published on the Civil War, in which he had served as a Confederate cavalryman. The two read them together, often aloud to each other. The son recalled that the elder man had frequently said that the surprising success of the Southern army was due in substantial part to the free hand given General Lee after an initial effort by Jefferson Davis to interfere with military operations, whereas the meddling of Secretary Stanton and Chief of Staff Halleck had been a serious handicap to Union commanders. More than three decades later Baker was to reflect that the lesson learned as a child was to prove helpful in affairs which neither the boy nor the father could have foreseen. When General Pershing left for Europe the Secretary told him that he would not interfere with his military decisions, nor would he permit military associates in Washington to do so. He therefore gave Pershing two orders: one to go, and one to return. He added: "If you make good, they will forgive any mistake. If you do not make good, they will probably hang us both to the first lamp-post they can find." To avoid this

ornamental denouement Baker knew it was essential to provide an adequate army. To do so, something was necessary
beyond volunteering because there was little glamour or
romance in the European war; it meant instead hardship,
dirt, and death.

Baker gave Leonard Wood credit for the initiation of the
draft of soldiers; from the General's idea a chain reaction
occurred. Wood took the proposal to Chief of Staff Hugh L.
Scott, who passed it on to Baker a month before the actual
declaration of war against Germany. The Secretary of War
gave his assent after studying the history of the draft in the
American Civil War as well as the British volunteer system
in World War I. He concluded that selective service would
not only prevent the disorganization of essential war industries but would avoid the undesirable moral effects of the
British reliance on enlistment only—"where the feeling of
the people was whipped into a frenzy by girls pinning white
feathers on reluctant young men, orators preaching hate of
the Germans, and newspapers exaggerating enemy outrages
to make men enlist out of motives of revenge and retalia-
tion." Baker took the plan to Wilson who said: "Baker,
this is plainly right on any ground. Start to prepare the
necessary legislation so that if I am obliged to go to Congress the bills will be ready for immediate consideration."
The result was that by secret agreement draft machinery was
actually ready long before the country knew that the device
was to take the place of the volunteering method which
Theodore Roosevelt favored. Before the Draft Act was passed
Baker had confidentially briefed governors, sheriffs, and pros-
pective draft board members on the administration of the
measure—and the confidence was kept so well that only one
newspaper learned what was going on. It was Baker, working through Provost Marshal Enoch Crowder and Major
Hugh S. ("Old Ironpants") Johnson, who arranged for a
secret printing by the million of selective service blanks—

again before the Act was passed—until corridors in the Government Printing Office were full and the basement of the Washington Post Office was stacked to the ceiling. General Crowder proposed that Regular Army officers select the draftees in cities and towns throughout the nation; it was Baker who thought of lessening the shock, which conscription always brings to a country, by substituting "Greetings from your neighbors" for the recruiting sergeant, and registration in familiar voting places rather than at military installations.

Even so, the Draft Act encountered rough sledding in its progress through the Congress. Democratic Speaker Champ Clark saw little difference between a conscript and a convict. Democrat Stanley H. Dent, Chairman of the House Military Affairs Committee, declined to introduce the bill. Democratic Floor Leader Claude Kitchin would have no part of the measure. In the judgment of Chief of Staff Scott it was ironic that the draft policy of a Democratic President, aimed at Germany, had to be pushed through the House of Representatives by the ranking minority member of the Military Affairs Committee—a Republican Jew born in Germany! He was Julius Kahn for whom the Chief of Staff thought no honor could be too great. After Kahn's death in 1924 Scott wrote: "May he rest in peace with the eternal gratitude of his adopted country."

In spite of powerful opposition the Draft Act finally passed Congress on May 17, 1917. In early June ten million young men registered by name and number. The day passed without incident in spite of the warning of Senator James A. Reed of Missouri: "Baker, you will have the streets of our American cities running with blood on registration day." On July 20, the first drawing of numbers occurred in the Senate Office Building before a distinguished group of congressmen and high Army officers. Secretary of War Baker, blindfolded, put his hand into a large glass bowl and drew the initial number of those to be called. It was 258. A man in Mississippi wired: "Thanks for drawing 258—that's me." He was the first of 2,800,000 called to the Army through the selective service system.[2]

It was one thing to call men to the colors; it was another to house, feed, and train them. The existing Army posts were wholly inadequate. In a matter of months the War Department built thirty-two camps, each one accommodating fifty thousand men—sixteen were under canvas in the South and sixteen with frame structures in the North. It was a gargantuan task; a typical cantonment in the North had twelve hundred buildings, an electric-sewer-water system, and twenty-five miles of roads. At Camp Taylor in Kentucky a barracks was built in an hour and a half from timber that had been standing in Mississippi forests one week before. The total operation was a construction project comparable in magnitude with the Panama Canal, but in 1917 time was in short supply; in three months the Army spent three-quarters as much as had been expended on the "big Ditch" in ten years.

In later years Josephus Daniels was to claim that World War I was the first in American history in which there was great concern for both the health and morals of our soldiers. It was the first American war in which the death rate from disease was lower than that from battle, due to the provision of trained medical personnel (of the 200,000 officers, 42,000 were physicians), compulsory vaccination, rigorous camp sanitation, and adequate hospital facilities. To the middle of September 1918, there had been fewer than 10,000 deaths from disease in the new army. This enviable record would have been maintained but for a great and unexpected disaster which struck the world with murderous stealth. It was the influenza pandemic of 1918–19. The malady was popularly known as the "Spanish flu" from the alleged locale of its origin. The world-wide total of deaths from "Spanish flu" was around twenty million; in the United States 300,000 succumbed to it. In mid-September 1918, the influenza-pneumonia pandemic swept through every American military camp; during the eight-week blitz attack 25,000 soldiers died from the disease and the death rate (formerly 5 per year per 1,000 men) increased almost fifty times to 4 *per week* per 1,000 men. In spite of this catastrophe the final mortality figure from disease in the American Army during World War I was 15 per 1,000 per year, contrasted with 110 per 1,000 per year in the Mexican War, and 65 in the American Civil War.

Both Secretary of War Baker and Secretary of Navy Daniels devoted much time and effort to the problem of providing reasonably normal and wholesome activities in camp for the millions of men who had been removed from their home environment. Their policy ran counter to the traditional idea that a good fighter was usually a libertine, and that in sex affairs "God-given passion" was a proof of manliness. Baker moved first; six days after war was declared he appointed Raymond Fosdick chairman of the Commission on Training Camp Activities (the CTCA). Fosdick, a brother of minister Harry Emerson Fosdick, was a graduate of Princeton, and a member of Phi Beta Kappa and the American Philosophical Association. His assignment was not a new one because Baker had sent him to the Mexican border in 1916 to investigate lurid newspaper stories about lack of discipline, drunkenness, and venereal disease in American military camps. Fosdick had found the installations surrounded by a battery of saloons and houses of prostitution, with *filles de joie* from all over the country flocking to San Antonio, Laredo, and El Paso to "woman the cribs." He also ascertained that many officers were indifferent to the problem, including Commanding General Frederick Funston who gave Fosdick the nickname of "Reverend." On the basis of the long chronicle of military history Funston and his breth-

ren assumed that the issue was insoluble and that anyone
interested in a mission like Fosdick's was an impractical idealist or a do-gooder.

During the brief Mexican venture Fosdick's report to the
Secretary recommended a definite stand by the War Department against the saloon and the excesses of prostitution. The
problem involved military necessity as much as morality, for
in pre-penicillin days venereal disease was a crippling disability. Fosdick insisted that a strong word was needed from
Washington, and it was immediately forthcoming. Baker put
the "cribs" and the saloons out of bounds, ordered the co-operation of military officers with local law authorities, and
told communities that the troops would be moved unless
wholesome conditions were restored. Both Baker and Fosdick
knew that a substitute was necessary, that the *verboten* approach was not the real answer. They were aware that soldiers
went to town, in more ways than one, because of the monot-
ony of camp life, to find the only release available in the
absence of movies, reading rooms, and playing fields with
adequate athletic equipment. Both knew that when trains
stopped at Texan crossroads bored soldiers would sometimes
enter to ask the passengers if they had any reading material
to spare, even a newspaper. There was no time in the short
Mexican encounter to evolve a solution but the area provided a proving ground for new departures in the near future.

When the United States entered the First World War
Baker made certain that the Draft Act of 1917 prohibited
the sale of liquor to men in uniform and that it provided
for broad zones around the camps in which prostitution was
outlawed. Even so Fosdick, as the new Chairman of the
Commission on Training Camp Activities, encountered strong
and vociferous opposition. New Orleans had a notorious red-
light district extending over twenty-eight city blocks, and
the business-minded mayor of the city journeyed to Washington to present the case for "the God-given right of men

to be men." In Europe, Premier Clemenceau, showing his
animal proclivities as the "Tiger of France," asked Pershing
by letter for the creation of special houses where the sexual
desires of American men could be satisfied. When Fosdick
showed the letter to Baker his negative response was: "For
God's sake, Raymond, don't show this to the President or
he'll stop the war." Ultimately Fosdick's "Fit to fight" slogan
swept across the country and every well-known red-light district in the United States was closed, a hundred and ten of
them. The result was that the rate of venereal disease in
the American Army was the lowest in our military history.

This was the negative side of the situation. Affirmatively
Baker worked on the premise that "young men spontaneously
prefer to be decent, and that opportunities for wholesome
recreation are the best possible cure for irregularities in conduct which arise from idleness and the baser temptations."
The wholesome activities were to be provided by many organizations including the YMCA, the Knights of Columbus,
the Jewish Welfare Board, the American Library Association,
and the Playground and Recreation Association—private societies which voluntarily performed the job that was taken
over almost entirely by the Special Services Division of the
Army itself in World War II. Over these voluntary agencies,
in 1917–18, the CTCA served as a co-ordinating body in
carrying out what *Survey* called "the most stupendous piece
of social work in modern times." Under Fosdick the first executive officer of the CTCA was Richard Byrd, whose name
in later years was to become synonymous with activities at
the polar antipodes. From the point of view of popularity the
best-known member of the Commission was Walter Camp,
the Yale athlete whose sobriquet was "the father of American
football." He was placed in charge of athletics, and among
other things adapted the type of calisthenics known as the
daily dozen. The CTCA program of activities was profuse:
William Farnum and Mary Pickford on the screen, Elsie Janis

and Harry Lauder on the stage, books provided by the American Library Association, full equipment for games and sports —except that no "bones" were furnished for the all-time favorite pastime played on any floor and known as "African golf." The CTCA distributed a khaki-bound songbook that provided the impetus for spirited renditions of the selections found therein, plus a number of others whose lyrics were more earthy—from "Johnny Get Your Gun" to "Keep the Home Fires Burning" to "Mademoiselle from Armentières." Most of the verses of the latter were unprintable but, no matter what was set to music, the first global encounter was certainly a "singing war" by contrast with World War II.[3]

Concern for the welfare of the soldier was not limited to his tenure in the Army; attention was also given to his status, and that of his family, after release from military service. Baker and Secretary of the Treasury William McAdoo have been given major credit for the War Risk Insurance Act of 1917, which insured the men against disability or death while in service and made provision for their rehabilitation when they returned to private life. Baker always insisted that Samuel Gompers, the President of the American Federation of Labor who was also a member of the Advisory Commission of the Council of National Defense, really deserved all the kudos for this plan. One day Gompers had told Baker that war risk insurance should be built upon the same principle as industrial compensation. His idea was that a system of compensation for war injuries, if laid down in advance, would make postwar pensions unnecessary and would do justice to all soldiers, rather than justice to some and less than justice to others, a situation that had been true of all previous military pension systems. The idea appealed to Baker, who brought in consultants from insurance companies along with Circuit Judge Julian W. Mack to draft the measure. Later the administration of the Act was placed, against Baker's wishes, in the Treasury Department with whose representatives Mr. Gompers and his associates continued to sit.

At the time of passage it was thought that the War Risk Insurance Act would end the lobbying for pensions and bonuses that had followed all of our previous wars. This fond hope proved illusory, but in later years Baker remained steadfast in his opposition to pension and bonus bills. He applauded the opposition of President Coolidge to the Bonus Act of 1924, and was disappointed when the measure was passed over his veto; one of the few enthusiastic letters he wrote to Franklin D. Roosevelt was sent in 1935 when he congratulated the President on his message in opposition to immediate payment of the same bonus. Baker felt that the bonus commercialized the calling of the soldier beyond the needs of the ex-servicemen, and would repeat in America "the principles of largesse to the army which grew up in Rome and became first occasional, then habitual, and finally destroyed Rome."

In later years Baker would speculate on the moral climate of the American Army as he read the realistic and naturalistic war literature that was appearing in the 1920s and 1930s. He liked the famous war play *What Price Glory* and thought everyone should see it, because it portrayed war as it is under modern conditions with all "its deep degradations and its pathetic nobilities." But he did not think Remarque's *All Quiet on the Western Front* or Arnold Zweig's *The Case of Sergeant Grischa* could have been written about American soldiers, and he was horrified that John Dos Passos' *Three Soldiers* drew a picture in which American doughboys were self-pitying neurasthenics and all French women were easily immoral. Baker had no illusions about the "old Adam" inherent in man whether he existed in war or peace, but he confessed to a "deep-rooted conviction that the American Army in France was at once the sanest, the soberest and the least criminal body of men ever gathered together as any army in human history." This conviction, he added, was based "not upon affection and prejudice in its behalf, but upon the unanimous testimony of experts, psychologists, psychiatrists, ministers of religion, social workers and earnest men and women who were associated with it and studied it." He was certain that Fosdick's work through the CTCA was the outstanding achievement of the War Department; other armies had been supplied with the spirit and implements of victory but for the first time, he felt, an armed force had been given a moral shield.[4]

During the war almost three million men were denied any choice about service in the armed forces of the United States; they were simply drafted as their numbers were called. Some were unwilling to serve as combatants, and their refusal raised the old and difficult question about the relationship between the laws of a sovereign government and the dictates of an individual conscience. The debate on this dilemma is both ancient and perennial. At the Diet of Worms Martin Luther spoke for individual autonomy when he said: "It is neither safe nor prudent to do aught against conscience. Here I stand—I cannot do otherwise. God help me. Amen." Socrates once stated the argument against conscientious objectors when he assumed the voice of "The Laws" in speaking to Crito: "Having brought you into the world, and nurtured and educated you, and given you . . . a share in every good that we had to give, we proclaim . . . the right of every Athenian that if he does not like us . . . he may go where he pleases . . . but if he still remains he has entered into an implied contract that he will do as we command him." Baker's voice was an echo of Socrates when he said:

> I was a public officer, sworn to enforce the written law of the nation, and to defend its constitution. The conscientious objectors were under a less explicit obligation, though they were

quite sure that they were entitled to all the liberties and immunities guaranteed by the constitution and the laws which they felt a conscientious obligation not to defend. They were, therefore, aggrieved that the War Department would not join them in setting aside laws and duties which they did not approve. . . .

The fact about the conscientious objectors is that they acquired a quite unwarranted importance in their own eyes. To each of them he and his cause became the pivotal and central thing in the world while, of course, as the case then stood, they were, frankly, relatively unimportant. The world was then deciding not whether a few individuals might for conscience's sake, assert a variant opinion from that all but universally held by the society of which they were a part, but whether any such thing as liberty was to be left in the world at all.

A sizable percentage of the conscientious objectors had religious scruples against all wars; they belonged to so many different sects that Baker concluded that nothing short of a comprehensive knowledge of Professor James's book, *The Varieties of Religious Experience,* would qualify a man for success as Secretary of War. Other "C.O.'s" were aliens who did not want to fight in a particular war against their national kinfolk. Some were humanitarians who held that all men are brothers and should not shed fratricidal blood. There were political objectors—among them anarchists, syndicalists, and socialists—some of whom were willing to fight in a "class struggle" but had no intention of serving in a "capitalist war." Wilson and Baker wanted conscientious objectors treated with humanity and consideration, but this benign attitude had little popular support in the frenzied war period. Millions of fathers and mothers with sons on active duty found it difficult to be sympathetic with men whom they regarded as shirkers. Baker noted that "the great body of our people, with their hearts overseas with their boys, were impetuously impatient that the War Department should waste their forms of law on men who would not even do the ministry of mercy in the hospital corps to their fellow men who, by reasons of their no less conscientious response, lay sick and wounded. Thus the friends wanted the conscientious objectors released as heroes while their enemies wanted them shot as traitors. Both were irritated that the War Department merely applied the law." In their effort to pursue a middle course the President and the Secretary of War could achieve nothing but unpopularity. The patriots criticized them harshly for the coddling of "cringing, skulking cowards." Those who favored individual conscience were convinced that Baker had sold out to the military, that "the voice was the voice of Newton D. Baker, but the will was the will of the chief of staff."

The original Selective Service Act made provision in noncombatant service for religious objectors only. It made no mention of those who had conscientious objections to war on nonreligious grounds, for whom both Wilson and Baker thought consideration should be given. In late 1917 the Secretary ordered that all men who had "scruples against war" should be considered as conscientious objectors, and asked military commanders to treat them with "tact and consideration." By executive order of March 20, 1918, President Wilson recognized both religious and nonreligious objectors, who might be assigned to noncombatant duty. This was essentially a policy of work or fight. In mid-July Baker wrote Wilson: "We are now doing absolutely all that public opinion will stand in the interest of conscientious objectors." These orders went far beyond the Selective Service Act but, in the prevailing situation, were frequently impossible to execute. They had to be carried out by military commanders, most of whom considered conscientious objection as recalcitrant resistance to authority. Many officers, though not all, treated the dissidents either with disdain or brutality. Among the sternest of the military disciplinarians was Major General Leonard Wood.

The question of sincerity presented a serious problem because, as Sidney Webb once observed, "it is even more easy to pretend to a conscientious objection than it is to pretend to sciatica." In June 1918, Baker established a board of inquiry to determine the sincerity of conscientious objectors. Its members—who went from camp to camp interviewing objectors—were Judge Julian Mack, Dean Harlan F. Stone of the Columbia Law School (later Chief Justice of the United States), and Major Walter G. Kellogg of the Judge Advocate General's Office of the Army. Approximately 3,900 men were recognized and accepted as conscientious objectors, of whom more than 3,300 accepted noncombatant service, largely in medical work or on farms. Five hundred and forty were court-martialed because their sincerity was questioned or because of their "sullen and defiant" attitude. Of this group Baker himself saw about two hundred, and he found most of them a "sad and unshaven lot." He asked one of them, a solemn and serious man, why he objected to going to war. With perfect assurance the fellow replied, "I am a brother of God." Baker told him that we hoped God was on our side, and that we were perfectly willing to include members of his immediate family. This rejoinder, logical though it may have been, made no impression.

Only one of those court-martialed was acquitted; there were 17 death sentences and 142 life terms. All of the death sentences were reversed, and on November 23, 1920, Baker released the last 33 conscientious objectors still in prison so that they could be home by Thanksgiving. This was two years after the close of the war but Baker was severely criticized for his lenience; there were many who thought that this "crowd of marplots and conspirators" should not be dumped upon an "already outraged nation." Early in the war a white-headed Dunkard leader, asking for the exemption of his brethren, had realized fully the difficult position in which Baker found himself. He said to the diminutive

Secretary of War: "The Lord has placed a heavy burden upon thee, son."[5]

The imposition of the death penalty in courts-martial presented one of the infrequent cases where Baker found it necessary to overrule General Pershing. Pershing asked for full authority to impose the death penalty without review by the Secretary of War and the President; Baker replied in the negative and Wilson concurred in his decision. The assumption of review authority, in cases where the general courts-martial had imposed the death penalty for military offenses or civil crimes, placed Baker in a difficult position because he did not believe in capital punishment.

There were four early test cases which resulted in the permanent denial of the death penalty as a means of enforcing military discipline. Privates Jeff Cook and Forest Sebastian had been asleep at their posts, slumbering while in a standing position and leaning against the trench wall; soldiers Stanley Fishback and Olon Ledoyen refused to obey an order to fall in for drill. All four were sentenced to death. Baker's recommendation for clemency in the Cook and Sebastian cases was typical. After citing their youth and their fatigue from exposure, he stated that he could not believe that the death sentence "ought to be imposed in cases which do not involve a bad heart, or so flagrant a disregard for the welfare of others . . . as to be evidence of disloyalty." He was certain that the men would consider the restored opportunity of their forfeited lives as a "challenge to devoted service for the future." The President sustained Baker, and in place of execution Fishback and Ledoyen were sent to disciplinary barracks for three years while Cook and Sebastian were restored to duty. In the latter cases Baker's forecast was fulfilled; Sebastian was killed in battle during the Aisne offensive, and Cook was twice wounded in action before the close of the war.

Apart from military offenses there were also cases involving civil crimes, such as murder and rape, which carried the death penalty under the law of the States in which the crime was committed. On review of these trials, Baker usually recommended clemency on sociological grounds, but his recommendations were not always accepted and some American soldiers were executed for these serious civil—as contrasted with purely military—offenses. He noted death penalties where the criminals were "little above the lower animals" but he observed that the men involved were uneducated, and he confessed a strong feeling "that the society that left them illiterate might well exact less than the extreme penalty which it would rightfully exact from men who have had wide opportunities of contact and appreciation of all the circumstances with which they are confronted."

Procedure in courts-martial is always a controversial subject in a democratic country, but the penal recommendations by the Secretary of War do not sustain the later charge by Senator George E. Chamberlain that in this regard Baker was an "exponent of Prussian militarism." On the contrary, Baker was proud that the United States had the happy distinction of being the first country, engaged in a large-scale war, to emerge from it without a single execution by capital punishment for the enforcement of military discipline. By contrast with British and French practices there were no "ceremonial executions" in the American Army, killing that was designed to frighten the survivors into obedience. Baker was certain that "the flower of American youth did not need to be stimulated by terrorism."[6]

Within the Wilson Administration there was no hesitation over the appointment of John J. Pershing as Commanding General of the American Expeditionary Forces, although he was selected in preference to five active major generals who outranked him. Before this designation was made, however,

Baker found it necessary to dispose of ex-President Theodore Roosevelt who wanted to take a volunteer army to Europe. Roosevelt was intelligent, dramatic, and belligerent; the English statesman and littérateur John Morley had once described him as an interesting combination of St. Vitus and St. Paul, a wonder of Nature comparable to Niagara Falls. He was so dogmatic that Elihu Root jocularly accused him of imagining that he had discovered the Ten Commandments, so patriotic that it was claimed that he really believed *he* was the American flag. Although Roosevelt was now almost sixty, was blind in one eye, and was intermittently bothered by poisoning resulting from equatorial fever, he still was a vigorous antagonist. Months were to elapse before Baker and Wilson convinced TR—and the rest of the country —that the war in France was no place for the traditional heroics of the "Charge of the Light Brigade."

As an advocate of the strenuous life the Rough Rider had begun to think of the European "Roosevelt Division" as early as 1914. Because of our neutral status at that time, he hoped to finance the enterprise from private sources but expected the War Department to provide arms and supplies and some of its better officers. He had in mind a force of cavalry and mounted infantry, seemingly unaware that warfare had changed since his Cuban skirmish in 1898 and that men on horses would be splendid targets for the machine guns that were so lethal in World War I. By 1916 he was making more active plans and wrote to Police Headquarters in New York City, of which he had once been the head, asking "in the event of war" for two horses, "horses with good manners who will stand fire and the like without making a fuss . . ." He mused that an "elderly Major General who had been President of the United States and who had broken all kinds of bones, needs a hardy and well-bitted horse." Thousands offered to serve under him, including Baker's own brother Julian and William Edgar Borah, later a Senator known as the "Lion of Idaho." Early in 1917 Roosevelt stated that if President Wilson refused to authorize the special expeditionary force under his command, he would muster it anyway in Canada. On March 19, 1917, several weeks before the actual declaration of war against Germany, Roosevelt asked Baker for permission to raise a division of volunteers for immediate service at the front. Baker denied the request on the ground that Congress had not authorized such a force, and that even if it had the officers for it would be drawn from the Regular Army. Roosevelt had fought as a Colonel of volunteers, but he was certain that he qualified as a Regular Army officer by reason of his position as a former President:

> I wish respectfully to point out that I am a retired Commander-in-Chief of the United States Army, and eligible to any position of command over American troops.

Baker's reply was polite and abrupt:

> I have the honor to acknowledge the receipt of your letter of the twenty-third. The military record to which you call my attention is, of course, a part of the permanent records of this Department, and is available in detail for consideration.
> The patriotic spirit of your suggestion is cordially appreciated.[7]

After war was declared in early April Roosevelt went to Washington to press his case personally. He saw Wilson at the White House; Baker went to see the ex-President at the home of his daughter, Alice Roosevelt Longworth. Both conversations were fruitless. On this issue both the President and Baker knew that they had additional support from our English allies; General Tom Bridges of the British Mission in Washington had told the President that the war in Europe was too serious for untrained amateurs. Bridges had warned the British Chief of Staff against any American volunteer

force, and had averred his opinion that the Germans would
ridicule, and the British and French would be depressed by,
a hastily organized expedition of nonprofessional soldiers
from the United States. Baker was also delighted to receive
the support of a prominent Republican, ex-President William
Howard Taft, who had broken with Roosevelt before the
presidential election of 1912. Taft wrote the Secretary of
War that it was hard for the public "to tear away from the
traditions of volunteering handed down to us from the various wars regarded only in the light of ultimate success, and
without the slightest analysis of the enormous waste and
useless slaughter due to such an illogical and really absurd
system." Baker sent the Taft letter to Wilson, who was pleased
enough with the commentary of the 350-pound former President to observe: "Taft is certainly acting in a mighty big
way."

When the epistolary combat was resumed Baker wrote
Roosevelt, with some confidence, that the War College had
recommended that no troops be sent until after an adequate
period of training, that these divisions would be commanded
by men who had devoted their lives exclusively to the study
and pursuit of military matters, and that this purely military
policy did not undertake to estimate "what, if any, sentimental
value would attach to a representation of the United States
in France by a former President of the United States." Roosevelt thanked Baker for his "frank and courteous letter" and
then disagreed vehemently with every argument in it. He
thought the policy outlined by Baker came from military
men of the "red-tape and pipe-clay school, who are hide
bound in the pedantry of . . . wooden militarism. . . ." He
thought Baker had forgotten that in Cuba he "commanded
troops in action in the most important battle fought by the
United States during the last half century."

It all came to nothing and Roosevelt finally disbanded his
unauthorized paper division. While doing so he fired a broad-

side at the President who, in his judgment, was only "tepidly hostile" to Germany but felt a "more active hostility toward Wood and myself"; he was certain that Wilson was more interested in keeping Roosevelt out of the war than in putting anyone else into it. His parting shot at Baker was to the effect that the Secretary of War was "exquisitely unfitted for his position." In later years Baker reflected on Roosevelt's personality and achievements; in the assessment he found good and bad features. With regard to Roosevelt as President, Baker approved of "much of his brave statesmanship." He realized that there had been a "fine but pathetic heroism" about Roosevelt's desire to go to France in 1917, but his presence there would have created two Presidents— "one in Paris telling Mr. Clemenceau what he thought the President in Washington ought to do; and the other in Washington trying to protect purely American interests against enthusiastic pro-ally concessions which our President in France would have made to keep things humming." Baker was never able to fathom TR's belligerence. During the presidential campaign of 1912 he had thought Roosevelt was insane enough to die in restraint, possibly in a strait jacket. Many years later he observed: "I never see anything from Roosevelt's pen without a sense of amazement. . . . He once threatened to bite General Miles. I have always been surprised that in the course of his stormy career we have no record of his actually having bitten anybody." Baker was amused when he heard that Roosevelt loved cats. He had no doubt that the former President, in his imagination, conceived of cats as all claws. Temperamentally the two men were so far apart that Baker finally disqualified himself as a witness; his conclusion was that "more than any other human being I have ever known, he seemed to lack humility."[8]

The choice of a commander for the American Expeditionary Forces was made in May 1917. Baker took the records of

all major generals to his home, and studied them alone. He
discovered that most were disqualified by age or illness; the
list was quickly reduced to two men—John J. Pershing and
Leonard Wood. Pershing was a West Pointer who had seen
service in Cuba and the Philippines, in 1906 had been
jumped from captain to brigadier general over the heads of
862 officers, and had recently led the Mexican punitive expedition against Villa. Wood was graduated from Harvard
as a physician, joined Roosevelt as a Rough Rider, became
Military Governor in Cuba, Governor General in the Philippines, and Chief of Staff in Washington. Both Pershing and
Wood were Republicans, a coincidence that appeared to
eliminate politics from the choice of one of them by a Democratic Administration. In actuality, political repercussions
from the appointment were inevitable because Wood was a
close friend of Roosevelt. In 1915–16 President Wilson had
been particularly displeased by the Roosevelt-Wood campaign for preparedness through the creation of civilian training camps, the best known of which was the "businessmen's
camp" at Plattsburg, New York.

Baker chose Pershing and presented the nomination to
Wilson, who approved it. Both were confident that Pershing
would be loyal to civilian authority, and were just as certain
that the opposite would be true if Wood were appointed.
Baker had admired Pershing's loyalty to Wilson's policy of a
limited invasion of Mexico, although the General personally
wanted to march to Mexico City. By contrast, the Secretary
of War knew of several occasions which had demonstrated
Wood's inability to be loyal to a political superior. He was
convinced that with Wood in France the cabal of Wood,
Senator Lodge, and Roosevelt "would have been a disaster
to our country and a boon to the Germans equal in strength
to fresh armies in the field on their side." Wilson agreed,
and told Baker by letter: "Personally, I have no confidence

in General Wood's discretion nor in his loyalty to his superiors."[9]

A year later Wood was again in Washington asking to be sent to Europe as an auxiliary officer in command of a division he had trained at Fort Riley, Kansas. Pershing did not want him under his command and preferred to see Wood retired, but suggested that a possible alternative was to send him into military exile, perhaps as American military representative in Russia! In Pershing's judgment it was high time that meddling, political generals be put where they could do no harm. He told Chief of Staff Peyton C. March that if Wood was sent to France he would be returned immediately to the United States. Baker chose to keep secret Pershing's wishes and directed all of the criticism toward himself. He said that he took the entire responsibility to prevent Wood from "agitating his friends into activity against Pershing, who was absent and could not defend himself." Baker's conclusion was: "Pershing has got enough on his shoulders and what's a Secretary of War for?"

Both Pershing and Baker believed Wood was physically unfit for service in Europe but the doctors did not agree with them. While on shipboard in 1898 Wood had struck his head on a low chandelier, and in following years a developing intracranial tumor caused numbness and weakness on the left side of his body. In 1910 the famous neurosurgeon Harvey Cushing removed a large meningeal tumor from Wood's brain by an operation that was fairly successful except that it left the General with a persistent limp due to residual spasticity of the foot. Baker had seen Wood at Plattsburg, limping badly and painfully short of breath after a short walk up a hill.

Except for the limp Wood's recovery appeared to be complete and a Medical Examining Board at Washington declared him physically qualified for active service in March

1918. Among other things the Board had made him hop about the room, first on one foot and then on the other. One of the examining physicians was heard to exclaim: "He don't hop the way I do but, my God, he *can* hop!" Because of Pershing's opposition there was no possibility of active service in France for Wood, but a certificate of physical disability would have relieved Baker of the embarrassing necessity of explaining the real reason for relegating him "to the woods" at home. Wood had been under the direction of the Secretary of War for two years, and in Baker's judgment was his most "insubordinate subordinate." He therefore told the General that he had many talents as a superior officer but was incapable of being a helpful subordinate. Many years later, in retrospect, he concluded that Wood's difficulties stemmed from an attempt to be a great soldier and a great politician at the same time. Baker was certain that this dual role was not possible in the United States because Wood's political activities made him unpopular among his military associates, while his arbitrary military point of view made him suspect among the politicians.[10]

Wilson was convinced that the American Army should be a separate unit in France, and Baker's first order to Pershing had been an instruction to keep the American Army intact. The Secretary of War did not believe American soldiers would be willing to fight under British or French flags, nor did he think they would react favorably to foreign military techniques and discipline. On the other hand Lloyd George and Clemenceau, confronted by the serious depletion of British and French ranks in 1917, pressed for the brigading of American troops with their own national units. Their argument was that brigading with veteran troops was the only practical method by which fresh American soldiers, who entered the war late, could gain the experience learned in previous campaigns.

On this issue Baker was compelled to use plain and force-
ful language in his conversations with both Lloyd George
and Clemenceau. The French leader told him that in Wilson
and Pershing the United States had produced the two most
stubborn men in the world. Baker replied politely: "Mr.
President, in that competition my country would have much
to fear if France entered your Excellency as a contestant."
The Tiger growled, readjusted his skullcap, and changed
the subject by asking, "How many air-plane engines can
France get on immediate delivery?" When Baker visited England in 1918 Lloyd George, angered by the insistence of the
Americans on a separate army, told him that American forces
had been of little use and that British shipping had been
wasted in transporting them to Europe. Baker immediately
called the bluff of the British Prime Minister. He said that
it was his assumption that American manpower was essential
to the winning of the war but that the British should feel
free to withdraw their shipping if they thought its use more
important in other channels. This thrust placed Lloyd George
in a neat cul-de-sac and Lord Milner, who was present as
a member of the British War Cabinet, was unable to conceal
his mirth. All were amused when Lloyd George excused himself with the statement that he and his associates had to go
off and fight the war in Turkey. The next morning Baker
received an indirect message from Lloyd George, the gist
of which was that the conversation of the previous evening
had best be forgotten. In later years, when Lloyd George
published his memoirs, it was Baker's turn to be amused.
He noted that the first four volumes were devoted to the
thesis that the British high command was inept, but that the
fifth continued the argument that it should have been given
the extra burden of mismanaging the American Army as
well![11]

In the summer of 1918, with Russia removed from the

war as a result of the Bolshevik Revolution, the United States
sent troops into Russia at two points: Archangel in the north
and Vladivostok on the Pacific. In the Far East the initial
motive was to assist the Czechoslovak Corps (consisting of
former prisoners of war and deserters from the Austro-
Hungarian Army) which was desirous of fighting on the
Allied side but was currently stranded on the Trans-Siberian
Railroad. In northern Russia the original idea was to protect large stores of Allied war supplies and to revive the
eastern front against the Germans. The dispatch of American
troops occurred after extensive soul searching on the part
of Wilson, the sixth of whose fourteen points had demanded
the evacuation of all Russian territory by foreign forces. In
both areas Wilson felt that the only legitimate object for
American or Allied troops was to guard military stores or to
render aid acceptable to the Russians in the organization
of their *own* self-defense. This fine distinction between military intervention and guarding military supplies was utterly
lost upon the British, many of whose leaders were convinced
that the Communist regime should be overthrown straight
away. They entertained the fanciful hope that a union of
the forces at Archangel with the distant Czechs would not
only re-establish the eastern front but would also accomplish
the destruction of the Russian Communist government.

Ultimately both expeditions failed. In Manchuria the
Allied force consisted of 9,000 Americans and 72,000 Japanese troops; when the Americans left in 1920 the Japanese
stayed for a quarter of a century. In northern Russia, after
the Armistice had removed the German menace, it was soon
evident that the British were as interested in fighting the
Bolsheviks as the Boches. From the outset the Allied force
at Archangel was involved in violent action against the Soviet government; none the less 5,000 American soldiers remained on the frozen Russian steppes for nine months under
the command of the gigantic British General Ironside, who

was appropriately elevated to the peerage in 1941 as Baron of Archangel and of Ironside. The Americans had been ready to go home when they found that the supplies they were supposed to guard had already been hauled off to the interior by the Communists; after the Armistice on the western front they were even more puzzled to know what they were doing in Russia and why they were doing it. In the attempt to find out the contingent suffered 2,000 casualties from temperature at 35 degrees below zero and Bolshevik shells before the remainder of the 5,000 men returned to the United States.

Baker was opposed to both expeditions and later said that the only real disagreement he ever had with the President concerned the wisdom of sending American troops to Russia. Wilson agreed with him on the military futility of the Archangel expedition, but felt obliged to send it because he had already refused so many British and French requests that they were beginning to think he was not a good associate, much less a good ally. Baker always regarded the North Russian campaign as a side show "born of desperation and organized for the purpose of keeping up home morale rather than because of any clear view of the military situation." General Bliss felt the same way. The British were talking about sending an expedition all the way to Irkutsk in the middle of Siberia not far from Outer Mongolia. When Bliss remonstrated that Irkutsk was too many thousands of miles from the eastern front to be of any help, the British reply was that it was nearer than Vladivostok! The astounded American General was reminded of the man who claimed he was nearer the moon when he stood on the top of his house. Bliss was certain that both the man and the proposed military expedition were still too far away to have any chance of reaching their objectives.

In the Far East Wilson was moved by sentiment. He had an emotional prejudice in favor of little countries, and his

feeling for the Czechs was extremely friendly. Although he
emphatically dismissed the idea of restoring an eastern front
by military action in Siberia, he ultimately concluded that we
should help the Czech Corps to get out of Russia by way
of Vladivostok. Baker could not agree, and as early as November 1918 told the President that the presence of our
troops in Siberia was being used by the Japanese as a cloak
for their own occupation, while the plight of the Czechs
was forgotten. When the skeptical Secretary handed sealed
instructions to General William S. Graves, who had been
chosen to head the American Siberian force, he said: "Watch
your step; you will be walking on eggs loaded with dynamite. . . ." He prophesied that some day we would be rudely
awakened by the realization that the Japanese, who went in
under our wing, had so completely mastered the country
that they could not be forced out of Manchuria by either the
Russians or the Allies. With the passage of time Baker's
early pessimism became reality.

The Russians resented the presence of foreign troops on
their soil, whatever the purpose of their presence, and proceeded to welcome them with shot and shell. Baker was
convinced that the United States was inconsistent; it would
not intervene in Mexico but was trying to justify intervention
in Russia. His own view was that except for the Russians
everybody should be removed from the country—diplomatic
and military representatives, political agents, propagandists,
and casual visitors—in order to allow the Russians to settle
down and run their own affairs. Our own military forces
should be ordered home by the first boat, with further assistance limited to economic aid only. Baker was free to admit
that he did not understand Bolshevism, and that he disliked
what little of it he comprehended. He had a feeling, on the
other hand, that if the Russians did like it they were entitled
to have it, and that it was not our responsibility to assume
that only 10 per cent of the Russian people were Commu-

nists and that we should help the other 90 per cent who were claimed to be resisting it. This point of view was echoed by General Bliss when the White Russian Admiral Kolchak, with ideological support from the Allies, was making an unsuccessful attempt to overthrow the Bolshevik Government. The commentary by Bliss may have as much pertinence in 1961 as it had in 1919:

> Some people say that there can be no disarmament while Bolshevism exists in Russia. But Bolshevism exists everywhere; and it will exist after we have killed the last Bolshevik. The trouble is that we are trying to kill Bolsheviks and not Bolshevism. The latter can be killed, but not by force of arms.[12]

VII. Secretary of A War—
Administration

IN THE CONDUCT of military operations Baker worked closely and amicably with the President and the Secretary of the Navy. Secretary Daniels thought the co-operation of the Army and Navy during World War I was "perfect," and quite a contrast to his strained relationship with Baker's predecessor Lindley Garrison. On one occasion Garrison had said to Daniels: "I don't care a damn about the Navy. . . . You run your machine and I'll run mine." There was a private telephone wire from Baker's office to the White House, and many observers believed the Secretary of War had closer relations with Wilson than any other Cabinet member, in part because the War Department was the largest of any branch of the Executive Office. Baker saw the President frequently, never found him too tired to consider any problem, and disagreed with him only once—on the Siberian expedition. The Secretary of War recalled that he had an "incredibly free hand" and that Wilson often supported his judgment even when he learned about the matter after the decision had been made. Once Baker, entirely on his own, granted permission to name a gigantic installation at Muscle Shoals in honor of the President. It was Wilson Dam. Later he sent a brief note to the White House reporting what he had done and explaining that the project would be the largest in the world, but not the longest. The reply from the President was quaint and characteristic: "Dear Baker: I am very glad to have the description of Muscle Shoals. Permit me to express my pleasure that I am at least not the longest dam in the world."[1]

The organization of the War Department has always been complex and confusing. A bewildered colonel once summarized the perennial departmental pattern with the remark: "It's just a can of worms; it's just a can of worms." Baker thought Elihu Root had been the greatest of Secretaries of War because he had established the position of Chief of Staff (assisted by the General Staff) in 1903; without this co-ordinating and supervisory body Baker was certain that the effort in World War I would have been no more successful than willingness to fight Indians "according to the traditions of the Custer age." There was spirited disagreement with this point of view. Seventeen bureau chiefs (such as the Adjutant General, the Judge Advocate General, and the Chiefs of Engineers and Ordnance) did not enjoy their subordination to the Chief of Staff and were resentful because they had been pushed down one rung on the organizational ladder. For more than a decade they had unsuccessfully claimed the right to report directly to the Secretary of War, and their persistent campaign for independence nearly succeeded in 1917—indeed it would have resulted in victory but for an interpretive decision by Baker supporting the authority of the Chief of Staff.

For their direct assault on the Chief of Staff the bureau chiefs thought they had found a powerful weapon in a clause

of the National Defense Act of 1916. Section 5 of this Act
stated that the General Staff would "not be permitted to
assume or engage in work of an *administrative* nature that
pertains to established bureaus or offices of the War Department." In interpreting this clause the Judge Advocate General rendered an opinion that emasculated the General Staff
of all workable authority and restored the chaotic decen-
tralization that had prevailed during the war with Spain
in 1898. This legal impasse was made to order for a lawyer
with Baker's training. He took the documents home with
him, studied the work of Elihu Root, decided that the word
"administrative" in the Act applied to routine affairs only,
and thus restored the Chief of Staff to his primary role as
a co-ordinating and supervisory official. It was an ingenious
decision, and it had momentous import when the United
States entered the First World War. Baker was to use the
Chief of Staff to the limit; and he recalled:

> Each day at two o'clock all other business was put aside, and
> the Chief of Staff and I held a conference frequently lasting
> hours. Memoranda, reports, recommendations of all kinds deal-
> ing with the military establishment were by my direction trans-
> mitted through the Chief of Staff, and before being presented
> to me were examined by the Chief of Staff and his aides. My
> practice throughout my whole incumbency was to have the Chief
> of Staff sit opposite me at my desk with baskets filled with
> papers of this kind. The Chief of Staff took them up one by
> one, explained to me the origin of the paper, its purpose and
> its recommendations. If the matter was important he further
> stated the extent to which it had been reviewed by his subordi-
> nates in the General Staff and what his own views on the ques-
> tion were. I frequently examined papers of this kind, and where
> there were controversies and differences of opinion endeavored
> to weigh both sides. Occasionally, for one reason or another,
> such a package of papers would be reserved by me for more
> careful reading and study. . . . For the most part, however, I
> decided the questions presented at the time. . . . The volume
> of the Department's business was too great to permit more de-

tailed personal study except in cases of great importance. . . .[2]

On this intimate basis Baker dealt with three Chiefs of Staff—Hugh L. Scott who reached retirement age in September 1917, Tasker H. Bliss whose military retirement became effective in May 1918, and Peyton C. March who served from that date until 1921. It was Baker's ultimate intention to designate as Chief of Staff a younger man, who had seen service in France and understood military problems on both sides of the ocean. This turned out to be March, but until his appointment the Secretary was happy to rely on the proven wisdom of Scott and Bliss, both of whom at sixty-four were within a few months of retirement.

Baker admired them all as military men; on the personal side he was particularly fond of Scott and Bliss. When Baker entered the War Department Scott, who was then Chief of Staff, told him that it was unnecessary to keep Garrison's "leavings," and that if Baker would indicate the name of the new COS, Scott would have him on hand in ten minutes. Baker's reply was reassuring and unlike the pacifist he was reputed to be: "I am going to look up to you as a father," he told Scott, "I am going to do what you advise me, and if either of us has to leave this building I am going first." Thereafter the Secretary would never call for Scott by buzzer, but always appeared at the door to summon him. When Scott asked him to use the buzzer Baker said: "You are older and wiser than I. You know all about the business, and I know nothing about it, and I cannot reverse the natural order of things . . . to call you with a push button." Statements of this kind were fine for morale in the Department, but they also provided ammunition for critics who blasted away with the charge that the pacific Baker was overly impressed with the alleged omniscience of the Martians. They were to claim that his determination to see the best in everybody made him a War Department "Candide," whose chief characteristic was an earnest but misguided desire to wage a conflict that would be the best of all possible wars.

Scott had made his reputation by direct observation of the Indians of the Southwest and the Moros in the Philippines. Scott was no scholar but in Baker's judgment he had a rugged common sense that was adequate for the operation of the War Department in peacetime. When the war came along the vitriolic Peyton C. March found Scott totally inadequate and said so in his usual forthright language: "[Scott] was deaf; preferred to talk in grunts and the sign language; and he went to sleep in his chair while transacting official business." But Baker had real appreciation for his first military mentor and after Scott's death attempted to raise funds, during the difficult 1930s, for his widow.[3]

Baker's real admiration was reserved for Bliss, the most scholarly person he ever knew and by far the finest intellect he encountered among military men. It was a reciprocal affection; as far as Bliss was concerned Baker was the great wise chief whom he "loved more than any man on earth." Bliss would have been an adornment to any university faculty; he knew geology, Oriental botany, wrote English with vigor, spoke it with force and beauty, and as a linguist—beyond a usable command of French, Spanish, and Italian—was an authentic scholar in Greek and Latin. Baker claimed that he read Greek as easily as "I read English"; in Latin Bliss had read all the books he could lay his hands on in the Library of Congress, including the patristic works of St. Augustine and St. Jerome.

Baker never had any occasion to learn whether Bliss knew anything about routine maneuvers, and was not at all sure that the General could have drilled a squad. On the other hand it was a certainty that Bliss knew more about military

Newton Baker as a boy. Even at this age he was wearing glasses.

Newton Baker as a young lawyer, practicing in Martinsburg, West Virginia, about 27 years old.

Peter Witt, Tom Johnson, and Newton Baker on December 31, 1909, Johnson's last day as Mayor of Cleveland. Baker continued to serve as
City Solicitor until his election as Mayor in 1912.

Mayor Baker, 1913.

Secretary of War Baker drawing the first numbers in the second
military draft, June 27, 1918, in the Senate Office Building.

Newton Baker leaving the White House on his way to be sworn in as Secretary of War. Forty-four years old, Baker was by far the youngest member of Wilson's cabinet.

President Wilson and Secretary of War Baker review the District of Columbia
National Guard, leaving for duty on the Mexican border in 1916.

The President and the Secretary of War on the reviewing stand at Fort Myer,
Va., November, 1916. Mrs. Baker and Mrs. Wilson
are on the stand behind them.

The Council of National Defense. Left to right, standing: Franklin Martin, Daniel Willard, J. Rosenwald, Samuel Gompers, Bernard Baruch, Howard Coffin, W. S. Gifford. Seated: David Houston, Josephus Daniels, Newton Baker, Franklin Lane, William Redfield, William Wilson.

The cabinet in June, 1916. Clockwise around the table: President Wilson, William McAdoo (Treasury), Thomas Gregory (Attorney General), Josephus Daniels (Navy), David Houston (Agriculture), William Wilson (Labor), William Redfield (Commerce), Franklin Lane (Interior), Albert Burleson (Postmaster General), Newton Baker (War), Robert Lansing (State).

Secretary of War Baker with General Pershing (front center) and officers
somewhere in France, spring of 1918.

General March, Newton Baker, King Albert of Belgium, and
General Pershing upon the presentation of the D.S.M.
to the king in October, 1919.

Newton Baker makes the nominating speech for James Cox of Ohio at the 1924 Democratic National Convention in Madison Square Garden.

Franklin Roosevelt at the start of his 1932 campaign in Columbus, Ohio. From left to right: James Farley, Newton Baker, James Cox, Governor Roosevelt, Governor White of Ohio, Senator Bulkley of Ohio.

history than anyone Baker had ever known. The Secretary recalled:

> In those long hours after midnight in the War Department, when we were waiting for messages from overseas on occasions of breathless anxiety—as, for instance, on the first night that our first convoy was in the danger zone, or when the *Leviathan* on her first trip was in the danger zone, and nobody who bore any part of the responsibility for sending them there could sleep—General Bliss and I would sit in my office and he would compare military arms and their effectiveness, their effect upon the size of armies, from practically prehistoric days down, never skipping a stitch, but noting each improvement in arms and knowing its results.

The midnight sessions were not restricted to Washington. In the course of one of Baker's trips overseas, he was in Paris during an air raid. The Secretary and General Bliss took refuge in a cellar full of high-priced wines; Bliss was convinced they were safe because the Germans would want to protect potables of such excellent vintage! Whatever the reason the building was not hit, and the two men told stories until the bombardment stopped.

Bliss was also a profound student of diplomatic and political history, and he was later to use his brooding intelligence to advantage as a member of the Allied Supreme War Council and as a delegate to the Paris Peace Conference. In a weary moment Baker once asked how long the current war in Europe would last. He was shocked to get the reply— "thirty years." Baker remonstrated that it was not humanly possible for the conflict to last that long. Bliss's reply was both acute and prophetic:

> Oh, no, of course not. This particular episode will be concluded in a year or two, then the war will take a new phase and will be waged for a little while, perhaps with economic weapons, until nations rehabilitate themselves and feel a fresh access of strength for another try on the military side. Unless

all the lessons of history are deceptive, thirty years would be
about the normal time for the generation that had the passion
to breed this way to pass off the stage and let others come who
have a new objective and a new point of view.[4]

Peyton C. March, who became Chief of Staff in May 1918,
was a decided contrast to his predecessors. In manner he
was a Richelieu—harsh, autocratic, and peremptory—once
characterized perfectly as pre-eminently *fortiter in modo* but
not particularly *suaviter in modo*. March had enjoyed his
early war assignment as commander of artillery in France,
and on his arrival in Washington Baker commented pleas-
antly that he supposed the order to return as Chief of Staff
had been received with mixed feelings. March's reply was
typical: "No, Mr. Secretary, it made me sick at the stomach."
Neither brought up the subject again.

The reorganization that followed March's arrival almost
turned the War Department upside down, and Baker found
it necessary to spend a substantial portion of his time making
the rounds with a cruse of oil and bandages to bind the
wounds of those damaged in the upheaval. He was willing
to do so because March's enormous energy and efficiency
provided the "mule kick" that moved men and munitions
overseas during the critical year 1918; he realized fully that
March would have been a disaster as Chief of Staff in peacetime but that his very ruthlessness got results during a war.
He had selected March originally in spite of advice to the
contrary from colleagues, and he never regretted the decision. Many years later Baker concluded that the victorious
decision in World War I was achieved by a matter of days
and that March's "energy and drive supplied the days necessary for our side to win."[5]

Beyond his Chiefs of Staff Baker found that military men
varied as much as civilians: there were the lazy and the dili-

gent, the ignorant and the educated, the capable and the incompetent, those with ethical codes of conduct and others who were at best amoral. When the Draft Act was written the Secretary respected General Crowder's military knowledge but found him woefully deficient in Freshman English; Baker was to grow weary "of the slaughter of cutting out rhetoric" from the manuscript as Crowder submitted it. Ex-professor Woodrow Wilson helped with the editing and agreed with Baker that it was hard work "clearing up the underbrush" of General Crowder's syntax and verbosity. On the other hand the Secretary was happy to observe the growth and steady advancement of an able young colonel named Douglas MacArthur. When Baker was trying to think of a name for the "interstate" 42nd National Guard Division that would carry with it "the pride, enthusiasm and affection of every part of the country," MacArthur happened to be in his office and remarked that such a division would "stretch like a rainbow clear across the United States." It was a perfect appellation for the division, the famous Rainbow Division which MacArthur was to command in France. In time Baker came to the conclusion that the higher command of the army, with its share of both the competent and those not so able, was genuinely patriotic and wholly without the taint of what the country feared might become an undemocratic leaning toward militarism. This was a decided contrast with the situation in Germany where the Prussian Junker and monarchist, General von Hindenburg, was so militaristic that (in Baker's judgment) he would have qualified as chief of staff for the Visigothic conqueror Alaric. Baker felt that the American Army only went into action when statesmen confessed their failure and he did not find any historical instance in which the United States had been urged to war by its soldiers. On the contrary, he found many examples of the responsibility of politicians for the outbreak of armed conflict: Charles Sumner, Thaddeus Stevens, John C. Calhoun, and Jefferson Davis in connection with the Civil War; Pulitzer, Hearst, Lodge, and Roosevelt in the preliminaries to the Spanish-American War; and the ineptitude of European diplomats, particularly Sir Edward Grey, with regard to the First World War. This judgment was hardly the one expected from a lawyer who was sometimes called the "pacifist Secretary of War."[6]

As Secretary of War and Chairman of the Council of National Defense Baker was responsible for both military operations and the co-ordination of industrial resources. In addition it was necessary to work closely with many collateral agencies such as the United States Shipping Board and the Emergency Fleet Corporation. The complexity of this situation, plus the military necessity for quick action, was productive of a bedlam. Ralph Hayes, who was Baker's private secretary at this time, tried to issue a War Department directory in early 1918 but met with little success. Hayes reported that if anyone should ask for a succinct statement on the organization of the Department, his only recourse would be to crawl under his desk.

To make a dent in the mountain of work many members of the Department, including the Secretary, worked from 8:30 in the morning until 11:00 at night—frequently on all seven days of the week. Baker claimed that one of his major war functions was that of "chief bouncer," driving out of the offices of the Department those who wanted to work twenty-six hours a day instead of sixteen! He recalled an attempt, at two o'clock in the morning, to persuade General Crozier to go home. Baker failed because he had no satisfactory answer to Crozier's interrogation: "Why, Mr. Secretary, you're not gone yet, so why should I go?"

Baker went to Europe twice in 1918, once in the spring and again in the fall, staying six weeks on each trip. He was the first member of the Cabinet to cross the Atlantic during incumbency. A third trip had been planned for the summer but Baker's inertia prevailed. He said that when he was in Washington there was so much to do that he could not leave, whereas in France he found himself so busy that he could not return; the consequence was that he was apt to stay where he was! His first journey was for the purpose of inspection of military installations so that he could "more intelligently read Pershing's needs from his cables"; the task on the second trip was primarily that of conferring with the French and British on shipping and military plans for 1919. Both journeys were undertaken with great secrecy, in part because England was still mourning the mysterious disappearance of Field Marshal Kitchener at sea in 1916. Baker therefore found it necessary to board revenue cutters stealthily on the outskirts of New York, to embark on "sealed" vessels far out in New York harbor, and to travel to Europe with curtained portholes and little illumination to prevent the attraction that stray gleams provided for lurking submarines. The whole business puzzled the Secretary who had never known whether his secret service attendants had been assigned "to keep him from being blown up, or from running away."

Baker visited the war front on both trips and happened to arrive at dramatic moments. On the first journey the great German offensive of March 1918 began while he was visiting the headquarters of General Pétain, Marshal Haig, and the King of the Belgians. On the second he saw the Americans go over the top at St.-Mihiel, and after the victory entered the town—which had been occupied by the Germans during four years of the war—with Generals Pétain and Pershing. On these trips "the little giant of the War Department" was known to American soldiers as "the little guy in the trick hat," apparently because he wore the only derby they saw in France. There were also moments of disillusionment. Once Baker's train stopped at a small station where a crowd was asking to see the Minister of War. According to Baker:

> I was very chesty about it. I was delighted to know that my fame had preceded me and traveled so far and so fast, and with great complacency and kindliness of disposition toward those who were thus honoring me, I got up and went out to the back platform to greet the crowd, permit them to see me, and bow my acknowledgments. Which I did. I did my part. When I got out I waved my hat and bowed, whereat the crowd, with one accord, set up a unanimous cheer: "Vive Monsieur Clemenceau!" Apparently the only Minister of War of whom they had ever heard was their own distinguished minister.

The Secretary's archenemy George Harvey was not sure whether the country suffered more from a Baker in Europe or a Baker at home; he observed simply that Baker was in France "seeing everything and comprehending nothing." Mrs. Baker was once horrified to hear a man on a train express a hope that Baker's ship would be torpedoed, but Harvey knew it was unlikely. He was confident that German submarines had been ordered to provide a safe convoy for Baker in order to assure the continuation of his inefficient and scandalous operation of the War Department. The feeling of the nation was more accurately expressed by Alfred Jay Nock, historian and littérateur, who told Baker that he was glad to see him back safe and dry in spite of a "diverting picture of you sprinting down a French turnpike, and old Hindenburg after you with a bungstarter."

It was a matter of wonderment to many of Baker's friends that he did not die in his tracks. Here was a man of frail physique, regularly consuming too much tobacco and getting little exercise, with his everlasting deskwork broken only by public addresses or trips of inspection. His nearest approach to a vacation was at sea, en route to France on a battleship or a transport, but on these occasions there was the omnipresent menace of the submarine and the voyages could hardly have been classified as a relaxation. Baker occasionally played tennis on the White House court, and thanked the President for keeping him "in fighting shape" (according to the *Washington Post*, Baker, after three "slashing" sets on the White House courts, would run to the Department where he was soon lost in a gargantuan bathtub built to accommodate William Howard Taft when he was Secretary of War). Once the worried Joe Hostetler, Baker's law partner in Cleveland, asked Justice Clarke to see Baker and to report on the state of his health. Baker ascertained the purpose of the visit and commented: "I think I satisfied the Judge that I am going to live forever." He claimed there were only two nights during the entire war when he was unable to sleep: the first when the first convoy was in the danger zone, the second when the *Leviathan* (the former German *Vaterland*) made her first trip loaded with American troops. Baker worried that these vessels and the men on them would be lost, and he knew a collateral consequence of disaster would be public reaction against the dispatch of the AEF. Fortunately no troop transport was ever lost on the eastward voyage, and Baker could sleep peacefully when he found the time.[7]

On the civilian level Baker was supported by a brain trust that included young men who later would become newspaper editors (Walter Lippmann and Eugene Meyer), a Supreme Court Justice (Felix Frankfurter), a President of Amherst College (Stanley King), an Executive Director of the New York Community Trust (Ralph Hayes), and a President of the Carnegie Corporation (Frederick Keppel). They wrote so much of his correspondence that Baker referred to *his* style during the war as "composite"; he longed for the time "when we will again sign the things we write and write the things we sign." One day Mrs. Baker told him, with considerable elation, that a professor of English wanted to include some of his letters as models in a book of epistolary composition. Baker observed that he would be at a loss to determine the true authorship until he saw the letters, which he had signed but had not written.

There was some disagreement on the magnitude of the task confronting Baker. His friends were certain that he was the busiest man in Washington and his colleague David F. Houston, who was Secretary of Agriculture, testified that the War Department presented the most difficult of all Cabinet positions during World War I. The Director of the Committee on Public Information, propagandist George Creel, distributed an effusive piece entitled "Around the Clock with Secretary Baker" in which the latter appeared as a dynamic precursor of Univac. In Creel's version Baker now had little time for his Theocritus or his Juvenal, kept five secretaries fully occupied, and following a day at the office, lasting from 8 A.M. to 11 P.M., took a full brief case home—after which it was "supposed" that he slept. This description of the Secretary's life and hard times was more than Baker's archenemy George Harvey could stand. He was delighted to go around the clock with Creel, in the following paraphrase on Baker's busy day:

> "Yes" or "no" comes with a decisive ring in his voice and hundreds of millions of dollars gush from the Treasury at his nod. . . . Five stenographers then rush in. He dictates to nearly all of them at once. Others linger in hailing distance as a reserve if some, perchance, should drop dead. Immense bundles of documents of state appear, in which he immerses himself, lost in a profound vacuum of sublimated thought.
>
> The shorthanders flee madly from the incarnated human tempest, waving their notebooks ominously. Now the landscape fades away in a haze of tobacco smoke. Gradually the scenery reveals a briar pipe, with the Secretary of War attached, curled up in a deep, soft-armed chair, revelling in his Theocritus and Juvenal or a biography of Tom Johnson and three-cent carfares.

Opinions might vary, but there was no question that Baker's schedule was hectic enough. The Council of National Defense met in his office three or four times a week, each session lasting from one to three hours. State governors appeared in an effort to prevent a favorite cavalry regiment of their own National Guard from being turned into a field artillery unit necessary to meet General Pershing's demands. Politicians fought bitterly over the location of military camps with an eye toward local rather than the national interest, with the issue frequently revolving around the question—according to General Bliss—as to whether the installation "should be built on an inaccessible mountain in one part of the state or in a swamp in another part." There were the daily conferences between Baker and his Chief of Staff. A procession of military advisers and civilian aides constantly demanded attention, the military arriving through one door and the civilians through another. Through it all the Secretary looked boyish and somewhat incongruous, particularly by contrast with the tall and bulky generals who crowded around him.

There was also the mob in the outside office—visitors of assorted sizes and importance, all of whom wanted to see the Secretary of War. To dispose of them Fred Keppel, who had been Dean of Columbia College, invented what he called a "battue," from the hunting term signifying the driving of game by beating the bushes. Keppel drove away all he could by diverting the callers to someone else. That left a residue, at the end of each day, of thirty to forty hardy customers who stood their ground. Keppel invited them to return the next day, all at the same time. They were placed, like sitting ducks, around the anteroom. Shortly after eleven in the morning Baker appeared, spoke to the first visitor, and if the matter was of importance made a later appointment with him. If the problem was of little consequence, which was true in nine cases out of ten, Baker glanced at the next man—who rose to the bait—and the first interview was over. In this manner Keppel and Baker managed to flush the busy room in time for the Secretary to drive home in his Maxwell for lunch.[8]

In later years Baker came to the conclusion that his functions as Secretary of War had really been consultative and deliberative, rather than executive in nature. He likened his role to that performed by evangelists in Southern camp meetings—one of "comforting the failing." He described his own military IQ as subnormal, but he believed he was a fair success in placing an encouraging hand on the shoulders of those who were carrying too-heavy burdens. It was, as he stated it, the "secret of using enthusiasm in others when it is not exactly your enthusiasm." Baker was content to select the wisest and most aggressive military men he could find and then stake his fate, and the country's, on their performance. It required great self-restraint to refrain from meddling but Baker was convinced that personal interference had been one of Secretary Stanton's great failings in the Civil War, and he proposed to profit from that bad example.

Because of this concept of his proper role Baker did not qualify as an orthodox administrator by the usual definition of the term. On some issues—the selection of Pershing, the disposal of Roosevelt and Wood, the Draft Act, and the orders regarding the Commission on Training Camp Activities —he acted quickly and conclusively; on these problems his decisions were peremptory although the language employed was scholarly and sweetly reasonable. But on many other matters he was very unlike the hard-nosed administrator who operates speedily and without time for consultation and contemplation; the Secretary lacked the desire to settle each problem as it appeared, with the finality and dispatch with which a terrier deals with a rat. He was inclined to establish "areas of planned neglect" because he was aware that many problems settled themselves with the passage of time.

One commentator, employing the parlance of baseball, observed that Baker arrived on first through a base on balls more frequently than any other figure in public life, but this practice had its drawbacks. It sometimes resulted in his being called out on strikes by the umpire of public opinion, with no evidence that he had lifted the bat from his shoulder.

By reason of Baker's innate kindliness plus his interest in people, he was inclined to allow unimportant matters and unimportant people to take an undue share of his time, and the inevitable result was a long working day. He sometimes dealt with minor affairs that could have been delegated to subordinates; he also let them handle and botch matters which he should have dealt with personally. His devotion to friends and his sympathy for a subordinate in trouble— both characteristics of a lovable nature and a gracious personality—were not always conducive to the prompt dispatch of public business. But this personal solicitude did produce great loyalty and *esprit de corps,* and an interesting debate might be developed over the managerial puzzle as to whether it is better for an administrator to possess deftness in designing organizational charts and following channels, or virtuosity in the art of mobilizing superlative efforts from many men for the attainment of ultimate objectives.

In the long run Baker's achievement as Secretary of War was not based on his reputation as a decisive administrator any more than, in later years, the reputation of Franklin D. Roosevelt was founded on administrative prowess. Baker possessed qualities that were more important and far rarer than administrative technique. He had brought to the War Department an unusual knowledge of and sympathy with the social problems of the nation. It was as the interpreter of the Army to the community that Baker played a vital role —unique because of his sincerity, his real intellectual ability, his patience and optimism, his belief in democracy, and his power of expression. He was among the first to realize, in

modern warfare, the relationship which the community must
bear to military forces. He saw clearly that the Army was
responsible to the American people rather than to the government or the Wilson Administration, and he served as an
eloquent interpreter and arbiter between two armies: the
military establishment on the one hand, and on the other
a civilian force composed of politicians, parents, and vociferous special pleaders. Here was the real Secretary, the one
who brought the community into the operation of the draft
law, who created a wholesome recreational environment for
American soldiers, who stood between the military and party
politics, and whose knowledge of labor conditions and understanding of labor leaders earned such esteem and confidence that there was no serious delay in war contracts
because of strikes or lockouts. When to this unusual ability
was added his willingness to select and support *à outrance*
aggressive military leaders like Pershing and March, and his
finesse in dealing with the British on shipping, it is apparent
that he was the head, not the figurehead, of a great and successful enterprise.[9]

VIII. Secretary of A War—

Supplies

BAKER'S FIRST RESPONSIBILITY as Secretary *of a War* had been to select the commanding officer of the American Expeditionary Forces in Europe, his second was to send an army of two million men overseas. His third task was to supply this gargantuan army, on which fifteen billion dollars was to be expended in less than two years. He was perfectly aware that modern war was a conflict of smokestacks—it was no longer a combat of "Samson with his shield . . . and David with his sling." Because of this new situation he observed that nations now began wars with the slogan of "business as usual" and ended them with civilians almost as militarized as the soldiers. In theory he believed that one of the greatest guarantees of peace would be the exclusive manufacture of war materials by the government itself. In actual practice, however, he was responsible for the co-ordination of private—rather than public—industry and resources through his position as Chairman of the Council of National Defense. This body consisted of six members of Wilson's

Cabinet, whose knowledge of industrial affairs was not great enough to impress business magnates. Because of this situation it was not surprising that much of the policy work at the top level was actually done by an advisory commission of civilians, headed by Daniel Willard, President of the Baltimore and Ohio Railroad. In actual day-by-day operations the major activities of the Council were carried out by the subsidiary General Munitions Board under Frank A. Scott, a prominent Cleveland industrialist, until it was superseded by the independent War Industries Board of which Bernard Baruch was later chairman. Baker thought Scott's work on the Munitions Board was "in many ways the most valuable single service performed by any civilian . . . performed with the unselfish devotion which . . . left his health . . . impaired." He respected Baruch's ability but early in the war had expressed to the President some question about the advisability of naming him to a prominent position in the Government. Baker doubted that "the country would accept as an ideal appointment a man whose success in life had been largely that of a Wall Street financier."

Baker paid so little attention to the politics of those who were engaged in the common effort that a Republican caucus could have been held in the War Department. Grosvenor Clarkson, the secretary of the Council of National Defense who was himself a Republican, testified that members of the "opposition" party comprised seven-eighths of the staff executives of both the Council of National Defense and the War Industries Board. It was an example of nonpartisanship that Clarkson would not have believed possible before he went to Washington—"something for those to ponder who attacked Mr. Wilson's administration for not establishing a coalition war government." There was E. R. Stettinius of the J. P. Morgan firm, a solid Republican who was named special assistant to the Secretary of War in charge of supplies. Samuel McRoberts, President of the National City Bank and one of the pillars of the Republican party, was made chief of procurement. Stanley King, a New England shoe manufacturer, was particularly valuable in supervising labor policy under Baker's direction, and for a year was his private secretary. King was a liberal Republican who had worked with Louis Brandeis on social projects in the Boston area. Republican Daniel Willard was for a time Chairman of the War Industries Board; Republican Julius Rosenwald of Sears, Roebuck was the chairman of an important committee on supplies and embarked on a special mission to France for the War Department. So many of the key officials in the War Department were members of the GOP that some of Baker's Democratic colleagues worried about it. At one time three top assistants were Republicans: Assistant Secretary Benedict Crowell was a Cleveland contractor in charge of munitions, Assistant Secretary Keppel had the responsibility for recreation and social work, and Special Assistant Emmet J. Scott (who dealt with problems concerning Negro soldiers) was a Republican who had been Booker T. Washington's secretary at Tuskegee. The bipartisan arrangement functioned very well; by the end of 1917 the supply problem had been solved so effectively that the Shipping Board was experiencing difficulty in finding enough vessels to carry the mountain of materiel to France. Ultimately the Board managed to provide the ships by the seizure or requisition of enemy and neutral vessels which were in our harbors at the outbreak of the war, by a gigantic construction program designed to furnish an Atlantic bridge of boats, and by borrowing merchantmen from our British ally.[1]

When World War I began Baker was charged with unpreparedness due to niggardly and penny-pinching expenditures; when the conflict ended he was accused of colossal extravagance, not excluding the allegation that he paid the French a rental fee for the trenches in which American boys were dying and that the AEF was oversupplied with well-constructed coffins but was given defective ammunition. The initial attack was mounted by Republicans who demanded a "coalition" Cabinet, to be achieved by the replacement of Baker and Daniels by Elihu Root and Theodore Roosevelt. Opponents of the Wilson Administration regretted there was no House of Lords in the American political pattern; promotion to such a quiet and contemplative body, they claimed, would have been a perfect "putting out to pasture" for a Secretary of War who was really a pacifist in ill-fitting warrior's attire. "Historian" Theodore Roosevelt was confident that the American chronicle showed no better example of "fatuous incompetence" than that displayed by the War Department during World War I. In the presidential campaign of 1920 the Republicans were to smear the Wilson regime through indictment of a number of individuals for alleged war frauds.

Baker read the newspapers during the war and concluded wistfully that they regarded him as a complex and paradoxical villain—their picture of the Secretary of War portrayed a "harsh, unjust, arbitrary, soft-hearted, mild, easy-going tyrant." He appeared to be imperturbable but the merciless attack left its mark. On one occasion the diminutive forty-five-year-old Secretary suggested that he give up his work in the War Department to enter active military service, but the President turned him down. When a friend remarked that he seemed to be unmoved by criticism Baker was quoted in reply: "If you took my heart out, you'd see the heel prints on it."

On the Congressional front the attack was bipartisan, and there was no abatement in the assault until the Secretary's dramatic counterattack which was to occur in January 1918. At first Baker resented the time consumed in answering Congressional inquiries, which took about one third of the General Staff's time during a period when the Germans were the active foe. Later he concluded that the investigations had been beneficial because they spread throughout the War Department the impression that anything done on Tuesday was likely to be investigated on Wednesday. As a consequence complete records were maintained, documents that gave Baker a comfortable sense of assurance and safety in following years. He was to recall that Senators, Republican and Democratic alike, hunted him "with dogs," and that the Democrats seemed to be more proficient in the game of hare and hounds. In later years he observed that Democratic Senators gave him almost as much work as the Germans, and that he had to fight enemies both foreign and domestic at the same time. When he talked privately with the legislators Baker said that he asked only that they "beat the Germans first and then beat me if I still seem to deserve it." He did not feel that the attacks were personal; any other Secretary of War probably would have been assaulted with equal fury because

> every malcontent, disappointed contractor, unjustified aspirant
> for high places in the military service, and overzealous partisan,
> wrote letters to Senators, which they read on the floor of the
> Senate, telling exactly how the war ought to be fought, and
> pointing out grave defects in the way it was being fought. This
> sort of thing took place in every country, and always takes place
> in every war. I was obliged to keep silent about most of it,
> both because we were absorbingly busy in what we were doing,
> and also because much that was being done could not be pub-
> licly discussed without lending aid and comfort to the enemy.[2]

The difficulties between the Administration and Congress were caused chiefly by the necessity for military secrecy and the rapidity with which expenditures had to be made. Field Marshal von Hindenburg was reported to be grateful for the information received about American preparations, and for that reason the War Department was anxious to keep its activities as secret as possible. This cloak around American operations had one unfortunate consequence: the electorate was mystified and restive from a lack of definite information, and this uncertainty was reflected in the Congress.

With regard to expenditures the United States had always assumed that the Navy, as the traditional first line of defense, would be at its best when war was declared. By contrast it had been customary for the Army to be at its worst at the beginning of a conflict, and at its best at the close of a war. For that historic reason preparedness in the Navy, vis-à-vis the Congress, had always been relatively easy; preparedness in the Army had always been difficult in peacetime. Because Congress was slow in appropriating money, during the early months of the war Baker personally authorized expenditures of several hundred million dollars for needed supplies before either House had voted a penny for the purpose. As a lawyer he did some worrying about such illegal expenditures, but finally concluded that the crisis was too acute and that the sums involved were too large for punitive action. "You can put a man in jail," was his comment, "for spending five dollars or fifty dollars, but three hundred million dollars passes anybody's sense of humor or propriety." The sudden increase in the size of the Army—from 212,000 to 4,000,000 men in eighteen months—meant that billions of dollars had to be spent with phenomenal speed for ordnance, clothing, army cantonments, transport, and all the other paraphernalia needed by a modern army. This required immediate expansion of industrial facilities already busy with war orders from our Allies in Europe, and the result was a considerable amount of waste and confusion. In fact that United States Government from its inception in 1789 to the day we entered the First World War in 1917 had spent twenty-four billion dollars for all purposes; to mount our war effort in 1917–18 we spent twenty-five billion dollars in eighteen months, not counting ten billion more that was lent to the Allies. The combination of hasty action and unlimited funds produced some dandy blunders. At one time the War Department could not understand the requisition, and Pershing was puzzled by the delivery in France, of lawn mowers and obstetrical supplies. The mystery was finally solved; Pershing's own quartermasters had ordered from the standard list for Army posts in the United States, oblivious to the patent fact that certain peacetime items were superfluous in European trench warfare. Once Baker went to the basement of the War Department and was unable to get through the corridors because they were piled from floor to ceiling with typewriters. In response to a query the Adjutant General reported that every available typewriter in the country had been purchased. Baker asked the reason, and received the prompt reply that if he had not purchased them the Surgeon General would have done so—and if both had been negligent the monopoly on typewriters would have passed to the Navy or the Treasury. Given human frailty, such possessiveness may be understandable, but the fact remains that it was frightfully expensive.[3]

Criticism of the War Department reached a climax in January 1918 when Oregon's Senator George Earle Chamberlain, who was Chairman of the Committee on Military Affairs, defied the Wilson Administration by introducing on his own account a bill to create a cabinet minister of munitions. In an address before the National Security League in New York, Chamberlain said:

> Let me say that the military establishment of America has fallen down. There is no use to be optimistic about a thing that does not exist. It has almost stopped functioning, my friends. . . . I speak not as a Democrat, but as an American citizen.

Theodore Roosevelt, who happened to be present, jumped to his feet and applauded loudly.

Josephus Daniels read the story and wondered if Chamberlain had suddenly lost possession of his senses. There was much speculation concerning the Democratic Senator's motivation. Daniels thought it arose from disappointment over federal patronage in the West; when Secretary of War Garrison had resigned in 1916 Chamberlain had told President Wilson that ex-Governor Oswald West, from his home State of Oregon, ought to be appointed to the Cabinet, but Baker had been chosen instead. Ray Stannard Baker was certain that Chamberlain's attitude was traceable to the great business interests of the country which were resentful of government controls, heavy taxation, and the growing power of labor. Whatever the provocation Wilson was so enraged that he asked Chamberlain for verification of the statement, and the Senator replied that he had been quoted correctly. The break with the Administration became complete with the President's prompt rejoinder:

> As a matter of fact, the war department has performed a task of unparalleled magnitude and difficulty with extraordinary promptness and efficiency. . . . My association and constant conferences with the secretary of war have taught me to regard him as one of the ablest officials I have ever known. The country will soon learn whether he or his critics understand the business at hand.

Baker accepted the statement with "infinite gratitude" but again offered his resignation; he told the President that "a time may come when you will find it possible to advance the cause and consolidate the sentiment of the country, by making a change either by sending me to other service or to none." Wilson declined the offer, and his generous support brought Baker to the conclusion that the moment had arrived for a well-publicized defense of his stewardship. He proposed to Administration stalwarts, particularly Senators Ollie James of Kentucky and Claude Swanson of Virginia, that he be allowed to address the entire Senate. He felt that a bad precedent had been established in 1790 when Congress refused eloquent Alexander Hamilton (who was Secretary of the Treasury) permission to appear before it; he wanted the privilege of appearing in the Senate for discussion of the "imaginary grievances and fanciful accusations" which arose from "accidental shortcomings in a vast and hurried enterprise." James and Swanson told him the proposal to overthrow a century-old precedent was impossible, and Baker compromised by agreeing to address the Senate Military Affairs Committee. He asked for an open session in a large room which would accommodate interested visitors. The Committee insisted on a closed hearing in their small chamber until Baker circulated through the press his original demand for a session open to the public. At this point, in Baker's phrase, "it finally dawned on the Committee that they could not have an executive session in a dark corner and turn the great crowd away." A large room seating three hundred was provided; even so there was standing room only and the corridor outside was packed.

Baker's five-hour speech before the Committee was heavy with detail in its point-by-point defense of the War Department and was extemporaneous except for occasional reference to slips of paper, handed to him by Ralph Hayes, on which statistical information had been noted. This marathon effort checked, if it did not crush, the attack on both the Wilson Administration and Baker; thereafter the assault was directed at specific individuals and incidents rather than in the general direction of the War Department. Daniels was enraptured with Baker's unstudied eloquence. "No such speech," he was sure, "restrained and fortified with logic and evidence, had been heard in the Capitol in a generation." Ollie James, a Senator of monumental proportions, sat anxiously in the front row "perspiring like the village-pump" throughout the hearing. At the noon recess he rushed for the exit, hurried to the White House, dashed past the doorkeepers, and explained to the astonished President: "Jesus, Mr. President, little Baker's eating 'em up." Even the Secretary of War, who was ready to admit that "one's judgment of his own performances is always untrustworthy," ultimately came to the conclusion that this speech was the best he ever made. In any case, the denouement was tragic for Senator Chamberlain. His reply to Baker lasted three hours but his bill to reorganize the Cabinet "died a-bornin'." In 1920 he ran for re-election, still criticizing the administration of the draft, the procurement of uniforms, the failure to build air-planes, and the "fossilized men" in the War Department who should have been retired. He was defeated, left the Senate, and according to Daniels—scarcely an unprejudiced witness—"never was heard of again." Daniels thought it was

This Denver Post *cartoon of January 29, 1918, pictures Secretary of War Baker's successful defense of his administration.*

a sad ending for a career which in the early years had given
so much promise of distinction.[4]

Baker's speech did not end the inquiries into the behavior
of the War Department. The American operation in World
War I was conducted by the Democratic party; it was investigated for eight years by the Republicans. Because of the
pervading selfishness of mankind there were many examples
of legal profiteering in wartime, just as there are numerous
instances of legal profiteering in peacetime in relation to

The Denver Post *of January 30, 1918, continued to support*
Baker's reply to his critics, Roosevelt and Chamberlain.

the income tax and other laws. There was colossal evidence
of waste and incompetence. On the subject of extravagance,
since all war is a waste, it proved impossible to convict individuals of profligacy. Probably the most eloquent testimony
for this truism was given by Republican Charles Gates Dawes,
who had been the general purchasing agent for the AEF. The
future Vice-President earned the soubriquet "Hell and Maria"
while testifying on behalf of the War Department in 1921:

> Sure we paid. . . . We would have paid horse prices for
> sheep if sheep could have pulled artillery. . . . It's all right
> now to say we bought too much vinegar or too many cold
> chisels, but we saved the civilization of the world. . . . This
> was not a Republican or a Democratic war; it was an American
> war. . . . Damn it all, the business of an army is to win a war,
> not to quibble around with a lot of cheap buying. . . . Hell
> and Maria, we weren't trying to keep a set of books. We were
> trying to win a war.

The data on incompetence was just as clear as that on waste
and profiteering. When all of the evidence was in, however,
it seemed apparent that the top men in the War Department
were honest, zealous, and competent, and that most of the
lesser men had been as honest and zealous but less competent.
Why this should have surprised anyone was a puzzle to Frank
Scott, the Cleveland industrialist who had been Baker's Chairman of the Munitions Board. He wrote:

> Naturally, mistakes were made. Do we not have something
> under 500 business failures in our country every week? If we
> do, in time of peace, does this not prove a tremendous per-
> centage of error and incompetence among business men who
> are not working under any special pressure nor perplexed by
> extraordinary conditions such as war introduces. Why should
> any one assume that a declaration of war would miraculously
> eliminate this weakness from our business personnel and sud-
> denly give us, for the Government service, prodigies of sound
> judgment and far-sightedness, even when dealing with wholly
> unfamiliar subjects.[5]

The most striking example of general ineptitude—an embarrassing combination of waste, incompetence, and some legal profiteering—was the airplane scandal. The charge was clear: huge sums of money had been expended for only 1,379 planes and 4,435 Liberty 12-cylinder motors. In its early stages the program was the responsibility of eminent Republican businessmen, particularly Howard E. Coffin, the builder of the Hudson automobile, and Colonel Edward A. Deeds, who had left the National Cash Register Company to work with Charles F. Kettering in the new Delco concern that made self-starters for automobiles. Coffin and Deeds became unduly enthusiastic about the American potential for production of fighting planes in a short time, and promised results that turned out to be impossible. Among the unanticipated and extenuating reasons were the unusually cold winter of 1917–18 which made it difficult to procure spruce for the planes, strikes among the lumbermen, and exasperating changes in Allied specifications which made it impossible to "set" the production of one aircraft.

The whole sorry business was thoroughly investigated by a number of Congressional committees, and by special inquiries conducted by Republicans Charles Evans Hughes and Gutzon Borglum. Borglum—an able sculptor, an enthusiastic aeronaut, a Progressive Republican, and a close friend of Roosevelt—was versatile and contentious. He was a powerful and eloquent fellow with a jutting forehead, who saw every issue in vivid whites and blacks; his opponents were not only wrong, they were crooked. Felix Frankfurter, who had several assignments with the War Department in this period, classified him as "one of those artists who had delightful incapacities for running government, but knew exactly how to do it." Borglum got the erroneous idea that President Wilson had appointed him a committee of one to investigate the mess, reported that most of the appropriation for aircraft had been absorbed by a conspiracy of profiteers, and made quite a journalistic splash before it was alleged that he too was interested in forming a company to manufacture planes. He countercharged that he was the victim of a plot, formed by Baker, Deeds, and others, to discredit his report. Baker had no respect for Borglum as an investigator, and when the sculptor filed a compensation claim for his efforts, the Secretary made an unusually acid comment: "When the Government of the U.S. begins to pay people at extravagant rates for constituting themselves nuisances, Borglum will of course be entitled to a very large sum."

The Hughes Report, submitted to the President on October 31, 1918, was thorough. The investigation had consumed twenty-two weeks and there were 17,000 pages of testimony. The evidence indicated that predominant reliance on automotive manufacturers had not been justified, and that a hundred million dollars had probably gone into the pockets of men who could skillfully extract it from the government without giving value received—although it was clear that all contracts had been made in open daylight for all to see. There was also enough circumstantial evidence to lead some critics to the conclusion that Colonel Deeds had been misnamed, except for his alleged partiality to former business partners. Deeds was subsequently tried by a court-martial, and was acquitted of "unlawful intent" or personal profit from his financial transactions for the government.

On matters of judgment Baker came in for his share of criticism because of the airplane fiasco. On February 20, 1918, he was pilloried for signing a misleading press release, prepared by a sanguine subordinate, which announced dramatically that the "first American-built battle *planes* are today en route to France." Actually one lone combat plane, a de Havilland, had been crated and started on its way. Even faithful friends of the Secretary thought he had carried his basic faith in humankind too far, especially where this trust concerned the production of airplanes. One of them questioned Baker's confidence in businessmen, and wrote:

> I have found mighty little patriotism in the average business man and when he comes offering something for nothing, I get suspicious of the Greeks bearing gifts. I think that if you had a little of my pessimism in that regard you would be better off. There is no class in the world so selfish and unpatriotic as the American business man. Everything is fish that comes to his net. He simply cannot help it. The capacity for making money is an instinct and he obeys an instinct—an uncontrollable instinct.

Others felt that he had relied too much on finesse in the treatment of Republican *particeps criminis,* especially in one instance where it was suggested that a "whack on the precise high Republican nose was the only effective quiescent."[6]

Altogether there were more than fifty Congressional investigations into all the activities of the War Department, in addition to a continuing inquiry by the War Transactions Division of the Department of Justice. The net result, after several million dollars had been spent on inquiries, was thirty-seven indictments for war frauds. Ultimately four of this number were convicted in minor cases; i.e., a man in Texas was incarcerated for stealing a secondhand truck worth $2,400, an Army officer got a kickback (and eighteen months in jail) for approving an order for skid chains, a man in Maine was fined $100 for pilfering property, and another in New York paid a similar fine for falsifying his application for a passport. In 1926 the Department of Justice dismantled the War Transactions Division, and its Director of Investigations accompanied his resignation with the observation:

> After four years of research under three Attorney Generals, it is a happy comment to add there were so few instances of deliberate attempts to defraud the Government of the U. S. . . .

> It was unfortunate that so many . . . charges of fraud were given circulation . . . involving reputable men.

Ralph Hayes summarized the eight-year inquiry by stating that "what had started with a whoop was abandoned in a whisper."[7]

IX. Secretary of War—

Demobilization

WHEN THE ARMISTICE was signed Baker and the War Department were going full speed ahead; with a clashing of gears the machine was now put into reverse. For automobile drivers backing is frequently a slow, painful, and potentially dangerous challenge; it was no easier to apply the brakes to a human military machine and to place it suddenly on a retrograde course. Billions of dollars in war contracts had to be canceled, but the negotiations over necessary financial settlements required time for arbitration. Millions of men had to be returned to their homes, but two million of them were in France and transport ships were in short supply. For the American doughboys who arrived at Brest on the morning of November 11, 1918, the solution was easy; they saw nothing of France except a harbor and were returned on the same transport, ironically to receive an enthusiastic welcome in New York as the first home-coming heroes from "over there." But for the veterans of the Meuse-Argonne, who had had more than enough of life in the trenches, any delay was exasperating. Actually the demobilization of almost three and a half million men was completed in one year, but this achievement was twelve months too long for many of the soldiers. The delay was to have a political effect. One of Baker's Congressional correspondents prophesied correctly that the sooner the men returned the stronger their appreciation of *Democratic* principles would be; Republican success in the presidential election of 1920 might be explained, at least in part, by the misunderstanding of the situation by two million American soldiers who were stranded in Europe.[1]

With the war obviously drawing to a close in the autumn of 1918 Baker began to think about a lasting peace, and he prayed there would be enough foresight to establish a new order for the long interests of the future. He wrote Brand Whitlock that he doubted if either of them would live long enough to see whether the days of wisdom would outlive the days of repentance, but he was optimistic enough to believe that the world was growing better, and he hoped that its peoples had learned the futility of aggregate wrongdoing under the guise of national aggrandizement. Within a few days of the Armistice the Secretary put his foot down when Ignace Paderewski, eminent both as a pianist and a chauvinist, asked for the release to a Polish Legion of all soldiers of Polish extraction in the American Army for the purpose of fighting the Russians. Baker said he would place his faith in international police rather than independent armies.

Wilson planned to appoint Baker as a member of the Peace Commission, and the Secretary would have accompanied the President to Paris had it not been for the surprising departure from the Cabinet of Secretary of the Treasury McAdoo within two weeks after the shooting had stopped. The resignation, for financial reasons according to the announcement, came as a bolt out of the blue to Baker, who first saw it in the newspapers. The incident irked him so much that years later he told McAdoo that the original press release had been most unfortunate, "particularly at a time when you and everybody else in the country were making sacrifices of a financial kind without thought of their effect upon your personal fortune." When McAdoo replied that financial considerations had been secondary to his run-down physical condition due to overwork, Baker's riposte was unusually blunt and mockingly deferential. He said there was such a thing as a leave of absence, that many officials in Washington were worn in body and mind at the close of the war, and that "any consideration for my own health or financial situation would have required me to resign on the 11th day of November. I did not feel free to do so and, of course, your presence in the Cabinet was vastly more important than mine." In his reply McAdoo countered with a third reason. As the "Crown Prince" (he was Wilson's son-in-law) he did not want the charge of a "family dynasty" made, and that might have happened with the President in Europe and McAdoo in charge here. Baker did not bother to reply.

Whatever the motive, McAdoo's departure effectively killed Baker's appointment to the Peace Commission. Secretary of State Lansing had to accompany Wilson to Paris, and the Treasury would now have an inexperienced head. Baker therefore told the President that the country might very well feel that the Cabinet should not be further weakened, during the critical period of domestic adjustment, by the withdrawal of the Secretary of War for diplomatic duty abroad. Wilson thought the matter over for three days, and one afternoon, as Baker reported it,

> came over to my office to tell me that he had been trying to see some other way out, as he was very anxious to have me with him, but he felt the strength of my suggestion so much that he was obliged to adopt it, although he was reluctant to do so. He was genuinely fine about it, and I am so sure that

this is the right thing to do that I have a real sense of relief
. . . about the whole matter.

One consolation for Baker was that the President accepted
his suggestion for a replacement on the Peace Commission.
The appointment went to General Bliss, whose vast knowledge was to be utilized scarcely at all by Wilson, occupied
as he was by demanding European premiers. Bliss saw the
President for personal interviews only five times during the
entire Peace Conference.[2]

From the vantage point of easy hindsight it appears that
Baker was fortunate in being compelled to stay at home.
While the war was still in progress his literary friend Alfred
Jay Nock had been dubious about the peace settlement; with
one eye cocked at the statesmen of the era, he had asked the
Secretary why he expected "this particular crop of thistles to
grow figs when none other in the history of the world has
ever done so." At first the prospects for a lasting peace seemed
alluring. Wilson appeared in Europe, the first Chief Executive to make the journey while President, and was idolized
by adoring crowds which regarded him as the King of
Humanity. But European leaders—the opportunistic Lloyd
George, the Irredentist Orlando, and the cynical Clemenceau
—had little regard for Wilson's League of Nations. They
were careful to keep the idealistic American President at
arm's length from the worshipful people for fear his popularity might bring about their own political downfall.

Bliss wrote Baker that he hoped the President was impressed by the fact that his strength lay in the hopeful crowds
rather than with the "people with whom he was riding" as
he greeted the multitudes, but the latter were to have little
voice in the peacemaking. Lieutenant Ralph Hayes (Baker's
secretary who had enlisted in the Army as a private) wrote
that Paris was overrun by a horde of men in uniform—"tin
soldiers" who wanted to make the city "a robber's nest of

social functions." At the Hotel Crillon on the Place de la Concorde Colonel House commanded a large group of experts, each one convinced of the supreme importance of his own contribution; the result was that the first struggle among Americans in Paris was not over the establishment of peace, but over suitable room assignments! Captain Walter Lippmann, now in the French capital, congratulated Baker on making the most humane army that ever decided a great war —but he was not sure there was enough statesmanship in the world to write a good peace, and was not certain that the people of the United States were very clear about the matter. By January 1919, Bliss told Baker, the French desire to bring complete ruin to Germany was little less than insanity, and he was feeling more strongly with each passing day that the wisest thing for the United States to do was to get out of Europe—"horse, foot, and dragoons." Bliss stated that we had entered the war to abolish *German* militarism, which had been accomplished, but *European* militarism appeared to be as rampant as ever. He did not think we should stay there indefinitely to untangle every knot that had been "wantonly tied in the skein of European politics."

This was the same point of view expressed by relief expert Herbert Hoover, who wrote Wilson in the spring of 1919 that if the Allies would not adopt peace on the basis of the idealistic fourteen points, the United States should retire from Europe "lock, stock, and barrel." Hoover knew that Wilson might have negotiated on a hard-boiled and pragmatic basis: he might have stopped the huge American loans on which Europe depended for its existence, and temporarily might have demanded America's share of territorial spoils and enemy reparations to trade them later for international concessions. But the future Republican President thought that Wilson, whom he admired, was too great a man to bargain in this way and that American idealism was "unfitted to participate in a game played with power as the counters."

By 1920 Raymond Fosdick, who had organized the recreational program of the American Army so well, was appalled that the United States could win a war so brilliantly and lose the peace so ignominiously. In melancholy prose he wrote Baker:

> We have proved ourselves unworthy of the sacrifices our soldiers made for us. Do you remember those boys we saw in that hospital in Paris just a year ago? And those other boys that were coughing their lungs out in that gas hospital? They didn't die to pave the way for a bigger and better war in which their sons would die. And yet that is where we seem to be heading.

Baker was not so pessimistic. He was certain that the treaty, while disappointing, was better because of Wilson's influence. "If the President had not been an international gentleman," he wrote, "the peace finally patched up in Paris would have made the looting of Peking look like a Sabbath School scolding. . . ." In later years he was ready to admit that Wilson's idealism was accompanied by a conviction, inherited from a long line of Presbyterian Covenanters, that he had been tapped on the shoulder by Fate to carry on certain providential purposes:

> I am perfectly certain that nobody ever led a crusade in the Middle Ages with more quiet conviction than he. The consequence of this was that whenever anybody opposed Mr. Wilson, he was more or less unconscious of the personal quality of the opposition, but disturbed that people should be foolish enough to thrust themselves in the way of Providential plans. None of this was consciously worked out in his mind. It rather took the form that when he thought anybody was wrong, he interpreted the word wrong to mean about what the preachers call sinful. . . . I told him once of a very annoying instance of political misconduct on the part of a senator. His comment was characteristic: "Baker, the Devil is a very personal and a very busy gentleman." In a vague way he felt that anybody who did anything wrong was possessed of devils. . . . I am quite sure he regarded Lloyd George as one of the most magnificent sinners

he had ever known. In like manner he was offended not by Mr. Clemenceau's paganism, but by the fact that all of his courses led clear off the map of the Divine purpose.[3]

Demobilization was made infinitely more difficult because the Democratic administration during most of the period was rudderless as far as domestic affairs were concerned. For months Wilson was in Paris at the Peace Conference, and in September 1919 he suffered his disabling paralytic stroke. Baker had always insisted there was no such thing as an indispensable man, but now he was not so sure. Wilson's absence, he thought, left a greater vacuum than any in history, rivaled only by the death of Charlemagne which turned an "orderly empire over to three squabbling sons."

The illness of the President presented the difficult problem as to whether he should be succeeded by the Vice-President, an issue which this country has also faced, but never solved, during the administrations of Garfield, Cleveland, and Eisenhower. When Secretary of State Lansing called a meeting of the Cabinet four days after the President's thrombosis, Wilson was irritated. He asked his personal physician, Admiral Cary Grayson, to ascertain by what authority the Cabinet had been convened. Baker told Grayson to inform the President that the only purpose of the informal session was both innocent and practical; they had met to extend sympathy and to consider business that had been in abeyance since the last meeting a month earlier. Baker's explanation appears to have satisfied the President about the loyalty of his Secretary of War, but the meeting intensified Wilson's suspicions of Lansing. The two men had disagreed over the League of Nations, which Lansing was reported to have classified as thoroughly bad. There was a new flurry south of the Rio Grande; Baker had been shocked by Lansing's belligerent desire to intervene with military forces in Mexico during a temporary crisis late in 1919 over the alleged kidnaping by bandits of an American consular agent there. There was some evidence to indicate that major support for armed intervention came from American oil prospectors south of the border who wanted the protection of the United States Government. The conservative Lansing claimed that the Mexican Embassy in Washington was spawning "red" propaganda; Baker was horrified to hear the Secretary of State say that "if we go into Mexico it will settle our difficulties *here.*"

Whatever the motive Lansing's proposal was hardly consistent with Wilson's steadfast emphasis on the right for all nations, large and small, to self-determination. When Lansing resigned early in 1920 the public assumed that the chief reason was Wilson's anger over the holding of Cabinet meetings. Baker never believed it. In his judgment it was a miracle that Lansing had stayed for five years with Wilson because no two men could have differed more widely in their approach to political problems. To Baker:

> President Wilson was an imaginative farseeing and foreseeing man, who realized that the World War had changed the basis of international relations. Secretary Lansing was a black letter lawyer who believed that after a temporary disturbance of a world war had subsided, the old rules of international law would be found entirely adequate. . . .

Someone had to take over the State Department for the year that remained in Wilson's Administration, and most of the *cognoscenti* assumed that the successor would be the able Undersecretary Frank L. Polk. If Polk was not chosen it was thought Baker would get the nod, although he wanted to finish the job in the War Department and was apprehensive about a temporary assignment which would end before the period of initiation was completed. To everyone's surprise Bainbridge Colby, a Republican-turned-Democrat who had been a member of the Emergency Fleet Corporation, was chosen. Baker never knew why. His colleague Josephus Daniels assumed it was because the President wanted to strengthen the merchant marine.[4]

A few months remained to the Wilson Administration after the Republican triumph in the election of 1920, and Baker stayed to the end in a position which he had accepted for one year but which he had occupied for five. As March 4, 1921, approached there was some denunciation of his tenure as Secretary of War. His old nemesis George Harvey, soon to become Harding's ambassador in London, was scurrilous in his judgment on Baker's "graduation" from a regular four-year course plus a postgraduate term of one year in the War Department:

> It was at an appalling cost, but Mr. Baker has been educated. It cost no man knows how many thousands of precious American lives. It cost hundreds of millions, yes, billions of dollars. That Mr. Baker might be educated, our patriotic young men were sent half-clad, unarmed, untrained into the worst war known in history. They shivered in unheated barracks; they died miserably in improvised unequipped hospitals. . . .

On the other hand Baker could take pride in subsequent statements from John J. Pershing and Douglas MacArthur that he was the ablest Secretary of War the country had ever known. The *New York World* said that his success in sending two million men to Europe in less than two years was the most remarkable achievement of its kind known to military annals. The well-known dramatist and confidant of politicians, Robert Sherwood, testified that Baker had kept both his head and his honor in the midst of a welter of bureaucracy, jingoism, and hysteria. Paderewski expressed his appreciation for the "gifted statesman" who had converted a peaceful democracy into a military power within a few months, and added his admiration for Baker's offer of a kind word and a friendly smile for all who importuned him during critical days. General Hugh Johnson, who was to become the NRA chieftain of New Deal days, was certain that the former pacifist had proved to be one of "the greatest Lords of War that ever trod the earth." The chances are that it was Wilson's evaluation that pleased Baker most. "I wonder if you know," wrote the President on Armistice Day 1918, "how genuinely and intensely I have trusted and believed in you and how happy I am that the trust and belief have been absolutely justified by the result."

When Baker left Washington in the spring of 1921 there was a send-off that threw the Union Station into pandemonium. More than a thousand associates appeared to say good-bye, including Pershing, March, the new Republican Secretary of War John W. Weeks, and an assortment of two dozen major generals. A few days later the Harding Administration gave him a commission as a colonel in the Reserves. In appearance and manner he was certainly the most unlikely officer in the armed services, and in later days opponents would take delight in using the incongruous appellation "Col. Baker." Baker himself would contend that he had been given the wrong title. He remembered that a general had once told him that he probably knew enough to be a colonel but was completely lacking in the knowledge and qualifications necessary for a second lieutenant. An honest pursuit of this theory, Baker thought, would indicate that he should have been made a major general! In 1929 he was awarded the Distinguished Service Medal. He had discouraged earlier efforts on the part of his friends who wanted the distinction for him, with the comment that the only decoration he craved was the confidence and good will of the men with whom he had been associated in the war effort. While he was Secretary of War, however, he had seen to it that the first DSM had gone to President Wilson, the second to General Pershing, and the third and fourth to Generals Bliss and Foch.

After five years in Wilson's Cabinet he left Washington without financial reserves for a growing family. His Secretary's annual salary of $12,000 had been inadequate for the official demands of his position, and he had refused offers of financial aid from affluent and generous friends such as Justice Clarke and F. H. Goff, who was President of The Cleveland Trust Company. His departure from the capital was stamped with considerable disillusionment because of the fall of Wilson and the failure of the Senate to endorse the League of Nations. Back in Cleveland he wanted only a "roof to keep out the rain, a few more windows to lock at night, and an additional dozen frail porcelain gods and goddesses which my romping babies may break." There was to be no more government service. He envisioned the earth as a round and occasionally joyous place with peaks near home; the flat and dreary surfaces were in and around all public offices.[5]

The Armistice was signed on November 11, 1918, but the literary war continued throughout the 1920s and 1930s. The belligerent participants were diplomats and generals who substituted pens for swords, drawing in memoirs and diaries a rosy portrait of their own superlative efforts in spite of a variety of hindrances contributed by men who were alleged to be their colleagues. During the Spanish-American War Theodore Roosevelt had written such an egotistical account of his own contribution that the quizzical Mr. Dooley, after reading the volume, had come to the conclusion that it ought to be retitled "Alone in Cuba." Thirty years later commentators thought Pershing's book of his war experiences might have been called "Alone in France," and that the companion volume by General March might have borne the title "By Myself Against the Boche." As the avalanche of books rolled off the presses Baker suggested a practical division of labor. He proposed that 10 per cent of the total number of authors continue their writing; the remaining 90 per cent were to study the building trades in order to construct enough libraries to hold the works of those who went on with their composition.

One of the major dialectical battles was fought between Pershing (whose *My Experiences in the World War* appeared in 1931) and March (who could hardly wait to get his *The Nation at War* off the press a year later). After reading the two volumes Baker concluded that his chief service in the war seemed to have been the achievement of preventing Pershing and March from committing mutual murder. March was so bellicose that Baker thought he should have been born in the twelfth century when he could have followed Richard Coeur de Lion with a battle-ax. He recalled the observation made by General Bliss when Clemenceau and Foch were belaying each other with literary invective. Bliss had growled: "It is infinitely pitiful that these old men, both facing the open door of the tomb, should be wasting their time abusing each other when they ought to be saying their prayers."

Baker was most exercised by war diaries, so much so that he concluded that all keepers of diaries should be incarcerated! He had no respect for the literary device because Tuesday's anxieties and suspicions were often dissipated by Wednesday's facts, but the diarist seldom went back to make necessary changes or explanations. Furthermore diaries, usually written at the end of a long day when the author was tired and sleepy, were more apt to contain half-baked musings than well-done judgments. Baker once started a diary but abandoned it promptly. On the third day he looked at the notation made on the initial page, and never made another entry.

The first volume of *The Intimate Papers of Colonel House,* the secretive Texan who was a close adviser of President Wilson until their dramatic quarrel in 1919, appeared in

1926. Baker said it was the meanest book he had ever read. He was disgusted that House would spend thirty years gaining the confidence of the great and the near-great, would write these interviews at the end of each day, and then, after most of them were dead, would publish a thousand pages claiming the credit for practically every good thing any of them did. In his judgment egotism ruined more men than any of the other vices, and House, like March, was one of those fellows whose natural habit it was to suppose that he himself had done everything he saw going on around him. Baker never knew House well, a coincidence which he concluded was "part of the general good fortune which has accompanied me through life." He had no more than three conferences with the Texan "Mr. Smooth-It-Away," and none of them concerned problems confronting the War Department. This was fortuitous, in Baker's opinion, because it relieved him of any future anxiety that House would claim credit for the selection of Pershing, the planning of the Meuse-Argonne offensive, the writing of the Selective Service Act, and the organization of the services of supply.[6]

During World War I little notice had been given to George Harvey's indictment of Baker as a "pacifist Secretary of War." The charge really drew national attention for the first time in 1922 when the *Encyclopaedia Britannica* published a biographical sketch of Baker so denunciatory in tone that new life was given to Harvey's accusation. Said the *Britannica:*

> After the outbreak of the World War he endorsed the Administration's peace policy, supported the League to Enforce Peace, and urged that the national guard be tried fully before compulsory service be decided upon. After America entered the war he recommended moderation towards conscientious objectors and forbade men in uniform to interfere with anti-conscription meetings. The charge of pacifism was often brought against him, and his career generally as Secretary was widely

condemned throughout the United States as lacking in energy, foresight and ability, and especially for his failure to prepare adequately in the months immediately preceding the American declaration of war.

Numerous and vigorous protests were heard immediately, demanding that the *Britannica* recant and revise the article. They came from persons who were prominent in a great variety of professional, political, and religious fields: from General Pershing and Admiral Sims, Presidents Angell of Yale and Garfield of Williams, Rabbi Wise and the Episcopal Bishop Brent, labor leader Sam Gompers and merchant prince Julius Rosenwald, Grace Abbott of the Children's Bureau and Dean Roscoe Pound of the Harvard Law School. General March gave the Editor in Chief in London a generous piece of his mind and an uncomfortable half-hour, while in America a group of the *Britannica*'s editorial contributors including President Hopkins of Dartmouth, Professor Irving Fisher of Yale, and Dean Guy Stanton Ford of Minnesota assailed the article. On the Republican side Dwight Morrow called the sketch "ridiculous" and Senator James Wadsworth (Chairman of the Military Affairs Committee) labeled it "utterly false." General Bliss wrote his own evaluation:

> From the 9th of March 1916 . . . to the end of the war I never knew Mr. Baker to fail to meet every situation that arose, in so far as political opportunism combined with every form of petty, sordid "interest" permitted him. He became the target of criticism of men who regarded the war as their one great opportunity for profit, of men of both parties who protected themselves by the cuttle-fish game of darkening the political waters in which they swam, and of honest but ill-informed men, Encyclopaedists and others, who do not take the trouble to listen for the low voice of truth amid the howling of the mob.

For months Baker's friends were engaged in what turned out to be a scoreless guessing game, for in spite of much speculation and effort they never succeeded in identifying the "enemy" who wrote the offensive biography in the *Britannica*. Josephus Daniels assumed that it was from the pen of the literary manager of the Republican Campaign Committee. Justice Clarke surmised that it was inspired by George Harvey. Baker himself had a suspicion that Republican Senator Henry Cabot Lodge was the author because of his reputation as a biographer and historian. The *Britannica* kept mum except for the exasperating observation that the writer was an American and a Democrat whose ancestors had fought in the American Revolution.

One principal witness who was largely unconcerned about the controversy was Newton Baker. He thought the article would have little weight when the time came to write the real judgment on the success of American participation in the war and he felt it unworthy to worry about himself when so many, who had given active and unselfish service, would find themselves unmentioned in historic records. The foolish side of the *Britannica* article, in his opinion, was the attempt so soon after the war to write a historical judgment about a person still living who was involved in as complex an operation as the War Department during a great conflict:

> The fact about the office of the Secretary of War during a great war period is that no one human being ever was born who could have a very intimate contact with or knowledge of many of the details of the vast business going on under his eye and in his name. I selected here and there a subject to which I could give personal attention and tried in a general way to stimulate and encourage all my associates and subordinates, praising them whenever I could and backing up their efforts whenever they seemed to me loyal and well-intentioned. No doubt tens of thousands of things were done by the Secretary of War of which I have not yet heard and I suspect that in the long run I am in more danger of getting credit for good work done by others than I am of being blamed for the shortcomings of others. . . . I obviously know more about the Secretary of War than any other living person could possibly know and I should have a very difficult time making up my mind if I were

called upon to express a dispassionate judgment upon his performances. I know that he wanted to do very much more than
he did. I also know that some of the things he did pleased
even him; that a wiser person would have acted more wisely I
have no doubt but nobody could ever convince me that anybody could have been Secretary of War and tried harder than I
did while I was there.

Baker was unconcerned about the article but he couldn't
help being pleased by the efforts of his friends and the favorable comments from so many quarters. He noted that Ralph
Hayes—whom he characterized as "my former secretary, a
very brilliant young man and finely loyal to his old chief"
—had made an issue of the matter with the result that so
many people wrote complimentary letters "that I really got
during my lifetime a lot of obituary generosity." Hayes admitted that he worked himself into a "lather" over the
article; the *Britannica* thought so too and charged him with
being a "person of no account, running about making an ass
of himself." Hayes would have appreciated a little more
help from Baker; he was disturbed but not greatly surprised
when he found that the Secretary (one of the few people in
the world who had read the *Encyclopaedia* from start to finish) had written philosophical and impartial letters which
amounted to a defense of the *Britannica,* citing the service
it had performed for learning and literature through a century and a half. Hayes concluded ruefully that during the row
he had encountered almost as much difficulty from Mr. Baker
as from the *Britannica!* The offending author of the article
was never identified but Hayes did bring the *Encyclopaedia*
to revise it in the 1926 and subsequent editions, and he was
delighted to present Baker with a unique Christmas gift in
1924. It was a morocco-bound volume in which had been
placed the fine testimonials, received from all over the country, to Baker's war service.[7]

X. Lawyer

IN 1916, WHEN BAKER WAS forty-five, he had left the
Mayor's office in Cleveland in order to devote the remaining years of his life to the private practice of law. He
took with him as partners two young men, then twenty-seven
and thirty years of age, who had been his associates in Cleveland's municipal administration—Public Service Director
Thomas L. Sidlo and Assistant City Solicitor Joseph C. Hostetler. The firm began its operations with high aspirations,
but without capital or clients. Within two months it lost
its prominent senior partner for five years of service in Wilson's Cabinet. In the early days what business there was could
be conducted in a small office, modestly furnished through
the economical assistance of the partners' wives.

When Baker returned to the firm from Washington in 1921
he found his office much as he left it. The partners had been
busy but opportunities for growth during the war had been
limited—in part because Baker had made it a rule that the
firm would accept no employment directly or indirectly re-

lated to business with the government. In the remaining sixteen years of his life he was to see the partnership he had established in such modest circumstances become one of the leading firms in the Midwest, with a national reputation and a country-wide practice.

As Law Director of Cleveland in the "Seven Years' War Against Monopoly" Baker had the extraordinary advantage of continuous experience before the courts as a trial lawyer. As Mayor of Cleveland he had followed legal matters closely, and as Secretary of War he had been selected partly because a talented lawyer was useful in negotiating contracts for supplies—contracts which ultimately involved billions of dollars. In these negotiations he had dealt with, and had come to know well, most of the prominent industrialists and financiers of the nation. In spite of these advantages Baker's colleagues in his law firm never knew him to accept employment which required the assertion of a position contrary to his principles. He was glad to take specific cases but refused to become general counsel for corporate clients, because such a commitment might involve him in obligations inconsistent with his beliefs or interests, or might embarrass him in the acceptance of special employment from other clients.

Like Charles Evans Hughes and John W. Davis, Baker never chose to specialize, with the result that his practice covered most of the varied fields of legal interest. In their generation these three men were probably the most versatile of the distinguished members of the American Bar, employed as counsel in major cases which concerned different fields of the law, at a time when most lawyers were specialists in one or two fields but made no attempt to master all of them. Baker himself appeared as counsel (usually as chief counsel) in important cases involving patent law, international law, varied phases of American constitutional law, business and corporate law, the law of estates, banking (particularly in connection with the new Federal Reserve System), munic-

ipal law, freedom of the press, and the development of zoning
law. He frequently expressed the view that all young lawyers should engage in general practice in their early years
at the very least, and he believed that lawyers who began
their careers in one of fourteen specialties (which was true
in some law offices) would inevitably spend the balance of
their lives wondering what the other thirteen were all about.
However, because of his historical interest in American constitutional law, and international law, he had a preference
for cases in these fields.[1]

Baker's law practice was so demanding that he came to
regret the time taken away from the civic activities which
he enjoyed so much. He found it exasperating to be compelled to wait in Washington for several days before the
Supreme Court reached a case on which he was to appear,
and he deplored the long hours spent on railroad trains going
from one city to another. On the other hand he had accu-
mulated no financial reserves during two decades of public
service, had returned to Cleveland and the practice of law
in March 1921 with an indebtedness of almost eight thousand
dollars, was not insurable because of a defective heart, and
in his remaining years felt a normal and proper obligation
to make adequate financial provision for his family. None
the less some of his partners thought Baker's general uncon-
cern about money matters amounted at times to naïveté,
and there were occasions when they were disturbed by his
lack of interest in, and his refusal to take, highly remunerative accounts. At his death the Probate Court of Cuyahoga
County found that the net estate passing to Mrs. Baker in
real and personal property, chiefly stocks and bonds (after
deductions of $81,708 for debts, expenses, and federal estate
taxes), amounted to $154,593. The Executrix' return also
disclosed, as required by law, the gifts made by Baker throughout his lifetime. In the aggregate these had amounted to

$380,779 to Mrs. Baker, including the home on South Woodland Avenue which he gave her in 1925 and stocks, bonds, and cash which he had given her with consistent regularity throughout the years following his return from Washington. There was a similar pattern of regular gifts over a period of years to the three children, amounting to approximately $115,000. After inquiry and consideration of the evidence regarding Baker's consistent program of making such gifts, and in consideration of the affidavit made by his physician Dr. R. W. Scott, the Probate Court held that none of these gifts had been made in contemplation of death and were therefore not a part of the estate for purposes of the inheritance tax. The net estate plus gifts represented a sizable sum, but it was considerably less than a lawyer of Baker's eminence might have commanded.

Because he received national attention as the legal representative of large corporate interests—among them companies controlled by the Van Sweringen brothers, and various electric companies—there were critics who classified him as a "Wall Street lawyer." This was disturbing to Ralph Hayes for a number of reasons, one of them his ambition for Baker as a presidential candidate. Hayes knew that the former Secretary of War was responsible for defending freedom of the press for the Scripps-Howard newspapers, had represented the Amalgamated Clothing Workers, frequently appeared as counsel for the publicly controlled Federal Reserve System, and that on the local scene he would represent the City of Cleveland (but not the utility companies) in rate cases. For these reasons it perturbed Hayes that Baker, in the public mind, was often associated with the defense of the rich and the powerful. Hayes did not "hold it against" wealthy clients because they wore "plug hats and smoked ten-cent cigars," but he hoped to add a "push-cart vendor and an old lady in a shawl" to the list of customers. They were on the list, but the public would never know of their presence. It was distasteful to Baker to seek credit for work that he performed for impecunious or nonpaying clients—of which cases he had more than his share, and which he never delegated to a junior in his law firm. There had been the same reaction, on leaving the Mayor's office, when it was suggested that he be given a testimonial dinner or an automobile. Baker's comment was that if he were conscious of a personal contribution to the achievement of Cleveland he would all the more want to suppress any recognition of it.[2]

Some of Baker's cases were extensively publicized, although he believed that a few of those less well known were more important from the point of view of the legal principles and difficulties involved. Two of the widely publicized cases concerned the defense of newspapers against judges—Baker represented the *Columbus Citizen* in its ouster suit against Probate Judge Homer Z. Bostwick, and he defended the editor and editorial writer (Louis Seltzer and Carlton Matson) of the *Cleveland Press* on a charge of contempt against Common Pleas Judge Frederick Walther. The Cleveland case concerned the basic democratic principle of freedom of the press, and attracted so much national attention that Senator Arthur Vandenberg of Michigan considered the advisability of federal legislation against miscarriage of law in contempt cases and William Randolph Hearst, who wasted no affection on Baker, editorialized:

> It is astonishing that in this Republic, which sought to abolish tyranny, there should still exist judicial tyranny, exercised through the power to punish for contempt of court. The tyranny of judges can be just as great as the tyranny of kings.

Although betting was illegal in Ohio it was going on at the Thistledown Race Track near Cleveland through what was called a "contribution" system. The county sheriff closed the track, in the face of Judge Walther's puzzling injunction which forbade him from interfering with the use of the contribution system "provided it was not illegal." The *Cleveland Press* said the court was controlled by racing moguls, and leveled both barrels at Judge Walther in a provocative query entitled "If This Be Contempt." The judge thought it was, and promptly cited Seltzer and Matson.

In the subsequent trial Baker's strategy was clear and his defense was both witty and effective. He had to prove that illegal gambling (disguised as the contribution system) was going on at Thistledown, and that hostile newspaper articles were not subject to contempt proceedings—although they might be punishable as libel if the criticism was not justifiable. To Baker it was as "plain as the path to the parish church" that unauthorized wagering was being conducted under the contribution system:

> A lot of men who own race horses lease them to an association which runs a track, and the association to which they are leased runs the horses, and the spectators, who used to bet, no longer bet, but, by putting up money in the form of a bet, they really buy a participating interest in the lease of the horse for the particular race. These are short-term leases. (Laughter.)
>
> And then, if the court please, the race is run, and the gentlemen who contributed, if they were lucky enough to have contributed on Horse A and Horse A is lucky enough to have won first place, get very much more back than they contributed; while, if they are so unfortunate as to have contributed on Horse D, a horse that does not get one of the first three places, then they are so unfortunate as to lose all that they have contributed for their share of the lease of that horse for that race.
>
> The net result is the creating of legal fictions through which it is the duty of the trained eye of the law to see. The net result of it is that the same people go to the same race track and put their money in the same window, on the same terms, and either win or lose as they did before the thing was rebaptized and called the contribution system.

In connection with freedom of the press Baker argued, in the course of a long historical review, that democracy as practiced in America included the prerogative of criticizing all

public officials, so long as the commentary did not constitute
libel or slander.

No matter how brilliant Baker's performance may have
been, it failed to impress Judge Walther. He found Seltzer
and Matson guilty of contempt, and sentenced each of them
to thirty days in jail plus a fine of five hundred dollars. The
Court of Appeals, however, sustained Baker's argument in
an opinion that was unusually scathing in its denunciation
of Judge Walther:

> Now the thought in the mind of the Editor of *The Press* evi-
> dently was that here was a situation which called for strong
> remarks; and one must admit that in the editorials they did
> give utterance to strong remarks—but when one thinks of a
> judicial officer exercising the strong power of injunction to
> prevent an officer . . . against performing his duty, one cannot
> help but think that such action did call for strong remarks.
> We think the court erred in sitting in this case and in hear-
> ing the evidence. He could plainly have sent in another judge.
> We think he was not in a fit condition to give unbiased judg-
> ment. He sought to wreak vengeance upon the plaintiffs.
> Whether the court's order was designed to befuddle the Sher-
> iff's mind we don't know. Many sheriffs would have been be-
> fuddled by such a writ. The order was not worth the paper
> upon which it was written, then how could a comment, how-
> ever severe, on the paper, be contempt.

Homer Z. Bostwick was fifty-five, married, and Judge of
the Probate Court of Franklin County in Ohio. He developed
an extraordinary interest in twenty-four-year-old Opal Walker,
and during the subsequent relationship not only saw her
frequently but bestowed a number of presents including a
diamond ring and an Auburn automobile. This liaison was
terminated suddenly when Opal Walker unexpectedly married George Eversole. Judge Bostwick then attempted to
repossess the diamond ring from Mrs. Eversole by what was
alleged to have been intimidation. At this point the *Columbus
Citizen* (a Scripps-Howard newspaper represented by Baker's

law firm) entered the altercation with editorials against Bostwick. It also managed to get fourteen hundred signatures on
a petition, which was legally filed, asking for the removal
of the judge on the grounds of gross immorality, misfeasance,
and nonfeasance. If the charges were sustained Judge Bostwick would be removed from office; if they were found to
be groundless action for damages could be brought against
the *Citizen* and the fourteen hundred signers of the petition.
The controversy was enlivened by a bitter newspaper feud
between the *Citizen* and the powerful *Columbus Dispatch,*
which was supporting Bostwick.

In his argument Baker established the responsibility of the
Probate Court and then proved that Judge Bostwick did not
measure up to the high office which he held. On the Court
itself he proved, by historical analysis, that its functions were
both parental and sacred:

> The probate judge is an ancient officer in our jurisdiction.
> His function derives historically from an ecclesiastical court.
> Under the earliest ancient jurisdiction the crown was repre-
> sented by a priest or a bishop in dealing with the matters that
> are the basis of the Probate Court's jurisdiction. The King of
> England, as the *parens patriae,* was the father of the fatherless,
> the protector of the defenseless, custodian of the estates of
> widows, the advisor of those who by death or misfortune were
> deprived of their natural advisers.
> When those were transferred to us, the state of Ohio . . .
> becomes the successor of the King of England and is made
> *parens patriae.* What was once the ecclesiastical court has now
> become the Probate Court. . . .

Because of its conclusion, Baker's indictment of Judge Bostwick was often called the "Tell It to Opal" passage:

> And if the guardian of a child finds himself with a wayward
> girl or wayward boy on his hands and his own admonition and
> influence are not adequate, he takes him to the probate judge
> and he says to the child, "Here sits the parental function of
> the state of Ohio, listen to what he says." . . .

And if I, being the guardian of a minor girl, find that she is disposed to wayward courses and that I am unable to restrain her and I take her to the probate judge, I take her almost to the altar, I take her to a sacred place.

Now let's suppose in the present case that I, being the guardian of such a girl, in this county, take her to Judge Bostwick, and I say to the judge in her presence, "Judge Bostwick, this child for whom I am responsible won't listen to me, she needs your counsel and advice," and Judge Bostwick does his duty and gives her advice and tells her what the experience of the race is in upright living and in morals, and being the representative of the state in the matter of juvenile morals, he gives her good advice, and she snaps her fingers at him when he is through and says, "Tell it to Opal."

What is left of the function of the custodian of the public morals?

Baker's argument was successful, in both the original and appellate courts, and Judge Bostwick was removed from the bench.

In the early 1930s Baker was involved in a prominent and interesting extradition case concerning a peripatetic mischief-maker, then resident in Chicago, by the name of John ("Jake the Barber") Factor. Factor had a dubious reputation and was wanted by Scotland Yard on charges of swindling British investors out of millions through the sale of dry oil wells and nonexistent glass casket companies, and of cheating the Prince of Wales at cards. In America his alleged associations with gangsters did not enhance the esteem in which he was held; among other things he was kidnaped, was freed on payment of a ransom, and identified as his abductors the "Terrible" Tuohy gang in Chicago, several of whom were subsequently sentenced to ninety-nine years at the Joliet prison.

Baker never met Factor, received no retainer, and was interested only in the principle involved in the case. This involved the important question of asylum, i.e., whether under the Webster-Ashburton Treaty of 1842 and established principles of international law Factor could be extradited by

Great Britain for an offense under English criminal law (receiving money known to have been fraudulently obtained) which was not a crime under the law of Illinois. In such cases, ultimate discretion to grant or deny extradition is vested in the Secretary of State. However, the accused may, and in the Factor case did, obtain a judicial decision on the question of extradition.

Baker did not enter the litigation until the Federal Court of Appeals for the Seventh Circuit, in a two-to-one decision, reversed the verdict of the District Court which had denied extradition. He accepted participation in the case only at the urging of Presiding Judge Evan A. Evans of the Seventh Circuit, who had dissented from the decision and who believed that the extradition of any person involved principles of international and constitutional law which should not be overturned because the individual concerned appeared to be a scoundrel. Judge Evans was also convinced that the important questions involved should be represented in the Supreme Court by a lawyer who was extraordinarily well qualified to argue them. In the subsequent appeal to the Supreme Court of the United States, however, the efforts of Judge Evans and Mr. Baker were unsuccessful. In the majority opinion Justice Stone held that the offense charged was an extraditable crime even if not punishable by the law of Illinois. Justices Butler, Brandeis, and Roberts dissented sharply, adhering to the traditional principle that extradition should not be granted for acts not deemed criminal in the place of asylum. Baker said that he was lawyer enough to bow to a decision of the Supreme Court, but expressed professional surprise and was unconvinced by the majority decision. So was his friend Manley O. Hudson, soon to be an American judge on the World Court, who wrote a learned critique on the decision in the *American Journal of International Law*.

After the decision went against him, Factor urged the Secretary of State to refuse extradition on the grounds that the construction placed upon the applicable treaties by the majority of the Supreme Court was contrary to that placed upon their language by both Great Britain and the United States for nearly one hundred years and that, if the Court's interpretation were followed by the Secretary, the United States and its citizens would be placed in an inferior and unequal position. No extradition warrant applying to Factor was ever issued by the Secretary of State.

Baker was also involved in two estate cases—those of the E. W. Scripps and Cyrus McCormick families—which attracted the curiosity of envious newspaper readers throughout the nation because of the millions at stake. The case of Stanley McCormick (a son of Cyrus), who was mentally ill, concerned his care and the disposition of the income from an estate valued at more than fifty million dollars. In *Scripps v. Scripps,* Baker successfully defended Robert Paine Scripps against paying six million dollars to his sister-in-law Josephine S. Scripps, who was represented by Charles Evans Hughes of New York and John Weld Peck of Cincinnati. Baker thought that Hughes's argument was a masterpiece of impressive reasoning, and he said that he never hoped to equal his power of presentation. Baker was also modest enough to admit that one of his junior partners had prepared the case so thoroughly that he himself was little more than a trumpet through which the medley of facts was presented.

In 1930 Baker represented the Youngstown Sheet and Tube Company in its proposed merger with the Bethlehem Steel Corporation. In this case there were so many sensational developments that even the tabloids found it difficult to keep pace with them, particularly in regard to startling revelations concerning payments of handsome bonuses to prominent executives. Many who were suffering from the national economic depression enviously read the testimony that Eugene Grace, the President of the Bethlehem Steel Corporation, had received a bonus of $1,623,753 in addition to a modest salary of $12,000 for his services in 1929. The sums involved in the proposed industrial combination were large enough to support the rumor that lawyer's fees alone would total a million and a half dollars.

To the newspapers the suit was a battle for control between the national steel titans Charles M. Schwab and Eugene Grace of Bethlehem and a group of local financiers led by Cyrus Eaton and Charles Otis of Cleveland, plus the Wick family of Youngstown. The legal issue was not monopoly but whether the stockholders of a business (Youngstown) had been kept in the dark by their directors, and had been sold out by them. During the proceedings the management of the Youngstown firm was charged with fraudulent withholding of information which would have proved the merger unwise. Mr. Baker, representing the Youngstown company, its officers and directors, claimed that the control of industry by bankers and brokers, as typified by the Eaton-Otis-Wick triumvirate, was an "evil thing," and stated that Eaton's charges against the directors of the Sheet and Tube Company were "cruel and unjustified." It was Baker's contention that

> . . . if financial interests are to impose counting room domination upon the basic industries of America . . . then if I may use a great phrase . . . of Huxley, when he was describing his own disillusionment with the amount of misery that goes on in this struggling world of ours, he said, "If no better thing awaits mankind than a continuance of what we see about us, I, for one, welcome the advent of some friendly comet that will come upon us and put an end to us." I say that about America.

The struggle was so spirited that Baker confessed that, although he had been Secretary of War, the Battle of Youngstown was fierce enough to have justified the award of several Distinguished Service Medals. The judge of the Common Pleas Court, before whom the case was tried initially, held that the merger should be enjoined on the ground, among

others, that there was one director who was a member of
both the Youngstown and the Bethlehem Boards. Both Youngstown and Bethlehem appealed from the decision, but before
the case was heard again the economic situation had changed
so drastically that it was inexpedient for Bethlehem to go
forward with the merger, and it withdrew in accordance with
an escape clause in the contract. The case was heard on appeal, however, because counsel for Eaton and Wick claimed
that they should be compensated by Youngstown for the
services they had rendered in preventing the merger. On the
basis of this contention, it was necessary for the Court of
Appeals to review the entire record of the court below. The
Court of Appeals held that no fraud or misconduct of any
kind had been shown, that the plaintiffs had no right to
maintain an action enjoining the completion of the merger,
and that neither the lawyers nor the accountants who had
spent substantially a year in attempting to enjoin the merger
were entitled to any compensation from Youngstown. This
was a victory for Baker, a complete vindication of the Youngstown officers and directors, and a reversal of the lower court's
decision on the merits. The Supreme Court of Ohio subsequently refused to review the decision of the Court of Appeals.[3]

When Baker represented wealthy corporations he was accused of primary interest in remunerative corporate practice.
His defense of "Jake the Barber" Factor brought the charge
that he was defending a crook who had fleeced Britons out
of some five million dollars. Baker's reply was that it was
a lawyer's duty to defend the guilty as well as the innocent, even though he was regarded as an accessory after
the fact for so doing. Whether Mr. Factor, for example,
had certain legal rights or not could be determined only
by the courts of the country; if the time ever came, Baker
said, when lawyers declined to represent men merely because ignorant people with no knowledge of the facts had

already condemned them, nobody's life would be safe. For this reason he confessed that the more unpopular a client's cause seemed to be, the more deeply he felt his duty to defend it. The same principle applied to business firms; he had no more respect for the lynching of a corporation by an excited and popular prejudice than he had for the lynching of an individual by a mob inflamed by passion. He had always been impressed by the remark made about the famous ophthalmologist, Dr. William H. Wilmer of Johns Hopkins. Wilmer's success had been attributed to the fact that he "respected his materials." An eye was an eye to him, whether it belonged to a duke or an outcast.

In court Baker employed the same technique that had given him national renown as an orator. He usually spoke without notes of any kind, and he never pounded a table or raised his voice. In 1926 during one phase of the Chicago diversion case Baker was unexpectedly called upon, before the United States Supreme Court, to finish the argument in a speech that continued for two hours. He did so without notes or any apparent preparation. When the Court adjourned Chief Justice Taft and Justice Holmes came down from the bench to express appreciation for his fine argument. Later one of Baker's colleagues in the Cleveland office asked him how he could make such a lengthy speech without even a few moments for reflection. Baker said simply:

> You know, the human mind is a wonderful thing. When you are called upon to make a formal argument in court, assuming basic preparation, it has the capacity to select out of its recesses the appropriate material, to organize it in some logical arrangement, as your argument proceeds to make the necessary corrections as to time for interruptions . . . and to do all of this automatically, subconsciously and without seeming effort, leaving your conscious mind free to translate your thoughts into words and to give your attention to the court which is your audience.

He confessed that every now and then, as he went "pelting
along" in some extemporaneous speech, he suddenly realized
that he might be using a thought or phrase of another, with
no opportunity to give credit. For a moment he supposed that
he probably reddened and glanced over his shoulder with his
"inner eye to see whether the literary policeman was standing there with a warrant. Then, of course, I go on, sighing
as I think, 'How hard it is to be honest in this world when
so many great trees grow beautiful apples!' "

Baker's restrained argument was addressed to principle
rather than *ad hominem;* he fought his legal battles with
the blade of reason instead of the bludgeon of abuse. The
presentation was both rational and gracious because Baker
had early learned the danger of positive judgments. The
more he knew about a situation the more difficult it was to
have a fixed opinion about it, and he was inclined to believe
that complete knowledge would obviate the possibility of
any opinion at all. On public issues this point of view struck
some liberals as unnecessarily conservative and compromising.
Once Peter Witt listened to a brilliant speech by Baker on
the theme of world organization, and observed that he would
have been more impressed had he not known that the orator
might speak with equal ease and grace on the other side of
the question. In turn Baker believed many progressives acted
too frequently and hastily on the assumption that "it is not
worth doing anything unless you can do everything." He
had the greatest admiration for Felix Frankfurter and Dean
Roscoe Pound of the Harvard Law School on some issues
but he thought they "like all other intelligent liberals, are
very often *ad hoc* to such an extent that accent on an incident blurs the larger outline of a cause."

Baker's learning, objective approach, and disdain of rancor
were generally commended by lawyers and judges. Justice
Clarke stated that Baker's study of the law and of his cases
knew no limit except his strength, and applauded the avoid-

ance of "that meretricious cunning which has brought re-
proach upon our profession, as well as that vituperative speech
which has made many men notorious but never really noted."
At the time of the court-packing proposal by Franklin Roosevelt, the Institute of Public Opinion polled 175,000 members
of the legal profession as to their preferences for new members
on an enlarged Supreme Court. Baker was among the seven
leading choices, along with Felix Frankfurter, John W. Davis,
Senators Wagner and Borah, Roscoe Pound, and Learned
Hand.

After hearing Baker's presentation in the Chicago water
diversion case Justice Oliver Wendell Holmes was heard to
say that Baker was the outstanding lawyer of his generation.
Baker was too modest to agree, but he reciprocated the admiration. In his judgment the Great Dissenter was a "pagan
. . . but a brave and beautiful pagan. I wish I were half
so brave and beautiful."[4]

XI. *Pro Bono Publico*

BAKER WAS ACTIVE on so many boards and committees—institutional, charitable, educational, and corporate—that he once commented that every time he stuck his head out of a door or window he became chairman of three more supposedly voluntary societies. Once his secretary amused herself by listing the organizations in which he was involved; it took two full typewritten sheets. Baker scrutinized the lengthy columns and was able to add several that had been overlooked. Ralph Hayes, who wanted Baker to concentrate his energy on an active bid for the national presidency, regarded many of these efforts as an unwise dissipation of talent, and occasionally Baker had a suspicion that he was trying to advise mankind on too many projects and reforms.

In connection with education he was trustee of half a dozen colleges and universities, President of the American Association for Adult Education, trustee of the Religious Education Foundation, Chairman of the American Youth Commission of the American Council on Education, a member of the editorial board of *Foreign Affairs,* and Chairman of the American Institute of Pacific Relations.

His interest in large endowments (which he thought should be required to distribute their funds within fifty years to avoid unwieldy accumulation of wealth) was reflected in his service as director or trustee of the Carnegie Corporation, the Twentieth Century Fund, and the Rotary, the Woodrow Wilson, and the Cleveland Foundations.

In public service connected with the national government in Washington, he was appointed by President Coolidge (and was reappointed by Presidents Hoover and Roosevelt) to the Permanent Court of Arbitration, by President Hoover to the Wickersham Commission on Law Enforcement and as Chairman of the National Citizen's Committee for Welfare and Relief Mobilization, and in the first Franklin Roosevelt Administration was Chairman of the War Department Special Committee on the Army Air Corps. The Air Corps committee, which included President Karl Compton of M.I.T. and the pilot James H. Doolittle, was to ascertain what had been done with almost a billion dollars poured into the Air Corps during the past decade. It listened to witnesses for three months and filed a 4,283-page report, which was controversial only in its conclusion that a separate department for the Air Force—long advocated by General William ("Billy") Mitchell —would be wasteful and unnecessary.

On the corporate side Baker was a director of The Cleveland Trust Company, the Baltimore and Ohio Railroad, of RCA and NBC, of Goodyear Tire and Rubber, and of the National Life Insurance Company (whose President was David F. Houston, a former colleague in Wilson's Cabinet).

On the legal front he was active in the American Arbitration Association, the National Crime Commission, and the National Society of Penal Information. He was President of the American Judicature Society—and even accepted an associate membership in the New York County Lawyers' Association.

To cite a few of his activities in his home city of Cleveland, he was prominent in the Welfare Federation, the Foreign Affairs Council, the Musical Arts Association, and the Cleveland Orchestra Association. He served as Chairman of the Executive Committee of the Cleveland Community Fund (then the largest in the nation), and was a trustee of Goodrich Settlement House—all with enough accomplishment that the Chamber of Commerce awarded him its Medal for Public Service in 1927. Among miscellaneous good works, *inter alia,* he was a member of the committee to raise funds for the Stone Mountain Memorial in Georgia, and of the Advisory Board of the Salvation Army in northern Ohio.[1]

Particular time and effort was devoted to the problems of consumers and labor, to the activities of educational institutions, and to the movement for religious understanding. The National Conference of Christians and Jews had been founded in 1928 through the initiative of Baker, Charles Evans Hughes, and S. Parkes Cadman, the Congregational minister who was President of the Federal Council of Churches of Christ in America. Ultimately there were three co-chairmen—Baker for the Protestants, historian Carlton Hayes of Columbia for the Catholics, and the philanthropic industrialist Roger W. Straus for the Jews.

Originally Baker had believed that people could not "be argued out of religious prejudices because they were not argued into them," and thought the best method of destruction was to let such biases shrivel from lack of attention. In time he came to agree with Santayana that "ignorant people are always being made dupes by the things they think they know"—such as allegations of sinister designs of the Pope or the Seven Elders of the Jewish world. He found it advisable

to encourage thoughtful people of various faiths to rub elbows
and exchange ideas in a gentle and tolerant atmosphere, and
this the National Conference promoted through round tables,
Human Relations Institutes, and Brotherhood Weeks.

In 1935 he presided over the Williamstown (Massachusetts) Institute of Human Relations, which lasted five days,
and assisted in the editing of a book about it entitled *The
American Way*. This activity drew denunciatory letters from
anti-Semites, one of whom wrote that Baker's potential election as President was undesirable because it would mean
two or three Jews in the Cabinet plus several more on the
Supreme Court. Baker's reply was both gracious and pointed:

> I propose that you pray for me and I will pray for you and
> the God in whom we both believe will probably then give the
> greater influence to that one of us whose spirit is most in
> accord with His Divine Will.

In actual fact it was animosity toward a Catholic that
once caused him to consider resignation from the organization. He was so disgusted with the demagogy of Father
Coughlin, the radio priest from the Shrine of the Little
Flower in Detroit, that he admitted a prejudice unbecoming
to his official position as co-chairman of a National Conference which required collaboration among Christians as
well as with Jews.[2]

The National Consumers' League had been organized in
1899 by social workers Josephine Shaw Lowell and Florence
Kelley. Their aim was to promote better labor practices by
organizing consumers to purchase only those articles approved
by the League's special label as having been made and sold
under good working conditions. The founders were horrified
by sweatshops, child labor, and the starvation wages and
long hours of "girls behind the counters," and decided that
consumers should use their power by following the motto
"investigate, agitate, legislate." The organization soon enlisted

the support of forward-looking men. Before their elevation
to the Supreme Court Louis Brandeis and Felix Frankfurter
devoted much time as unpaid legal counselors for the League.
Baker belonged to the organization for thirty years, served
as a volunteer counsel, and during most of this long period
was either vice president or president.

As a young solicitor in Cleveland Baker had won the
League's applause by enforcing to the letter all the provisions
of the Ohio child-labor law. During World War I Sidney
Hillman, President of the Amalgamated Clothing Workers,
and Florence Kelley told Baker—who was both Secretary of
War and President of the National Consumers' League—that
many army uniforms were being made in the tenements by
"mushroom" contractors who paid frightfully low wages,
frequently to children under fifteen years of age. Baker followed the League's rule of "investigate, agitate, legislate"
and acted with celerity. His investigating committee was
appointed on July 20, 1917, and reported on August 11.
Immediately thereafter Baker appointed a United States
Board of Control of Labor Standards for Army Clothing,
with Mrs. Kelley as its Secretary, to enforce minimum labor
conditions in the production of uniforms. It was apparent
that the Secretary meant it when he told a group of young
American officers that the struggle for liberty was going on
both in France and at home. "We are in the business of
making the world safe for democracy," he said, "but we are
also in the business of showing the world . . . that democracy
is safe for the world."

For Florence Kelley, the impatient crusader who was General Secretary of the Consumers' League, Baker had such
high regard that he said she was intellectually the greatest
woman he had ever known. The daughter of an eminent
Republican protectionist from Philadelphia, a congressman
best known as "Pig Iron" Kelley, she repudiated everything
in her family background except its Quaker tradition. A Phi

Beta Kappa from Cornell and a graduate of the Northwestern
University Law School, she became a socialist while continuing her studies in social reform in Europe, joined Jane
Addams at Hull House, and was Chief Inspector of Factories
in Illinois under Governor Altgeld. During the First World
War Mrs. Kelley was President of the Intercollegiate Socialist
League, and came under attack as a dangerous radical. Baker's
comment was that the Consumers' League struck a fortunate
balance with a pacifist socialist as its secretary, and the
Secretary of War as its President! He admired her "fierce
fidelity to the things that are true and beautiful" and the
monumental courage that was so pervasive that "everyone
was brave from the moment she came into a room." When
organizations such as the DAR and the Lusk Committee in
New York published lists of undesirables headed by Mrs.
Kelley and Jane Addams, Baker's observation was that any
list containing such names was a roll of honor. When Florence Kelley died in 1932 it was not surprising that her friends
and associates asked Baker to deliver the memorial address.

As long as Mrs. Kelley was active in the League her influence kept Baker interested in the organization, in spite
of her Marxian criticism of production for private profit
and her desire for national regulatory legislation. With her
death, and with his basic conservatism augmented by ad-
vancing years and what he considered to be the nationalistic
menace of the New Deal, Baker finally resigned from the
League in 1937—after more than three decades of membership. There had been a presentiment of this step in 1923
when Mrs. Kelley engineered a change in Baker's official
status from active president to honorary vice president, because of his current position as chief executive of the Cleveland Chamber of Commerce and his advocacy of the open
shop for labor. At the time he had told Mrs. Kelley that as
the years went by he became more and more a follower of
John Ruskin because he had less confidence in the finality

of victory won by either side in industrial contests of strength. He said that when he was young it was his belief that every improvement of mankind had to be made during his lifetime, and had been impatient about any process that "took longer than the insurance actuaries were willing to guarantee that I would live." As he grew older he began to realize that time would go on after he stopped living, and perhaps the best work was accomplished by those who "help along the slower fundamental processes which form the future." There was no doubt in his mind that the pace of the New Deal was much too fast, and in the last year of his life he regretfully resigned from the League because it sponsored a constitutional amendment to give Congress the power to regulate wages and hours without restriction to interstate commerce. It was the old question of national versus local authority, and Baker's liberalism on domestic issues seldom went beyond the home environment. He was willing to admit that the "due process" clause of the Constitution had been unduly restrictive on the power of the States to act on social questions, but there was a greater danger:

> The tendency toward centralization in our national government is a thing Thomas Jefferson foresaw and against which he warned posterity. The accelerated pace of that tendency in the last few years fills me with genuine alarm. Just what sort of a government we will have when the states have been further enfeebled and power over our domestic and local concerns is transferred to Washington I confess I cannot foresee, but of one thing I am certain—it will not be the form of government under which for one hundred and fifty years we have had an indestructible union of indestructible states, with local police powers preserved to the states, and the intervention of the Federal Government restricted to international and obviously national concerns.[3]

As Secretary of War Baker had been a good friend of organized labor. He had insisted on union wages and hours in the construction of army cantonments, that labor disputes be settled by mediation rather than force, and that army uniforms should not be manufactured in sweatshops. Late in 1917 he wrote the President that in the control of wartime industrial relations he had found labor more willing to keep step than capital. He favored minimum wage laws and was to speak feelingly about the heartlessness of employers who were willing to have girls "sew their lives" into garments at wages so pitifully inadequate as to be a disgrace to the industrial civilization in which they were struggling for existence.

Labor was therefore astounded in 1922 when Baker made a public statement favoring the principle of the open shop. There had been those who were unable to fathom the contradiction of Baker as a fighting pacifist in 1917; five years later laboring men were puzzled by the paradox of a man who believed in both trade unionism and the open shop. In a public letter the *Cleveland Federationist* charged that one could not very well be a friend of man when "with one hand extended . . . you pose with a stiletto in the other—prepared to strike immediately that his back is turned." Union men thought Baker's pronouncement was not unrelated to his recent election as President of the Cleveland Chamber of Commerce, and could not agree with his own insistence that the office would not change his beliefs and activities, or with McAdoo's hope that he would be able to alter the purely materialistic philosophy of the organization.

The controversy attracted national attention with the publication of correspondence on the issue between Baker and A.F. of L. President Sam Gompers, with whom he had worked so closely and amicably during the First World War. The arguments employed by the two men constitute a preview of those heard three decades later in the national debate over right-to-work laws. Gompers defined the A.F. of L. as a "large body of fighters surrounded by enemies," stressed the existing

class struggle between capital and labor, and said that in practice the open shop meant that union members could not get
jobs. He could not understand why inactive nonorganized
laborers should gain the advantages of higher wages and better
hours won by the sweat and blood of union members. Although Baker claimed that he had been a trade unionist for
thirty years, and would be happy to join one, he believed
that every man should have the right not to join a union.
The idea of warfare between employer and employee shocked
him, although he recognized that a state of hostilities was very
much in existence. Unions collected "war funds" and employers set aside a certain amount of their gross income to
hire spies, strikebreakers, and *agents provocateurs;* because
management refused to recognize unions the latter spent
their strength, not in improvement of their craft, but in a
fight for survival. The result was a war like that declared
by Congress except that it was an unauthorized one between
civic groups within the nation. Baker admitted that he had
never had to depend upon his pay envelope for the next
day's food for his family and he had never been confronted
with the problems of involuntary or seasonal employment,
but he had great sympathy for those who did. He was inclined to blame employers more than labor for the impasse;
until those who managed industry made more "direct and
hopeful" efforts to adjust these problems he might disagree
with the means but he could not criticize the impulse that
drove unions to practices which they hoped might lift their
burden.

There was a forgotten man in labor controversies—the
consumer—whose voice should in future become dominant.
Baker insisted there were three parties to every labor struggle
—employer, employee, and the public—and that the public
interest was the one most frequently neglected. No one, he
thought, would want to live in a society controlled by organized wealth in the interest of its own vulgar ambitions,

or one dominated by organized labor in its own interests. He denied the right of either labor or capital to exploit each other, nor did he believe that management and unions had a right to bargain by themselves on issues which were really public in character. He could not support agreements dictated by either "money or muscle" because he was convinced that an arrangement between "the finger man and the gunman omits the interests of the victim." His comments to the Chamber of Commerce in Cleveland stressed the "common service of the common good" and could hardly have been pleasing to all of his auditors:

> Here is a community of a million people which, year after year, sees its substance wasted, its public peace destroyed, its employers on the one side embittered and its employees on the other side in despair and embittered, and both sides at times resorting to violence, while we the people . . . who pay the bills, have in our hands the only corrective. We must build up as the foundation of any labor policy in Cleveland, an attitude of mind on the part of the middle class, based upon the fact that we are the paymasters in this struggle. It is our heads that get cracked. We must build up a determination to find out what the right and wrong of each controversy is, and if anybody declines, employer or employee, to appear before us when we are properly assembled and inquiring into a controversy of that kind, let judgment go against him by default.

The correspondence on the open shop had been incisive but friendly although partisans of labor and capital took dogmatic points of view on the issue. Baker assured Gompers that in solving the complex problems of industrial relations he would rather have him "as an ally than any man in the U.S. . . . I should more correctly state my feelings if I were to say I should rather be your ally and work under your leadership in that cause." The statement was typical of the cordiality between the two men. When Mrs. Gompers died shortly after the war Baker had gone to the funeral. There were no religious obsequies because Gompers had changed from the Jewish religion of his father to a rationalistic worship of labor. During the ethical service Gompers sat unmoved and expressionless. At the close Baker was asked to say a few words. Gompers was shaken with sobs as he listened to Baker's compassionate and eloquent testimonial to the youthful struggle and the long companionship of a husband and wife who were now separated by death.[4]

The academic role was an accustomed and pleasant one for Baker. In the early years of the century he had taught in the Cleveland Law School and had suffered the usual pedagogic worries over the grades he was assigning; the marks for one class in constitutional law were so high that his conclusion was that "either I taught these young men too much or gave them too easy an examination." Three decades later he was teaching international relations at Cleveland College. At one time in the 1930s he was a trustee of seven universities—among them Western Reserve and Ohio State University, his two alma maters (Johns Hopkins, and Washington and Lee), and Tuskegee Institute. He received so many honorary degrees—Harvard, Yale, Princeton, Oberlin, Michigan, Brown, and Dartmouth were included in the long institutional inventory—that he found it impossible, in later years, to identify all of the gowns and hoods by color. He was offered the presidency of several institutions—Michigan, Johns Hopkins, and the University of Virginia—in the latter instance the tempting offer was to "occupy the pulpit of Thomas Jefferson." Baker considered a university presidency as the most useful and appealing of occupations because of the opportunity for association with and influence on great bodies of young people. He thought there was no tie in the world comparable to the academic bond between scholars in every country, and no peacemaking effort comparable to that performed by the college professor who taught students a love of justice and a constructive desire for peace. He refused the

offers with the greatest of reluctance, for the reasons that
he did not want to leave the law plus the feeling that his
educational theories were too "old-fashioned" for the modern age.[5]

The academic institution in which Baker had the greatest
interest was Cleveland College in the downtown area of
his home city. In 1925 it had begun its educational life modestly in 20,000 square feet of automobile loft, and was certainly no ivy-covered establishment of the traditional mold,
for it was designed to meet the needs of part-time scholars
considerably older than the usual college student. At its
inception there had been an acting director, one full-time
professor, little equipment, and no endowment, but its eight
hundred original students had increased to more than seven
thousand by 1930. Along with many other institutions the
college suffered from chronic deficits during the depression
years, and would have succumbed but for the protective
efforts of Baker as Chairman of the Board of Trustees. He was
tireless in his efforts and generous in his contributions; as
he phrased it he was scratching not only his head but the
bottom of his pocket in an attempt to keep the college alive.
In another figure of speech—unlike Baker because of its col-
loquial character—he referred to Cleveland College as his
"baby," and he added that he experienced the distress of
an anxious mother when he heard the educational infant
crying from severe financial pains.

Baker regarded the new departures in adult education at
Cleveland College as the most significant educational project
with which he was connected. In the light of his many national activities and his own traditional education at Johns
Hopkins, and Washington and Lee, the intensity of this interest at first glance appears puzzling. A partial answer to the
paradox is found in Baker's developing educational philosophy
as it was influenced particularly by two events in which he

was an active participant—the tent meetings of Tom Johnson, and the University of the American Expeditionary Forces in France at the close of the First World War.

In the first decade of the century Cleveland's Mayor Johnson had been elected four times by taking every issue directly to the voters. His vast tent seating five thousand people, which was moved from one part of the city to another during campaigns, had been an authentic public forum and had provided a rostrum where community issues were debated and decided. As an early example of adult education Tom Johnson's canopy made a great impression on Baker, and he was to use the device in his own campaigns for mayor. One of Johnson's great services, in Baker's judgment, was that he kept the whole of the population fully informed on his purposes and plans, with the result that Cleveland had the best-informed body of citizens to be found anywhere in America. Later Baker wanted Cleveland College to perform a similar service on a larger scale, to create a situation in which it could be said that every adult in Cleveland understood the large outlines—economic, social, and political—of modern international relations. Such a body politic, he was sure, would act from wisdom rather than impulse, and the ideal of democracy would be realized.

The tent meetings with Johnson had introduced Baker to adult education; his experience with the University of the American Expeditionary Forces solidified his belief in the concept. As a "pacifist" Secretary of War Baker had amazed his martial critics, who initially questioned the wisdom of his appointment, by moving more than two million American soldiers to France within eighteen months. After the Armistice there had not been enough ships to return that many armed men immediately, and the time of monotonous waiting had to be filled. Most of the commanding generals thought the answer was to drill men until they nearly fell in their tracks, so fatigued that the brain was numb. Per-

shing's staff, with an immense army at its disposal at the
close of the war, was actually contemplating a program of
intensive drill and tactical training—to correct the errors of
the Meuse-Argonne offensive! Finally some of the boys themselves supplied the answer. They said: "We don't want to
drill. The war is over. We want education."

The result was the University of the AEF, and Post Schools
that provided education at the elementary and high school
levels. Nothing like it had ever happened in the history of
the world; here were soldiers laying down their bayonets and
taking up books. Many realized that they had not been promoted because of ignorance; they now demanded education,
and got it. In Baker's opinion it was a splendid example of
the democratic principle at work. Democracy, he thought, was
both the best and the most difficult form of government, and
its performance depended on the process of continuous education. Among others, poet Edgar Lee Masters was enthusiastic
about Baker's program because he believed that an army with
ideas would ultimately make an army with guns superfluous.

Before the AEF University was terminated it had 11,000
students (the Post Schools had 130,000 more) in eleven full-
fledged colleges and correspondence schools teaching the liberal arts, law, medicine, and dentistry. It had none of the
paraphernalia, including the elaborate buildings, of a long-
established college; for example, the Khaki University at
Beaune, France, was housed in temporary shacks and its total
equipment consisted of blackboards, platforms, and chairs.
In one of the shacks Baker saw a learned private teaching
integral calculus to twenty men, including majors, captains,
lieutenants, and doughboys. Here there was no hierarchy except the aristocracy of the mind.

On its ultimate return to the United States the Army
brought back news of its discovery of the importance of
education, and Baker believed that the great national demand for scholastic training for adults stemmed from this

experience. He was idealistic enough to hope that the future Army would be accepted as an educational institution, refusing recruits unless they were willing to take scholastic and vocational training. In World War II the educational program of the Special Services Division was to be built on the foundation that Baker had laid.[6]

Out of these experiences, extending from northern Ohio to Burgundy, Baker developed a strong conviction that a common core of knowledge—a common intellectual heritage among peoples—was essential for the successful functioning of both democracy and international peace. He corresponded with Mrs. Chester C. Bolton (later a congresswoman from Ohio) on the possibilities for a universal language, such as Basic English, to encourage international understanding. He loved to tell the story of the valedictory address to the House of Commons in which the Younger Pitt quoted fourteen lines in Latin from Horace. There were two verses in the quotation in which the Roman poet, writing in the first person, spoke of wrapping himself in the divine dignity of his own achievements. Members of the House waited breathlessly to ascertain whether the speaker would include this self-laudatory passage, but Pitt, from a nice sense of modesty omitted them without comment, reciting the balance of the quotation. Instantly the whole House rose and applauded the orator's judgment and finesse for the omission. In Baker's opinion such an incident could have occurred only in England, where there existed a common irreducible minimum in the education of every cultured man. He was envious that in England college students could write, read, and speak with greater facility than their contemporaries in the United States, because he regarded this ability as the ultimate foundation of all culture.

This common core of knowledge was essential, especially in the United States, to give our cosmopolitan population the homogeneity that characterized older European nations. A despotism need only educate the despot, and an oligarchy the ruling class, but a democracy had to educate the whole body of its people—and the greatest danger would come from a failure to endow citizens with an indispensable body of common knowledge. Baker felt that traditional colleges, because of overemphasis on the elective system and specialized education, were turning out graduates whose educations were so unlike that there was almost no body of knowledge common to all of them. He was particularly disturbed by collegiate overspecialization along narrow vocational lines, which enabled a student to complete the necessary hours for his college degree with little education outside the branches of his specialty. To Munson Havens, a scholarly friend who was Secretary of the Cleveland Chamber of Commerce, he lamented:

> The idea of anybody supposing that a course in "Business Administration" could be any part of an education! Of course a systematic study in Business Administration is a most excellent thing to have, but a man should be educated first.
>
> Now of course all this is as old fashioned as Noah and if I were to say it out loud the ungodly would cite Mr. Tuck (Dartmouth) and Mr. Wharton (University of Pennsylvania) and a host of other proofs that the important thing in this world is to make a living, or a fortune early.

These developments had led many college students to believe that the primary purpose of education was to lengthen the acquisitive arm, to believe that the chief value of attending a college was to "get there first and faster in competitive industrial occupations." College men had once been identifiable because they possessed a common liberal education—and because of this liberal training an educated class had been entrusted with leadership in the moral concerns of society. This was no longer the case; specialization in colleges had deprived mankind of the cement of partnership in a great body of common knowledge. It was the responsibility of adult education, Baker believed, to provide this common core—to give men and women the liberal education they were not getting from colleges that had become degree factories.

Baker could be critical of traditional colleges, including some he served as trustee, not only for academic overspecialization but for overemphasis on athletics, which he characterized as an "unmitigated social evil." One of the reasons for this strong opinion was that college physical education usually developed the well-trained body to the exclusion of the well-trained mind; when a boy went to college to find trustees, president, townspeople, and fellow students unaware of scholarship but thrilled by athletic prowess, it was natural for him to change his scale of values about the important things in the life he had entered. In addition Baker thought college athletics exercised the wrong men; in his judgment the stout fellows with big muscles got on the teams while the flat-chested chaps sat on the bleachers "with ribbons on their hats eating ice cream cones and cheering when the leader directed." But he was also disturbed by current trends in adult education. He thought that this movement in the 1930s seemed to have two characteristics, neither of which served its primary purpose. The first was to teach everybody everything—from bookkeeping to bricklaying—as long as it helped them make a living. The second mistake of adult education was what Baker called a pathetic effort to get anybody to study anything—from Greek mythology to the chemistry of the sun—if it saved them from jazz or the movies. The result was not the social asset of a disciplined and lean intellect; he saw instead a disordered mind artificially crammed with commercial or esoteric pabulum. It reminded him of the synthetic production of *pâté de foie gras* by stuffing a goose with chestnuts. He thought it would be wiser to stress a common core of knowledge, by which he meant the study of language in all its forms, the social studies, and the sciences. He was convinced that it was better to have all Americans know one fact, than to have each of 120,000,000 people possessed with a different fact. He believed that the trunk of the tree of knowledge should grow as high as possible above the ground, before it began to spread into special branches.

To Baker education was vital to a democratic society but he never minimized its importance to the individual as well. He was certain that the principal aim of education was not the making of careers, important as that might be, but the creation of individuals with broader sympathies, deeper appreciations, and a braver outlook on life. The associations of an individual with others were casual and temporary, but he had to live with himself throughout all his waking hours. In order to do so he needed the inner resources that only a liberal education could provide; the alternative was a disappointing search for external excitement. In middle life particularly Baker thought it was a pathetic thing to look back over one's mind as a bit of waste land in which one could see the faded stems of a thousand beautiful plants that failed to grow because the individual was too busy with trivialities to water them. Among the trivialities were dancing and card playing; he had no religious objections to these diversions but regarded them as useless pastimes that took valuable time away from better things. He was afraid that the art of conversation, which distinguished our ancestors, had now become the possession of the bore and that the good bridge player was considered a more estimable person than a "spirit steeped in the poetry and art of the ages." Baker never allowed his own inner resources to wither. Surrounded by a howling mob at a political convention he was once found absorbed in a volume by Browning; many Clevelanders knew their Mayor as a small figure on a streetcar, his nose deeply buried in a book. It was his method of "cultivating the fence corners of the mind."[7]

Knowledge was one mark of an educated person but good manners were equally distinguishing because they exhibited the inner man. Baker went out of his way to tell college students that they were introduced as much by their behavior as they were by a presentation of diplomas or grades. If their manners were good they were well introduced, if their behavior was bad the result was the same as if they had borne a letter of introduction that said: "This man is a terrible boor!" On this subject Baker was not thinking primarily of the Greenwich Village variety of nonconformity, although he told students that they might be erecting undesirable barriers between themselves and others if they held their knives and forks extraordinarily (the "old banjo grip" on a fork and the "Davy Crockett lunge" with a knife) or donned eccentric clothes or wore their hats pronouncedly on one side of their heads. By good manners he was really thinking of an intellectual quality defined as warm human sympathy, consideration of other people's feelings, and an unexaggerated sense of one's own importance. A humble person gained the confidence and trust of others because he did not insist that his opinions were infallible and admitted that a good argument could be made on the other side; by contrast a bumptious assertion of opinion led to the inevitable conclusion that noise was being substituted for knowledge and conviction. Consideration for the feelings of others came only when a person realized that his colleagues knew as much or more about many things as he did; in Baker's judgment far too many young men had derived the notion from some fatal place that it was their responsibility to "tell the world," without realizing how impatiently the world received such gratuitous advice.

Good manners were important in college students; they

were vital characteristics of faculty members because it was their responsibility to lead by example rather than precept. From his experience in various universities he was disturbed that in making appointments to the faculty much more emphasis seemed to be placed on the fact that a professor had published extensively on some aspect of the dative case in Greek or on a mysterious impediment affecting the blood circulation in the feet of frogs than on his ability to inspire and stimulate students. As a college trustee Baker was confronted from time to time with cases involving academic freedom, and he was convinced that most of the trouble came from professors who lacked good manners and intellectual humility rather than from pedagogues with dangerous ideas. He guided his life as trustee by never interfering with sincere and earnest scholars however wrong he thought them to be, but he found himself completely out of patience with professors who were truculent and assertively dogmatic in manner, even when he agreed with their conclusions. As a result of wide reading and experience he had come to the belief that limitations on freedom of speech were much more destructive and damaging than abuses of this basic right; in the long run it was better to let academicians say what they really believed so long as they were sincere and honest persons and not demagogic poseurs. Ironically in 1923 an educational institution barred from its campus an organization with which Baker was closely identified. It was the League of Nations Non-Partisan Association which was denied the use of an auditorium on the campus of the University of Michigan, where the regulations prohibited the use of buildings to partisan political organizations. The university decided that the association was misnamed because it was really a partisan body, but in Baker's judgment the definition of "partisan" was not the basic issue. He thought that the university ruling was pedagogically unsound because it denied students freedom of choice in their quest for learning. On this issue Baker said that he had always admired the position taken by his friend President Ernest M. Hopkins of Dartmouth College when he was criticized for bringing Emma Goldman, the well-known anarchist, to the campus for talks with students. Baker agreed with Hopkins' wisdom in thinking it much better to have his young men hear Emma Goldman with him so that he could point out possible defects in her philosophy, rather than hearing her in some other place where there was no critical analysis of the discourse.[8]

One of the great formative influences in Baker's education in the days at Johns Hopkins and during the following years was his college fraternity Phi Gamma Delta. By his own admission he entered the university as a green country lad; the fraternity not only inspired him scholastically but gave him invaluable training in manners and the social amenities. At the chapter house lasting friendships, which he considered priceless, were formed with men who subsequently achieved prominence in many fields. It was certainly an outstanding fraternal group; half of the fourteen charter members (the chapter at Johns Hopkins was established in 1891) later made the pages of *Who's Who in America*. They were, along with Baker, Elmer Peter Kohler, chairman of the chemistry department at Harvard, David Kinley, president of the University of Illinois, Edward Allsworth Ross, the sociologist at the University of Wisconsin, political scientist Frederic Howe, W. Calvin Chesnut, who became a federal judge in Baltimore, and engineer Charles E. Phelps.

After his college days Baker was unusually active as a national officer of the fraternity serving at various times as treasurer, member of the board of trustees, and president for five successive terms. He regarded fraternal conventions as "sentimental journeys" and attended as many as he could; in the twenty-two years from 1891 to 1913 he was present at twenty of these national reunions. As time went on the de-

velopment of certain habits and practices among fraternity
men caused him great concern. In 1898 he led a successful
movement for greater democracy in the national organization of the fraternity. The repeal of the Prohibition Amendment in 1933 brought with it the problem of unrestricted
liquor; Baker regarded an occasional drink among gentlemen
as consistent with temperance, but chapter houses stocked
with booze would develop a perilous barroom atmosphere
in which the intellectual purpose of a college education
would be forgotten. Hazing at initiations he classified as
undignified horseplay which denied the theory of brotherhood and the beauty of fraternal relations. He was convinced
that the solemn and beautiful ritual of the fraternity was
falsified whenever it was preceded or followed by humilia-
tion, chagrin, or pain inflicted upon an initiate.

In spite of these worrisome practices Baker felt that fraternities could play a major role in modern education. In a
small college, fraternal association could be of great value;
in a large institution he believed it was essential. As universities acquired thousands of students, the influence of the
president lost most of its inspirational quality as that officer
became more and more remote from the student body; in
this situation a social substitute was necessary for the loyalties
of college men in earlier days. In Baker's opinion fraternities
could provide one substitute if they ceased to be "mere foci
of madcap exploits and ephemeral social distinctions," and
instead performed their vital function with dignity. He was
confident that his own fraternity, through the influence of
most of its chapters, was proving to be "the shadow of a
great rock in many a weary land." As a testimonial to his
high ideals Phi Gamma Delta to this day awards the Newton
D. Baker Cup annually to the chapter that has excelled in
ethical and social service.[9]

XII. Treaty of Versailles and

the League of Nations

B<small>AKER RESUMED</small> his law practice in 1921 but he spent the rest of his life as such a strong and active advocate for the League of Nations that there was newspaper speculation in the 1930s that he might be appointed its Secretary-General in Geneva. As an accomplished orator he was in constant demand, and he spoke frequently, but regardless of the occasion or the title of the speech he usually stipulated in advance that the subject would be the League of Nations. When he addressed the Cleveland Advertising Club the title was "Publicity and Peace," when called upon to make impromptu remarks at a marriage ceremony he spoke of the beauties of union and of leagues of peace, and he maintained that he would not vote for a street constable unless the gendarme stood for world conciliation. There was a rumor that he had made a deathbed promise to Wilson never to make a public address without endorsing the League. Baker characterized the canard as both romantic and absurd. He spoke because of the debt he owed to those who died in the

late conflict and because the strongest nation, under present
conditions, would die like a bee when it used its sting. He
was certain that modern war was a cocked pistol aimed at
the heart of civilization itself, with its hair-trigger held by
an unsteady hand. For his pacific efforts Baker was listed in
the *Red Network* compiled by the superpatriot Mrs. Elizabeth Dilling, and the Daughters of the American Revolution
blackballed him as a speaker before any of their chapters.
He was amused when he found himself a poor third on the
DAR list—behind ex-President Taft and Elihu Root![1]

After World War I the Treaty of Versailles might have
been either a peace of vengeance or one of reconciliation
with the fallen foe. It tried to be both, and was condemned
by disillusioned liberals who thought it was too hard and
by frustrated imperialists who found it too soft. President
Wilson was among those who were acutely dissatisfied, but
he was hopeful that the League of Nations would wipe out
the inequities. In the United States the opposition to the
treaty came chiefly from Republicans who disliked Wilson,
the Irish who hated Great Britain, the Italians who wanted
Fiume, the Germans who were convinced that the Father-
land had been betrayed, and the superpatriots who loathed
the League of Nations.

In spite of this discontent a substantial majority of the
American people appeared to favor the treaty when Wilson
brought it home from Paris. Henry Cabot Lodge, the Harvard scholar who had become chairman of the Senate Committee on Foreign Relations, calculated that time and money
were both necessary to change public opinion. Delay in the
progress of the treaty through the Senate was easy for the
"ambassador from the Bay State to the United States"; among
other things he consumed two weeks in reading the entire
264-page treaty aloud during committee sessions. Money,
necessary for speakers and printed material, was a little
harder to come by. Ultimately it was found in the reserves

of steel magnate Henry Frick and financier Andrew Mellon. Baker's old nemesis George Harvey was the first to approach Frick, and was delighted with his success. Said Harvey: "The desired reservoir has been found and it was deep and full."

Baker loved both Wilson and the League, and for their enemies his contempt was profound. Of the two Pennsylvania capitalists who financed the anti-League propaganda he was to say: "One of them knew how to make steel and both knew how to make money, but neither up to that time had ever been known to contribute a political idea to the common good or to cherish a political ideal except the protective tariff, which is now spawning its countless brood of ill, economic and political, over the world." For Lodge, the "ruffian of the Senate" who "kept us out of peace," his feeling came close to hatred—an attitude most unusual for the serene and impersonal Secretary. Matters were not helped when the frail Wilson suffered a paralytic stroke on a pro-League barnstorming tour, while Lodge—who hated the President as "the devil hates holy water"—gained ten pounds and seemed to thrive on the struggle. In 1920, after a quarter of a century in public life, Baker said that Lodge was the worst man he had ever known: "Seeing the light he sinned, knowing the truth he denied it, trusted as an associate, he betrayed the trust, followed he misled those who trusted in him. . . ." When Raymond Fosdick was about to make a commencement address Baker suggested that he tell the students that the average of human intelligence could never be high until Lodge had been taken to his Heavenly Father (Fosdick replied that he could compile quite a list of people with the B.A. degree—Below Average). Even the death of the Massachusetts Senator did not alleviate the bitterness; when Lodge passed on in 1925 Baker wrote:

> Since Senator Lodge is dead, I limit myself nowadays to hoping that he has found somebody to write a brief for him in the court in which he is now a litigant. I would not like the job.[2]

Baker played a minor role in the presidential campaign
of 1920, which Wilson had hoped to make a solemn referendum on the League of Nations. But the reaction against
a strong President, as Wilson had been, was apparent both
in and out of Congress; the public was tired of progressivism,
making the world safe for democracy, crusaders and prophets,
wheatless Mondays, porkless Thursdays, and gasless Sundays.
The times called for the nomination of second-rate men un-
burdened by a program of reform or anything resembling a
social philosophy. It was a disappointing prospect, and early
in the year Baker observed that it seemed reasonably certain
that there would be no political candidate for whom he
could vote on any party ticket. He thought he would "probably go to the Orient and see what the President of China
looks like while my fellow citizens are selecting a ruler for
me."

The confident Republicans held their convention in Chicago. With Wilson broken and discredited, and the wayward
Bull Moosers back in the orthodox camp, it was believed
they could nominate a rag baby or a scraggly dog and elect
him. The conservative Old Guard, spearheaded by a senatorial cabal that included Henry Cabot Lodge, was again
in the saddle. After considering the always hopeful Leonard
Wood, the aspiring Governor Frank Lowden of Illinois, and
the isolationist Hiram Johnson from California, the Republicans finally nominated Ohio's Senator Warren G. Harding
following the famous preliminary session in George Harvey's
suite at the Blackstone Hotel. During the campaign Harding
was vague on the question of international organization, intimating that he would support an undefined *association* of
nations, but not *the* League.

Baker reported the Republican maneuvers to his friend
Brand Whitlock, who was still the American ambassador in
Brussels (and who had a private worry of his own—he was

afraid the Single Taxers would nominate *him* for President
and asked Baker to stop the movement). According to Baker
the Republicans would nominate a man of the McKinley
type, and the winner would be Harding or Lowden because
they were favored by the bosses. Wood had the financial support of Colonel William C. Procter of the soap company,
but little else. Baker was amazed that the evidence of Wood's
physical disability was publicized by his own supporters during the campaign. Mrs. Douglas Robinson, a sister of Theodore Roosevelt who was active for Wood, had gathered a
number of ladies at her residence in New York and had read
medical certificates concerning Wood's brain tumor which
proved that "there was no longer any danger of his going
insane." This information, in Baker's version of the affair,
had greatly pleased the applauding ladies but the announcement had an unexpected result:

> . . . a very great number of people who had never heard of
> General Wood's brain tumor got their first apprehension of
> the possibility of insanity from this denial, so that the net
> effect of Mrs. Robinson's endeavor seems to have been to take
> all the buttons off the General's clothes to make them lighter
> for him to carry, but with the consequence that a good many
> of them are falling off.

There was much speculation about Herbert Hoover, who
was popular but couldn't decide whether he was a Democrat
or Republican. As early as 1917 Whitlock had characterized
Hoover as a great liberal who lacked charm but otherwise
qualified as another Tom Johnson. In 1920 Baker reported
that Hoover's friends were boosting him "for any old nomination that might be lying around loose"; some thought the
Republicans ought to nominate him, a few believed the
Democrats should do it, while still others suggested that if
neither party were sufficiently enlightened he should run in-
dependently and beat them both. Although Justice Clarke
believed that Hoover was the only man the Democrats could

elect, Baker was certain that the bosses of both parties would turn thumbs down on an aspirant who was a political schizophrenic.

On the Democratic side Wilson, prostrated though he was, unsuccessfully angled for a third term. His son-in-law, William Gibbs McAdoo, was a leading contender but suffered from the increasing public aversion for either Wilson or his relatives. Baker had no enthusiasm for McAdoo, observing in a curious mixed metaphor that he was a genius but an "uncomfortable genius, with a fierce energy, a fiercer temper and . . . a capacity for keeping every accessible hornet's nest violently agitated which would make the four years of his administration a fiery furnace." Attorney General A. Mitchell Palmer, noted as a "Red-hunter," had some support from federal officeholders but none from liberals; Baker thought his only qualification was based on the fact that he was the noisiest candidate. William Jennings Bryan was making coy gestures in the hope that he might get a fourth nomination, but lost because of his insistence on a strong prohibition plank in the party's platform. The question of Prohibition or repeal of the Eighteenth Amendment was to perplex the Democratic party for the next twelve years; to Baker it was a foolish diversion from real issues. He thought Prohibition was wrongly conceived and wrongly executed, and observed that a substantial part of the nation was "like a fellow who has sworn off and keeps walking up and down in front of a saloon cussing himself for his impetuosity." Within the Democratic Party there was Mr. Bryan, who favored beverages with zero alcoholic content, along with Governor Edward Irving Edwards of New Jersey, who wanted 3.2 per cent if he couldn't get four. In Baker's opinion "the present outlook is that Ivory Soap, 99 per cent pure, will win. . . ."

When a number of people told Baker that he should present himself as an active candidate, his answer was a decisive no. He said that he had always avoided partisanship in the War Department, and that political aspirations would jeopardize the successful completion of his Cabinet assignment. At this disappointing stage in his career he was certain that a Moses who asked him to take another public office would be required to bring the "fiat of God himself" plus a "reliable witness on Mt. Sinai when he gets the message . . ." This negative response, however, did not mean that Baker would refuse to work for the League and Democratic success in the campaign, with just a little "Old Testament revenge upon the Republican Amalekites" thrown in for good measure. This service he was glad to perform for his old Ohio friend James M. Cox, who finally got the Democratic presidential nomination. Cox had been Governor of Ohio for three terms and was one of a galaxy of newspaper giants in the first half of the twentieth century, a constellation that included Hearst of San Francisco, McCormick and Knox of Chicago, Josephus Daniels of Raleigh, and William Allen White of Emporia, Kansas.

Baker wrote the conciliatory planks in the Democratic platform dealing with Mexico and labor, and during the campaign spoke for Cox in Boston. He castigated the Republican candidate for his ambiguous stand on the League and was hypercritical of Harding's pompous phrases which the Sage of Baltimore, H. L. Mencken, characterized as a "string of wet sponges" and the worst English he had ever encountered. The intellectual Baker recalled Browning's poem "A Grammarian's Funeral," and concluded that Harding had not only been reading it but had decided to go Browning one better. When the sad news arrived that Cox had been decisively whipped in the election, Baker was as philosophical as he had been when Tom Johnson was rejected in 1909. During the war the country had been ideologically exalted;

it had now resorted to its normal condition, one in which it would cease to "harvest any spiritual grain or grow any wings. . . ." Mankind frequently presented an unkempt and unpleasant appearance; one should never forget, he mused, that "this is at best a naughty world, which washes its face and combs its hair *occasionally.*" The tragedy of Wilson and Tom Johnson had been that they overestimated the people's capacity for righteousness, but none could forget that both were great souls who by their faith paid the populace an undeserved compliment.[3]

For several years Woodrow Wilson, bitter and unforgiving because of the defeat of the Treaty of Versailles, refused his sanction to any collaboration with Republicans on behalf of the League of Nations. In 1922 he wrote Baker that he was hobbling along from day to day with as stout a heart as possible but was treasuring "the unchristian hope that I may still have the pleasure of doing up certain particular enemies of mine in a way that will make them permanently unpresentable in polite society." This stubbornness irked Baker who wanted to "get into the League *now* and if not to-day, to-morrow"; he did not think Wilson would live long enough to "get even" with all his enemies and, for his own part, he would not consent to "a day's delay to punish every enemy I have or ever had." At long last Wilson relented and in 1923 the League of Nations Non-Partisan Association was established with Democrat John H. Clarke as president and Republican George W. Wickersham, who had been Taft's Attorney General, as president of the council; among other prominent supporters were Judge Learned Hand, President Lawrence Lowell of Harvard, Wendell Willkie, Raymond Fosdick, Arthur Krock, and John Foster Dulles. As an ex-member of Wilson's Cabinet, Baker thought it best to remain backstage in a national nonpartisan production, but he played a prominent local role as secretary of the

Cleveland chapter of which industrialist Samuel Mather was president and chief contributor at the rate of five hundred dollars monthly.

Clarke was Baker's close friend and mentor; as a handsome, courtly, and wealthy corporation lawyer and co-owner of the *Youngstown Vindicator* he had been a devoted supporter of Tom Johnson. Liberal and progressive in politics, at the Ohio Democratic Convention he had supported the direct election of United States Senators as early as 1894—the first argument for this reform heard in an Ohio convention of either party. Justice Clarke had received strong support from Baker when Wilson appointed him to the Supreme Court in 1916, but by 1922 was ready to resign because he wanted to carry the banners of the League and because he was bored with the writing of inconsequential opinions dealing with a carload of mules or a petition of *habeas corpus* from a roustabout in California. "Neither of us," he wrote Baker, "would look for a moment, as practicing lawyers, at one half of the cases that engage the attention of the 'greatest court in the world.' " In addition to serving as president, Clarke paid his own expenses and gave the Non-Partisan Association $5,000 in 1923; he said he was willing to make it $50,000 if necessary to keep the organization alive.[4]

At the Democratic National Convention of 1924, which met in New York, Baker's role on behalf of the League was both prominent and unsuccessful. This was the year in which the party was split into two irreconcilable wings. The Southern Democrats, representing Property, Protestantism, and Prohibition, had William Gibbs McAdoo as their candidate. The Northern contingent was the party of the Common People, Catholicism, and Repeal—a curious combination of idealists and big-city political machines—whose idol was Governor Alfred E. Smith, formerly from the sidewalks of New York. The two factions staged a brawl in Madison Square

Garden that was every bit as dramatic as some of the prize
fights that were held in that pugilistic amphitheater.

Baker went to the Convention with one purpose in mind;
to fight for a pro-League plank in the Democratic platform.
In his judgment the alternatives were the League or chaos;
by comparison domestic issues were of minor significance.
The prohibition of alcoholic beverages seemed relatively unimportant and the issue of the Ku Klux Klan, which caused
so much hard feeling between the McAdoo and Smith forces,
was to Baker completely absurd. He had seen one Ku Klux
parade, which boasted a sheeted band whose instrumentalists
were blowing horns that protruded from their awesome hoods.
A man had asked Baker what he thought of it. His reply was
that the strange musical assembly resembled the "Sheet and
Tube Company" on parade.

Baker was a member of the Resolutions Committee, which
was to frame a platform, and it was there that he made his
first stand. The majority was hostile to immediate entry
into the League and favored a delaying action that called for
a national referendum under an act of Congress—*"after ample
time for full consideration."* Baker wrote the minority report
that asked for immediate commitment to the League. He
was disgusted with the stalling procedure devised by the
majority of the Committee; in his opinion the next war
would be over before the national referendum could be completed, and the boys who perished would be under tomb-
stones with a simple inscription: *"Died in battle after ample
time for full consideration."*

In 1912 Baker had been successful in convincing a national
convention that it should adopt a minority committee report,
and he made a second attempt in 1924. In his introduction
he admitted that he would attempt to arouse emotions, because no subject on earth was of such great importance to
him:

Why? I am a middle-aged man and I shall never be called upon again for any useful service in any other war, even though one were to come tomorrow. I am past the military age, but I have memories. On battlefields in Europe I closed the eyes of soldiers in American uniform who were dying and who whispered to me messages to bring to their mothers. I talked to them about death in battle, and oh, they were superb and splendid; never a complaint, never a regret; willing to go if only two things might be,—one that mother might know that they had died bravely and the other that somebody would pick up their sacrifice and build on earth a permanent temple of peace in which the triumphant intellect and spirit of man would forever dwell in harmony, taking away from the children of other generations the curse and menace of that bloody fight.

He censured the majority report because it substituted leadership of the malevolent Senator Lodge for that of Woodrow Wilson, who had been dead but a few months. He could imagine Wilson looking over his shoulder at the majority report, and the contempt on his face when he realized that his own Democratic Party had "dumped the League of Nations into the street . . ." and had left it "houseless, friendless, orphaned in an unfriendly world." In his peroration Baker said that he owed a debt to Wilson and that he intended to pay it:

> I served Woodrow Wilson for five years. He is standing at the throne of God whose approval he won and received. As he looks down from there I say to him, "I did my best. I am doing it now. You are still the captain of my soul." I feel his spirit here palpably about us. He is standing here, speaking through my weak voice.

It was a skillful forensic effort, perhaps the greatest of Baker's many speeches. Hardened newspaper correspondents were reported to have brushed tears from their eyes as they leaped to their feet. William Allen White, a veteran journalist and Republican, wrote Baker that he had attended every major national convention since 1896 but he had never seen

> a prophet lifting his voice before the king so righteously, so beautifully, so terribly as you lifted yours when you stood before King Demos that hot June day. You revived my faith in man and God like a great tragedy in which the human spirit rises clear and free above the most devastating calamity.

For a moment Baker had revived the exaltation of 1919 and the audience cheered wildly, but within a short time the parochial mood of 1924 returned and the same delegates who had applauded so recently were soon to vote down the Baker minority report by a plurality of more than two to one.

In later years Baker had an uneasy feeling about this speech; he came to the conclusion that the emotional content was too high while its argumentative effect was less than the subject deserved. He remembered that he had been so near physical collapse, as a result of two hours of sleep a night because of extended meetings on the party's platform, that his "intellectual hip was out of joint"; he also had been compelled to pull out all the emotional stops to hold an audience that was "eager to desert me for a sandwich with which to sustain themselves through the Klan debate to which it had been looking forward eagerly." He was tremendously moved, however, by the report about two people in Washington who listened to his address over the radio. One was Charles Sumner Hamlin of the Federal Reserve Board who had been an intimate friend of President Wilson. According to Baker:

> At the time I made the speech . . . he was at the house with Mrs. Wilson sitting in the room which the President used as an office. A radio . . . stood on the President's desk facing his empty chair with Mrs. Wilson on one side and Mr. Hamlin on the other, so that I was, in effect, speaking to President Wilson's empty chair with Mrs. Wilson and Mr. Hamlin deeply moved on either side of it. If I had imagined any such picture

when I was talking, I am not sure I should have been able to go on.[5]

After this traumatic experience the selection of a presidential candidate was secondary. Because of his preoccupation with the League issue Baker took relatively little interest in the candidates who were presenting themselves. When Rabbi Stephen Wise and Harold Ross (then editor of the *American Legion Magazine*) suggested that he become a candidate himself, Baker dismissed the proposal with the statement that they were "wickedly plotting against his happiness." The early proposal of isolationist Henry Ford brought from Baker the comment that Ford was the least qualified candidate in his recollection; to nominate a man because he made a cheap motorcar was no more rational than to name the patent-medicine king Dr. Jonas Kilmer because he manufactured the household remedy Swamproot. He considered his former Cabinet colleague, W. G. McAdoo, as an authentic but erratic genius; he was also opposed to his candidacy because the former Secretary of the Treasury showed little concern for foreign affairs. Al Smith stood for Catholicism and Repeal of the Prohibition Amendment, but those issues were not important for a country "that had been losing the World War ever since it ended in November 1918." Baker found it a sad spectacle to witness a great body of delegates inflamed by the religious issue; he knew a few who were surprised as they awakened each morning to find that the Pope had not built a residence in their back yards over night.

Baker came to the early conclusion that the deadlock between the McAdoo and Smith forces would be irreconcilable, and that a dark horse would be nominated. There were three compromise candidates who had his endorsement: David Houston, John W. Davis, and Carter Glass. Houston had been a colleague in Wilson's official family,

serving as both Secretary of Agriculture and of the Treasury;
Baker had always thought he was the ablest member of the
War Cabinet. Glass was the architect of the Federal Reserve
System and a peppery Senator from Virginia, for whom Baker
had always had great admiration. Davis was a fellow West
Virginian and an eminent lawyer, so capable that Baker said
that if he could be born again he would ask to be given
Davis's legal mind. Because Davis had resisted woman's suffrage and was a Wall Street lawyer who numbered J. P.
Morgan among his clients, there was concern about his il-
liberality on domestic issues, but the West Virginian was so
prominent a pro-Leaguer that Baker was willing to hazard
his nomination.

As a member of the Ohio delegation Baker went along
with the agreed strategy, which was to stop McAdoo by voting
for the former Ohio Governor James M. Cox (whom Baker
placed in nomination) until a switch could be made to
either Glass or Davis. Actually Cox withdrew his name on
the sixty-fourth ballot and the delegation voted for Baker
from the sixty-fifth through the seventy-third ballot, after
which increasing support was given to Davis, who finally
won the nomination on the one-hundred-and-third round.
The temporary swing to Baker was an attempt on the part
of the Ohio delegation, supported by a strong editorial from
Walter Lippmann's *New York World,* to swing the convention to the former Secretary of War. This maneuver never
had Baker's endorsement, and after the pro-League speech
the delegates showed little interest in him as a compromise
candidate.

In spite of the nominee's handicaps (Mencken dubbed
him the Honorable John W. Davis of Wall Street, West
Virginia) Baker thought that excepting Wilson he was the
best qualified candidate presented by either party in two
generations. He had no sympathy at all for the isolationist
Robert M. La Follette, who was the third-party Progressive

candidate. For the immobility of the Republican nominee, "Silent Cal" Coolidge, he had nothing but contempt; he believed that American patience with the do-nothing President was comparable to the stolidity of Englishmen who spent their time staring at the lions around the Nelson monument in Trafalgar Square. When the tumult was over and the Republicans had won again, Baker could only be amazed at the public indifference to the scandals of the Harding regime, including the infamous Teapot Dome affair. He thought the victorious Republicans had placed their ethical sights on the level established by Pennsylvania's Senator George Wharton Pepper who had claimed during the campaign that "70% of honesty in public affairs is a fair average." To Baker this was the most cynical and degrading public utterance of his lifetime.[6]

In 1924 Baker had been mortified by the failure of the Democratic Party to take a strong position on international co-operation. In the national campaign four years later the continued indifference of the party to foreign affairs again brought bitter disappointment. This was the election in which the ex-fish peddler Al Smith, sporting a brown derby and a long cigar, ran against the "Sage of Palo Alto," Herbert Hoover. During the campaign the League was shunted off the stage as the positions in front of the footlights were pre-empted by Prosperity, Prohibition, and Popery.

Because of popular opposition to what was called the "League Trap" Baker had changed his mind on the wisdom of a plank calling for immediate entry into the international organization. He regarded the public attitude as both ignorant and stupid, but was forced to admit that a "mountain" of prejudice actually existed. He had favored going over the mountain in 1924; in 1928 he proposed going around it. Before the Resolutions Committee at the Democratic Convention, which met in Houston, Baker switched the emphasis to the World Court; he argued for immediate entry into that tribunal along with a declaration of hearty and sympathetic co-operation, but not membership, in the League. On this stand he was supported by his former Cabinet colleague Josephus Daniels and Senator Carter Glass. The Committee voted them down by a vote of two to one. Baker decided against carrying the fight to the floor of the Convention, as he had done in 1924, because he knew the attempt would result in a disastrous second failure. He felt that the Convention was so completely dominated by isolationists like the pro-Irish David Walsh of Massachusetts that it would have been impossible for a minority to include even the least offensive of the Ten Commandments in the platform.

The Democratic platform, as it was finally endorsed by the Convention, followed the Republican lead in omitting any reference to either the League or the Court. Actually it catered to the dominant spirit of isolationism by a declaration of "freedom from entangling alliances" and by taking a position on the tariff that was pleasing to protected industries. Baker characterized the whole thing as abominable; he was sure that McKinley could have run on the tariff plank and that Senator Lodge would have been quite happy with the one on international relations. This was a great pity because Baker was hopeful that the time had arrived, as foreseen by Napoleon, when nations would fight their battles not with big guns but with big ideas before courts and tribunals. There was a sense of helplessness in his rhetorical question "Why are we so dumb?" It was Baker who had been saying: "A Republican President is a President of things as they are. A Democratic President is a President of things as they ought to be." When the Citizens League of Cleveland asked him for an evaluation of Harold Burton, then a candidate for State representative and later a justice of the Supreme Court, it was Baker who testified that Burton was a man of character, intelligence, courage, and public spirit—but added,

"He is a Republican and, therefore, ought not to be elected."
After Smith had been drubbed by Hoover in the November
voting he concluded sadly that it was the inevitable result
of the Democratic attempt to be more Republican than the
Republican Party. Among other things he had been perturbed that the Democratic campaign was managed by John
J. Raskob, a millionaire with connections in General Motors
and Du Pont, who had lately been a Republican but was
selected because he was a personal friend of Smith and would
contribute heavily to the campaign chest. Under the circumstances it was not surprising that the Democratic platform
had abandoned the low-tariff tradition; Baker noted that
Raskob had made his millions in industries sheltered by
Republican high-tariff walls.[7]

Baker manifested little interest in Al Smith as the party's
standard-bearer, and gave no support to friends who had
wanted him to make a try for the nomination himself. He
thought Franklin D. Roosevelt made a good nominating
speech for Smith, but found the sobriquet "The Happy Warrior" more interesting than accurate because he believed
Smith to be "more happy than warrior." His devoted friend
Ralph Hayes had long been working on ways and means to
make Baker President, a plan of operations that was to be
intensified in the campaign of 1932, but he found the ex-
Secretary of War exasperatingly disinterested. Baker said that
he was "almost hopelessly unavailable" because he was unwilling to sacrifice his freedom to say what he pleased, and
added that he derived more satisfaction from the "affectionate
prejudice" Hayes and Justice Clark had in his favor than he
would from living in the White House and "looking around
in its dark corners to see how many pennies Calvin has se-
creted there." In 1926 when Colonel House had suggested
that he run for Governor of Ohio as a steppingstone to the
White House, Baker's reaction was in the form of a dis-

concerting question: "Now I ask you, is any job in the world
from Pope down worth getting at the price of living . . .
in Columbus?" In 1927 the *Birmingham Post* started a boom-
let with the frightful slogan, "The country kneads Baker to
save the people's dough." His amused observation was that
the statement was Pickwickian because no one person in the
Federal Government had ever spent a third as much money
as he had, with expenditures in the War Department at the
rate of one million dollars an hour day and night—Sundays
and holidays included. Early in 1928 there was a rumor that
Governor Vic Donahey would appoint him to the United
States Senate as the successor to Senator Frank Willis, who
had died in office. Baker said he was glad the "duty call" had
never come because if he left the law profession once more
he would never be able to return to it, and because he had
not yet established sufficient financial reserves to care for his
family.

During the Houston Convention a resolute effort was made
to place Baker on the Democratic ticket as candidate for the
Vice-Presidency. It was engineered by the ever-active Hayes
and editor Walter Lippmann of the *New York World*. Most
of the preliminary work was done in New York, where Lippmann was in conference with Governor Smith and his political advisers Judge Joseph Proskauer and Belle Moskowitz.
Lippmann told Smith that Baker should be nominated because he was a brilliant speaker, was identified with the
Wilsonian tradition, would have the support of women's organizations and of reform associations, and would carry the
important State of Ohio. In a personal letter he added another reason: he told Baker he was the only man fitted to
be President, and that the Democrats should start a new
tradition by nominating a Vice-President capable of being
President; this opinion reflected the judgment of some that a
Smith-Baker ticket would be like the Old Star Bicycles—with
the little wheel in the front and the Big Wheel in the rear.

Lippmann found Smith noncommittal, Mrs. Moskowitz enthusiastically favorable, and Judge Proskauer fearful that Baker would not accept the nomination.

Proskauer was right. Hayes testified ruefully that Baker "bit everyone who tried to urge his acceptance." His immediate reasons, half in jest, were that Mrs. Baker wouldn't let him in the house if he came home a candidate, plus the fact that the penalty attached to the position was too great —as presiding officer of the Senate he would be forced during four long years to listen to Alabama's "Tom-Tom" Heflin, who was continuously beating the drums for King Cotton and race prejudice. In actual fact his real reason went much deeper, as he wrote Hayes:

> I am afraid you think me a very intractable and difficult fellow, but I was never clearer in my life than I was in my decision about the vice-presidential nomination. I hope I was courteous to everybody who approached me about it in Houston. . . . The fact is my dear Ralph, that I will never again run for office or accept an appointive office unless I believe some cause in which I am deeply interested will be furthered by my doing so. I need not tell you that I never wanted to hold office from my boyhood up to now. Those I have held I have accepted reluctantly and each experience has demonstrated to me that out of the one life allotted to each of us, the years spent in public office are deliberately sacrificed out of the sum total of possible happiness. That sacrifice I have in the past made because it seemed to me that the compensations in the way of opportunities for service justified it.[8]

During the campaign Baker was as disturbed by Smith's preoccupation with the Prohibition issue as he was with the Governor's silence on foreign affairs. He thought the wet-dry controversy and golf had done more to lower the tone of conversation among cultured people than anything since the "Pig Woman" murder case, and he could not develop much enthusiasm for the right to get drunk. He had never believed in the wisdom of placing the Eighteenth Amendment in the Constitution because that document ought to "declare great principles" while leaving legislative power to Congress. He recalled with amusement Gilbert Chesterton's remark that the inclusion of the Eighteenth Amendment in the American Constitution made him ponder how a British Constitution would look if it read, "The Government of England shall be by a hereditary king, a House of Lords and a House of Commons, and there shall be no dogs in Wimbledon Commons." He also believed temperance through self-restraint was a more effective solution than prohibition by legal fiat, and in the long run he was convinced that education was the only answer to intemperance in its three main forms—liquor, drugs, and prostitution. On the other hand Baker was never impressed by the personal liberty argument because he believed social progress was based on the surrender of individual rights for the general good, and he could think of no personal appetite he would surrender more willingly for the commonweal than the right to drink intoxicants. He was horrified by the gay manner in which the educated and propertied classes were violating the Amendment, and he thought the time might come when economically oppressed groups would rationalize their own contempt for the Constitution when it interfered with their necessities, because they had seen the educated and the wealthy flout the law when it interfered with their appetites. The upshot of Baker's pro-con attitude on the Eighteenth Amendment was that few derived any comfort from his position: he was too dry for the wets, and too wet for the drys.

Baker's caveats about Al Smith extended all the way to brown derby hats, although he was the first to admit that many people were not particularly fond of the black headdress which he himself affected "for some strange reason." As late as August of the campaign year he affirmed that he had resolved to be for Smith, but admitted that he was still "trying very hard to find out why." In spite of a variety of reservations about both the Democratic platform and the candidate Baker not only supported Smith but gave some speeches for him. He could take pride in Smith's record as a four-term Governor of New York, and he wanted to oppose the prevailing religious prejudice against a candidate who happened to be a Catholic. He certainly could not vote for a Republican nominee, Herbert Hoover in this campaign, although he knew him well and applauded his previous record on behalf of the League and the Court. But Hoover had sat by, silent, as a member of Harding's Cabinet while the League and the Court were jettisoned, and in addition was suppressing his beliefs on these questions in the current campaign, which to Baker was worse than having no beliefs at all.

In October Baker debated with Republican Theodore Burton in Cleveland, made a political address in Ashland, Kentucky, and was scheduled by the Democratic National Committee for additional speeches in Missouri and Oklahoma. En route to St. Louis, with what he described as "fire in my eye," he was taken from the train at Lima (Ohio) in great distress because of a "coronary accident," the first of several which were to occur in the remaining nine years of his life. In 1924 he had been able to boast that during his first fifty-two years there had been but one day of illness, and in that case he was obstinate enough to believe that his consignment to bed had been the result of a conspiracy between Mrs. Baker and certain Army doctors who wanted him to take an enforced rest. None the less he thought the indisposition at Lima was to be expected; forty years earlier at Johns Hopkins the physical director had told him that his heart was second-rate—"and at 57 I was still trying to use it as I did at 17." He wrote General Bliss that a month's rest had been prescribed, which he enjoyed because he could sit in the library and talk to friends; after the period of idleness he would be allowed to move about on the promise that he would not lift heavy burdens, run upstairs, "or chase street cars." He could read the many letters from friends expressing concern and sympathy, and he could laugh over the communication from a lady in the W.C.T.U. which expressed different sentiments. She had prayed that Baker might be disabled to prevent his speeches for the "wet" Al Smith, and could not resist the temptation to write him that her petition had been answered. Baker regretted that "she did resist the temptation to tell me her name," with the unfortunate result that he was "unable to thank her for her diagnosis of a trouble which has baffled the *regular* physicians." He claimed one disappointment in the whole "experiment." He had always supposed that when one approached "the river's brink . . . one would pass in review the full story of his life, add up the credit and debit columns and be finely amazed at the lightness of touch with which he had in his healthier days treated his grosser transactions. None of that took place with me at all. The experience was prosaic, disappointing and I have not the least desire to repeat it."[9]

Baker had no confidence in the idea of outlawing war by simple declaration, which was supported during the 1920s by advocates as disparate as Senator Borah and educator John Dewey, and which came to fruition in the illusory Kellogg-Briand Peace Pact of 1928. He thought of the concept as a sentimental abstraction and was inclined to agree with those who sneered that it was nothing more than an "international kiss"; as a device to prevent war it would be no more effective than the balance-of-power idea which was "as dead as Tiglath-pileser." Much more practical as a step toward international understanding would be the cancellation of war debts which he advocated during 1926 in an article appearing in *Trade Winds,* the monthly publication of The Cleveland Trust Company. In his judgment the war-debt settlements based on "capacity to pay" had not represented the magnificent achievements that everyone thought them to be; in actual fact they were magnificent disasters. Baker said it was time to stop

making faces at European nations, he agreed with Secretary
of the Treasury Andrew Mellon that a prosperous Europe
was the prime consideration, and he doubted that the debts
were collectible in any case. He was the first American of
political prominence to take this position, and the article not
only attracted comment by newspapers all over the world but
encouraged letters to Baker informing him that he was a
"damn fool" who ought to be deported. President Coolidge
averred that it was much easier for a private citizen like Mr.
Baker to give away the taxpayer's money than it was for the
President to do so, and during the presidential campaign of
1932 Senator Wheeler of Montana was to claim that the
"secret" support for Baker's nomination was being financed
by international bankers on Wall Street who stood to profit
by the cancellation of the war debts incurred by the United
States in the First World War.

Baker wanted American participation in the World Court
as well as the League of Nations. In the mid-1920s when a
promising prospect for the achievement of this goal was
changed into one of gloom and doom through crippling reservations submitted by Senator Borah, Baker said that Borah's
knowledge of the Court reminded him of De Quincey's con-
fession on political economy—he not only knew nothing about
it but was obstinate in keeping his ignorance intact. In 1930
another encouraging effort supported by President Hoover
was stymied by a Senate that regarded the Court as a tool
of the League of Nations; Baker's comment was that the Senate was suffering from an attack of hemiplegia, and that its
entire foreign-relations side was paralyzed. In 1935 American
adherence to the World Court seemed assured until journalist William Randolph Hearst and the Detroit radio priest,
Father Charles E. Coughlin, went to work. In Baker's opinion
Hearst was the worst influence in American society and
Coughlin, undisciplined by a superannuated bishop, was a
demagogic phenomenon who summoned all the discontented
to enlist under the enveloping banner of the Church of the

Little Flower in Royal Oak, Michigan. Baker appeared, to
no avail, on the radio against Coughlin; the isolationist telegrams that flooded Washington only made Baker think of
"the voices of the dead and of the children who now play
in our streets who may lie on the war-torn hills as I saw others
lie, unless we are brave enough to make this gesture for
peace." While all this was going on he had been appointed
by President Coolidge to the Hague Tribunal, a panel of international arbiters (distinct from the World Court) from
which jurists could be selected by nations that wished to submit disputes to its jurisdiction. At the time the other American members of the Tribunal were Elihu Root, John Bassett
Moore, and Charles Evans Hughes.

The intransigence of the Senate on the League and the
Court issues brought Baker to the conclusion that the august
upper chamber should either be abolished or limited in its
power. In his judgment foreign policy was not administered
by the President but by ninety-seven persons, ninety-six of
whom were Senators; this meant that the check and balance
system established by the Constitution was all check and no
balance. He suspected that shrewd diplomats from other
countries were more zealous to ascertain the opinion of Senator Borah than of the Secretary of State, although plain
American citizens were under the illusion that the State Department conducted our foreign affairs. He said he was no
specialist in what chemists called refractory substances but
he did know the composition of the United States Senate; for
that reason he favored its abolition and the substitution of
the British system of parliamentary responsibility. Because this
was not immediately possible Baker proposed a compromise
ad interim; it was the ratification of all treaties by a simple
majority of both houses, in place of the current requirement
for a two-thirds vote in the Senate.[10]

During the 1920s Baker had supported the co-operation of

all nations in the League in order to avert any war that might be imminent. Confronted with an impotent League and with the growing power of Hitler, Mussolini, and the Japanese war lords during the 1930s, he reverted to the position taken by Wilson in 1917—that of choosing friends and denouncing enemies. He declared that the situation was so grave that America must now place major emphasis on her own national interest, and he was in favor of war if necessary to restrain any or all of the aggressive powers from acquiring military or economic supremacy in the world. Although he knew that war was an irrational way to settle international controversies he believed there had been justifiable wars in the past and probably would be others in the future; as for himself he would not willingly "unfight" the American Revolution or the Thirty Years' War, which consolidated the Protestant Reformation. Because Germany, Italy, and Japan denied free speech, free thought, and the basic principles on which civilization rested, he would regret the necessity of choosing war in order to preserve them, but would not hesitate for a moment in doing so.

With this point of view, which was the same as that expressed by President Roosevelt in his "Quarantine Speech" of October 5, 1937, Baker's position on major issues during the 1930s is readily understood. In 1932 he joined President Lowell and Jane Addams in a petition asking for an economic boycott of Japan. He thought the neutrality laws of the 1930s, designed to limit our commercial relationships with belligerents on both sides of any war, were immoral and unrighteous. It was our ethical duty, he asserted, to aid an innocent belligerent even if it imposed the burden of naming the aggressor; as for himself he admitted that he was "neutral only to the extent that it permitted me to be pro-British." He wrote Senator Vandenberg that the alternatives were either complete economic isolation during a world war or co-operation with nations trying to keep the peace of the world from being disturbed; he chose the latter, believing that those who chose the former would face difficulties as great or even greater. When college students, at Oxford and in American universities, took a pledge never to engage in another war Baker said he did not underestimate their courage or undervalue their sincerity, but he thought the resolutions would not be much more effective than sealing the windows of a cottage would have been against the Johnstown flood. For this judgment he was criticized severely by Oswald Garrison Villard, the militant editor of *The Nation,* who told three thousand students at Western Reserve University (of which Baker was a trustee) that Baker might become the American fascist dictator because he was a "ruthless ex-liberal" who had become one of the greatest militarists in the country. Baker's bland rejoinder was that different men, with equal earnestness and equal sincerity, saw things differently.

By 1937, in spite of twenty years of effort on behalf of a League to enforce peace, Baker had gone full circle and was in the same situation that confronted him as a "pacifist" Secretary of War in 1917. He said in 1936 that nearly all the peace work with which he was connected seemed like "chasing butterflies on a battlefield" in view of the grave European and Asiatic situations. In spite of the fact that he felt our entry into a second world war was necessary under the circumstances, the prospect was frightening and disillusioning. He noted that Sir Oliver Lodge, the eminent British physicist, had predicted that scientists were on the verge of unleashing the power in the atom, which Baker understood would create enough power to "lift the German fleet from the bottom of the ocean at Scapa Flow and set it up on a Scotch mountain." He could only pray that science would not find the secret until there was enough moral intelligence in the world to deal with such colossal destructive force.[11]

XIII. Reluctant Candidate

For a decade Ralph Hayes and Justice Clarke had been pondering ways and means to elect their Cleveland associate President of the United States. Clarke and Baker had been attorneys in northern Ohio at the turn of the century, and had always trusted each other "without shadow of reserve." As a young man recently graduated with honors from Adelbert College of Western Reserve University Hayes had timidly asked Baker to speak at the City Club in Cleveland in 1915; he said later that in planning a luncheon for the Club he did not realize that he was arranging a life for himself. Despite the disparity in age the two men became the closest of friends, and Hayes was to say that if greatness ever walked this earth it was shod in Baker's shoes. Clarke and Hayes decided that the big push for the White House should occur in 1932, with the Justice providing the money and Hayes doing the "politicking." The plan was to keep Baker's name before the country so that the delegates would know where to find the right man after the avowed candidates had worn themselves out of contention.

Hayes arranged support from newspapers; by early 1932 Baker's nomination was being urged by the *Cincinnati Enquirer*, the *Richmond News-Leader*, the *Des Moines Register-Tribune*, and the *Cleveland Plain Dealer*. He worked through prominent individuals whose discretion could be relied upon in each of twenty-five to thirty States. There were promises of support from groups of lawyers, professors, ministers, and college clubs in every part of the nation. In Georgia Robert Woodruff, the tycoon of Coca-Cola, was trying to bore into the State delegation on Baker's behalf, although Hayes reported that he could scarcely imagine that "even a ticket consisting of Benito Mussolini, with God Almighty for Vice-President, could crack the Georgia lineup." In Jersey City Hayes talked with Mayor Frank ("I Am the Law") Hague, but found the boss exasperatingly noncommittal. In Virginia John Stewart Bryan, the editor of the *Richmond News-Leader*, advertised the recent survey by *Outlook* magazine proving that Baker was the first choice of editors who had been interviewed in thirty-four States. The *Portsmouth* (Virginia) *Star* came out for a ticket of Baker and Byrd with the winning slogan "Two B's and honey." Senator Glass was quoted as saying there were but two men capable of handling the nation's serious problems—Baker and Owen D. Young. In Ohio Senator Robert Bulkley and ex-congressman Martin Davey (soon to be Governor) advocated Baker's nomination. The *Cleveland Plain Dealer* used the occasion of Baker's sixtieth birthday (December 3, 1931) to endorse his candidacy, and the city's Mayor Ray Miller not only announced his support but referred to Baker as "the Jeffersonian apostle of the North." Correspondents suggested amazing slogans and sobriquets such as "New Deal (Diehl) Baker," "Root for Newt," and "Pat-a-Cake, Pat-a-Cake, Baker's Man"; one had written a campaign song entitled "Shootin' Straight with Newton." What passed for poetry appeared in the following verse:

It may be Roosevelt, Ritchie, or Al,
Robinson—Joseph—or even some gal,
But the Banshee, regarded by some as a faker
(By others upheld as a candidate maker)
Is inclined to believe that an Eminent Quaker
Will race with a gent known as Newton D. Baker.

In New York City Hayes was happy to report the support

NEWTON D. BAKER

"Here is the man the Nation needs." The Cleveland Plain
Dealer *of December 3, 1931, supports Baker for President.*

of Professor James T. Shotwell, dramatist Robert Sherwood, lawyer-politician-economist Adolf A. Berle, and journalist-historian Mark Sullivan. Walter Lippmann, whom Baker considered "a modern Erasmus," wrote that he and Hayes had their heads together frequently; one of the results was that Lippmann wrote a column for the *New York Herald-Tribune* stating that Baker was the inevitable candidate. Journalist Roy Howard indicated that he hoped Baker was not only nominated but elected, although he did not believe the Scripps-Howard papers should spearhead the boom because Baker's law firm represented them on legal matters.[1]

There was one major obstacle in the path of all these tactical maneuvers. It was provided by the proposed candidate, who had no desire to become a presidential nominee. Baker enjoyed telling the story about his parents:

> My mother wanted me to be a preacher. My father wanted me never to enter politics. And I have been trying to follow their advice ever since.

He said that he never went to Washington and looked at the White House without seeing it as a glorified prison, where "the sentence is for four years, without benefit of clergy or even the mollifying ministration of a parole board." There was one position as Chief Executive in which he *was* interested at the time, but it was the Presidency of the University of Virginia, which was offered to him in 1932. When he was invited to have a meal with Tammany sachems in New York he missed the opportunity because he was lunching with four college presidents at the Century Club. On the question of his alleged presidential aspirations there was an interesting exchange of one-sentence letters between Baker and an opponent. When the antagonist wrote "You don't have a chance," the equally laconic Baker reply was "I don't want one." It was no wonder that Lippmann concluded that the Clevelander was "almost perversely unhelpful to his enthusiastic friends," and that Hayes said if strategy were left to Baker "we would be going around with blinkers on our eyes, gags in our mouths, handcuffs on our wrists and chains on our ankles."

The central point was that Baker was less interested in the party's candidate than he was in its philosophy and program. By contrast with the Houston platform of 1928 he hoped the Democrats in 1932 could recapture some of the idealism of 1912 and 1916; in that case he would be found shouting, but indifferent whether he was the cheer leader or a member of the rooting section. In his judgment Owen D. Young was the best-qualified *person* to be President, although not the best-qualified *candidate* because of his close connections with General Electric and the Radio Corporation of America. He could think of others—Franklin D. Roosevelt, Ohio's Governor George S. White and Senator Bulkley, or Maryland's Governor Albert C. Ritchie—who were Wilsonian enough to fill the bill. But it was the philosophy of the Democratic Party that should be clarified first; after that he was in favor of letting events take their course. He could agree to consideration only if obstacles got in the way of other suitable candidates, and "if the impossible situation were to arise of my being the best qualified, I would ruefully subject such a judgment to a candid examination, and, if I agreed with it, act accordingly." It was this indication that Baker would respond to a duty call, although he phrased it in careful legal phraseology, that gave Hayes some hope; his statement was that he didn't object to Baker's shutting the door so long as he didn't slam it! In a letter to Baker, Roy Howard phrased it in another figure of speech. "I am not at all in favor of your putting your head and shoulders above the parapet," he wrote, "but the sight of just a suggestion of a pompadour would be encouraging . . . if it did nothing more than indicate 'that our flag was still there.' " Hayes

believed Baker's stubborn unavailability might in itself produce a cumulative insistence that he be nominated; he meant
to persuade Baker—preferably by "non-violent means"—that
there were too many people who would not accept a negative
answer.[2]

In 1927 Baker had dropped his advocacy of American
membership in the League of Nations. For the next five years
he said in speeches and letters that membership unsupported
by an informed public opinion would be worse than remaining outside the international organization, and that even if
he were President and could take the United States into the
League by his own fiat he would not do so. In spite of these
oft-repeated statements, the public still associated him with
immediate entry into the assembly of nations at Geneva.
After the League of Nations Association met in Philadelphia
early in January 1932 the *New York Evening Sun* reported
that the idea "rippled" through the assembly that if Baker
were elected President he would take the United States into
the League "right quickly." The *Columbus Dispatch* ran a
cartoon showing the League pictured as a European diplomat
who was holding Baker on his lap as he said:

> Patty-cake, patty-cake, Baker, man,
>   Make Uncle Sam, just as fast as you can,
> Send young Americans over the sea,
>   To settle the troubles of Europe for me.

Hayes was anxious to correct this erroneous impression and
at his insistence Baker made a statement on January 26,
1932, as he was embarking from New York for a "romance
with Mrs. Baker" in Mexico. He said that he was not a candidate for the Presidency, that the United States would go
into the League some day but should not do so until there
was an informed nonpartisan majority favoring it, and that
he did not favor a League plank in the Democratic platform.

The pronouncement was widely publicized in the press, which misinterpreted it as an indication that Baker's hat was in the presidential ring because he had welshed on his previous unpopular support of the League. Columnist Heywood Broun thought it apparent that Baker would rather "be a candidate than be candid," and the *St. Louis Post-Dispatch* said, "Like all the rest, he has put political expediency ahead of the welfare of nations and the peace of a world heartsick of war." Baker was surprised at the journalistic reaction and observed that it would have made him unhappy if he had really made the statement to affect the Democratic nomination. In spite of the unexpected result he did not regret the pronouncement because it merely repeated

The Democratic donkey disapproves Baker's drum-beating for the League. Cartoon in the Washington Star, *January 19, 1932.*

what he had been saying for several years; i.e., that thoughtful
Democrats and thoughtful Republicans should both work
for the League, not as a party issue but as a national policy.[3]

There were some who wondered whether Baker's activities,
political and otherwise, might have alienated certain blocs
of voters whose support would be needed in a national campaign. In May 1932, only a month before the nominating
convention, Franklin Roosevelt wrote Josephus Daniels (perhaps with tongue in cheek) that Baker "would make a better
President than I would," but he thought Baker's candidacy
would be handicapped by the loss of support from progressives
who did not like his wealthy legal clients, laborers who disapproved of his stand on the open shop, German-Americans
who remembered that he was Secretary of War in 1917–18,
and the Irish because of his advocacy of the League of Nations. One of the issues that particularly worried his friends,
and which Jim Farley and Louis Howe were to exaggerate
in order to make Roosevelt's nomination more appealing,
was that Baker was the candidate of the "financial crowd."
It was charged that he was the candidate-in-reserve of the
plutocrats, and that since his Tom Johnson days Baker had
"imperceptibly . . . warped out of the storm-tossed seas of
liberalism into Wall Street's snug harbor." In *The Nation*
Oswald Garrison Villard pondered the young man who had
enlisted under the banner of Tom Johnson and had now
topped his career as the paid attorney of the Youngstown
Sheet and Tube Company, Electric Bond and Share, and of
the Van Sweringen brothers—the Cleveland financiers who
through holding companies controlled a four-billion-dollar
empire in railroads. It was Villard's contention that this
new devotion to corporate interests had induced Baker to
spoil a marvelous waterfront development by placing the
new Union Station in Cleveland's Public Square, in desecra-

tion to the monument to Mayor Johnson which was not far away. In Villard's judgment Baker had the ability to "persuade himself at any moment that the position he assumes . . . is not only exactly the right one . . . even though it may be at the opposite pole from the position which he originally held, but that his taking it is quite consistent with his earlier beliefs and position." The editor of *The Nation* thought that the Baker type of political mind was the most dangerous in existence; he much preferred the conscienceless but undissimulating political pirates like Matt Quay, Boies Penrose, and Reed Smoot.

Equally troublesome was the allegation that Baker, who had once been a strong advocate of municipal ownership of electric power, was now chief counsel for power interests in suits challenging the constitutionality of the Federal Power Act. Many believed that if this charge was sustained Baker would become as unavailable for the Presidency as Owen D. Young, who happened to be the President of General Electric. Even Clarke wondered whether Baker's association with big business had blunted the edge of his former zeal against "the privilege doctrine of Alexander Hamilton." It was disturbing that long-time liberal friends, such as Felix Frankfurter and Fred Howe, were supporting Roosevelt rather than Baker.

By contrast with his constant harping on international problems Baker maintained public silence on domestic issues, with the result that an impression was created that he must be conservative on these matters. In private correspondence he made some effort to explain his position. He said he had never been general counsel to the Van Sweringens, although he had represented them on specific cases from time to time. He believed that water power, as the last great natural resource unmonopolized by private hands, should remain under government control or ownership, and he pointed with pride to his advocacy (as Secretary of War) of public ownership

and operation of Muscle Shoals long before Senator Norris
of Nebraska had introduced the first bill to make it possible.
On the other hand he did not believe in Federal control of
water power on nonnavigable streams, and his legal services
had been retained to test this extension of national authority. He also believed that the Federal Government should
produce power only, leaving distribution to private lines
under government regulation; on this issue he admitted he
was less radical than Senator Norris or Franklin Roosevelt.
On the general subject of Wealth versus Commonwealth Baker
believed some modified form of capitalism would evolve for
reasons which he stated in a letter to Hayes:

> I do not want to pronounce a credo at this moment, but I
> will admit to you that I am heartily ashamed of the ineptitudes
> of our present industrial arrangement and have no idea of
> being hush-hushed about them. If the captains of industry in
> the United States have not sense enough to organize industry
> upon a plan which will prevent the disastrous and cruel unem-
> ployment which we have at this time, then they ought not to
> be permitted to organize it at all.
>
> This does not mean that I believe either that industry can
> always be kept at the flood tide of peak production, but it
> does very definitely mean that industry has no right to impose
> upon labor the vicarious suffering caused by making it bear
> all the consequences of maladjustments and peaks and valleys
> in the industrial system. I am sure that I have no patent medi-
> cine remedy for the existing situation, but I do know that the
> responsibility for finding a remedy rests upon the employer
> class and is at this moment not being met or even considered
> with any genuine concern.
>
> If this sounds a bit radical to you, I assure you it is the most
> conservative thing I have ever said in my life, for he is, after
> all the true conservative who best realizes the extent to which
> the preservation of an economic system depends upon the
> justice with which it distributes rewards and imposes burdens.
> If I may counterweight this piece of wisdom with the definition
> of a radical, I would say a radical is one who realizes that there
> are injustices and is willing to cure them by imposing the op-

posite injustice. The truth of both of these definitions, if there be any truth in them, lies in the long view of their operation as principles rather than the immediate effect which occurs to one when they are stated.

Unfortunately for Hayes all of these judgments appeared in private correspondence rather than public statements, with the inevitable result that the electorate was left in the dark regarding Baker's position on domestic affairs.[4]

Among the active candidates there was great concern in 1932 about Prohibition or Repeal. There may have been reason to worry about Baker's attitude on many issues, but liquor was not one of them. Hayes was a "wet" but agreed that the issue should be played down; he did not think any candidate deserved to ride into the White House on a brewery truck. For some unknown reason the bartenders' union had presented Baker with a certificate of membership, an honor amusing to Hayes who had never seen him consume an "authoritative" drink or hook his heel over a brass rail. As a member of the Wickersham Commission in 1930 Baker had taken a stand for Repeal, but two years later hardly thought the matter was a paramount issue. He was certain that bread rather than beer should be the chief subject of discussion in 1932, and he believed it more important to find jobs for people than to find drinks for them. He thought it a great pity that the Democratic Party appeared to be more interested in gin fizzes than international problems, and asserted that he would take no interest in political proceedings if the chief issue was between a raging thirst on the one side and the Sahara Desert on the other. The platform ultimately endorsed Repeal, a stand Baker thought "wetter than wise."[5]

Because of the prevailing uncertainty regarding Baker's position on domestic issues Clarke and Hayes made every effort during the early months of 1932 to persuade him to make "the speech" that would put him in the public eye. Clarke wanted him to deliver a "Party speech on a Party occasion"—preferably on Jackson Day—because many had the impression that he was more interested in literary than political affairs. Hayes not only wanted the speech but asked that it stress domestic affairs:

> More people are hungry in this country today than ever before. . . . More workmen have no work. More farmers are smothered and impoverished under mountains of unmarketable crops. Industry languishes . . . behind a barrier designed to stop imports. . . . From no quarter does hope for a teacher and a prophet appear. You are the one person who could give inspiration to a people who cry for a leader. And, yet, instead of addressing yourself to the issues that so urgently weigh upon the mind and conscience of the country, you spend your strength in expounding upon a possible Twenty-first Amendment to the Constitution designed to realize the apportionment of power between the Executive and the Senate in relation to the ratification of treaties. Unanswerable as your argument is, isn't that subject far out of focus . . . in this winter of discontent? Men ask for bread—newer, fresher bread —and you are the only baker who can give it to them.

Having gone so far, Hayes added: "One day, after a particularly brazen letter like this, you will exile me—or decapitate me."

The speech was never made. On the one hand Baker believed that President Hoover's efforts to meet the Depression, belated and inadequate as they might be, were of such a character that public criticism at that moment would constitute bad citizenship. From another point of view he was more interested in the League and world peace than he was in the Democratic Party, and in this regard he felt he could exert a greater influence as a private citizen than as President. Hayes countered with the observation that it would be better to discuss today's issues instead of those that were fourteen years old, and suggested that when the League was mentioned

again in a public meeting the chairman should be instructed
to "grab his gavel, sock the speaker, and dismiss the crowd."
It was particularly despairing to find that Baker was speaking
frequently, but not on the "right" topics. As Hayes phrased it:

> In one incoming batch of clippings today, I find news-
> paper accounts describing engagements made by you to address
> some institute at Severance Hall on February 19 on Disarma-
> ment, to dedicate a church window in Detroit on February 21,
> to speak to the Daughters of the American Revolution at
> Hotel Statler in Cleveland on February 23, to appear before
> a conference on religious amity in Washington on March 7
> and to speak before the Builder's Exchange "immediately fol-
> lowing the Lenten Season." God only knows how many other
> similar engagements you have let yourself in for they do not
> happen to be mentioned in today's grist of clippings. If I knew
> any way under Heaven to dissuade you from agreeing to make
> this endless succession of speeches, I should certainly limit your
> circulation.[6]

As the time for the nominating convention approached
there was great concern, particularly on the part of Mrs.
Baker, over her husband's frail health and whether he had
the physical stamina to withstand the rigors of the Presidency.
As he became more convinced of the probability of Baker's
nomination and election Justice Clarke enjoined him to
guard his physical resources, especially to "cultivate deep
breathing." Hayes was more practical. Following a procedure
later pursued by Dr. Paul Dudley White with President
Dwight D. Eisenhower, Hayes asked Dr. R. W. Scott, the
famous heart specialist at Western Reserve University's School
of Medicine, for his judgment on Baker's heart condition
and his ability to withstand a presidential campaign. Baker
suddenly found himself submitting to a series of physical
examinations, reporting to Hayes that Dr. Scott was "examining me up hill and down dale because of the letter
you wrote him."

Dr. Scott sent his findings to Dr. E. P. Carter, the eminent cardiologist at Johns Hopkins Hospital, and consulted him before issuing his report on the matter. He stated that in his judgment Baker could, with reasonable safety, undertake the obligations imposed by a presidential candidacy "provided that it be not too strenuous." He went on to say that he had

> observed that Mr. Baker can do an extraordinary amount of mental work without apparent mental or bodily fatigue. Public appearances and important decisions made in the course of his work appear to cause him no worry either at the time or afterwards. However, in the event a political campaign should force Mr. Baker to undertake considerable physical exertion —a two-month tour of the land with several speeches each day, shaking the hands of multitudes, etc.—I would advise him, as I would many men of his age, not to do it.

Hayes was exultant as he envisaged a "front porch" campaign. With the medical "Nihil Obstat" in hand he told the unwilling candidate that Mrs. Baker had been left in a "pretty small minority." For many years her face had become radiant when she listened on the radio to speeches by *other* candidates. Her husband once asked her if she was particularly pleased by their political philosophy; the frank reply was "No, but I am thanking God that I am not listening to you." She was opposed to the prospect of Mr. Baker "batting" around the country on political tours.[7]

At the Democratic Convention of 1932, which met in Chicago, the leading candidate was New York's Franklin Roosevelt although he did not initially command the two-thirds majority necessary for nomination. His chief opponents in the early stages were Al Smith and Speaker John Nance Garner from Texas, who had support from California in William Randolph Hearst and his mouthpiece William Gibbs McAdoo. In a New Year's broadcast Hearst had dismissed Roosevelt, Owen D. Young, Smith, and Baker as "all good men in their way but all internationalists." He had settled on Garner as "another Champ Clark" and the one candidate whose motto would be America First. Most observers felt that Smith had no real chance for a second nomination and that his candidacy would be useful only to stop Roosevelt. Actually his entry into the race had an opposite effect on the dry and Protestant South; its delegates voted for Roosevelt, not because they were enthusiastic about him, but in order to stop Smith. A deadlock seemed to be in prospect, out of which a compromise candidate might emerge. Baker's friends expected him to be that dark horse—the John W. Davis of 1932. Before the voting started Walter Lippmann expressed their point of view in a widely syndicated statement:

> My impression is that he (Baker) is the real first choice of more responsible Democrats than any other man, and that he is an acceptable second choice to almost every one. Although there is not a single delegate instructed to vote for him, he is the man who, once preconvention pledges have been fulfilled, could most easily be nominated.

Hayes put a copy of this optimistic declaration in the hands of every delegate.

Hayes arrived in Chicago four days before the Convention opened, and established modest working quarters in two rooms just upstairs from "Candidate's Row" in the Congress Hotel. One of his facetious reports to Baker was that he had become a person of some influence as an Honorary Assistant Sergeant-at-Arms for the Convention, and he intimated to the reluctant Cleveland candidate that "if you play your cards right I may be persuaded to deploy my strength in your direction." Baker remained in Cleveland, working at his office by day and attending the summer opera at Cleveland Stadium in the evening. Hayes hoped that either Joe Hostetler or Tom Sidlo, who were Baker's law partners, would come to Chicago to be his direct representative. Baker refused to send either because he did not want the impression created that anyone was authorized to make agreements of the kind common to political conventions. Ellery Sedgwick, the editor of the *Atlantic Monthly,* was "candescent" in his anxiety to have Baker himself brought to Chicago to save the situation by addressing the Convention. Hayes dropped the proposal quickly when Baker announced that he would irrevocably eliminate himself as a candidate in the first paragraph of his speech.

Although neither Baker nor one of his law partners was on hand Hayes had able assistance in Chicago. From Cleveland there was Colonel Leonard Ayres, a vice-president of The Cleveland Trust Company who had been Baker's chief statistical officer in World War I, along with Burr Gongwer, Maurice Bernon, and Mrs. Bernice Pyke from the Cuyahoga County Democratic organization. From Indiana Ralph T. O'Neill, a former National Commander of the American Legion, was the active chairman of an ex-servicemen's organization for Baker composed of delegates to the Convention —a group of some potential importance since 25 per cent of the 1,154 delegates had seen military service in 1917–18. John W. Davis was loyal from first to last and Judge Samuel Seabury of New York was a Baker man and a willing one. John Stewart Bryan, the editor of the *Richmond News-Leader,* was busy coralling Southern delegates. In Hayes' modest judgment Wendell Willkie performed more prodigies of valor than any of the other "young Turks." After the Convention Baker would thank Willkie for his efforts, reminding him of the days when they sat next to each other at the Baltimore Convention of 1912—"filled with missionary zeal and determined to do a great service for the country."

The Hayes headquarters bore no visible sign of any connection with Mr. Baker, but none was needed. Its emis-

saries were busy with incoming delegates telling them what
Hayes called the simple truth, "that we were admirers of
Baker who were doing what we could to lay our hands on,
but without the remotest authorization from him." John
Stewart Bryan was busy sending telegrams to every editor
of his acquaintance against the attempted abrogation of the
two-thirds rule, which would have benefited Roosevelt. By
prearrangement from all over the country thousands of telegrams began to arrive in Chicago; the gist of their common
message was that if a deadlock appeared Baker was the candidate who could fuse the party and sweep the country. This
telegraphic fusillade, which had been planned weeks before
the Convention, produced some undesirable backfire; without
any supporting evidence the Hearst papers insisted that the
telegrams came from bankers and utility corporations which
were backing Baker. Just before the Democratic Convention
began its balloting for a nominee isolationist Hearst, who
really disliked Baker because of his stand on international
issues, would introduce himself editorially to a large audience: "Ladies and gentlemen of the Democratic Convention:
There are in the United States of America approximately
125,000,000 persons and among the least desirable of these
as a candidate for President is Newton D. Baker of Ohio."[8]

The first three Democratic ballots were taken during an
all-night session that left the delegates exhausted when ad-
journment finally came at nine o'clock on the morning of
July 1. On these initial tests three candidates had maintained
their strength with Roosevelt averaging 675, Smith about 200,
and Garner around 100 votes. Among the scattering ballots
Baker who had not been nominated received 8 Indiana votes,
and Governor George White who had been formally placed
in nomination received Ohio's 52—with the understanding
that they would be shifted to Baker after a few complimentary

ballots for the Governor. The coalition was holding firm
against Roosevelt, who was considerably short of the 770
ballots necessary for nomination under the two-thirds rule.
Roosevelt himself was so discouraged that shortly after five
o'clock in the afternoon (the Convention was to reconvene
for the fourth and decisive ballot at eight thirty that evening)
he put through a telephone call from Hyde Park to Baker
in Cleveland. As Baker recalled the conversation Roosevelt
said, "It now looks as though the Chicago Convention is in a
jam and that they will turn to you. I will do anything I can
to bring that about if you want it." Because arrangements had
already been made for a "deal" that would result in Roosevelt's nomination within a few hours after his call to Cleveland, in retrospect Baker concluded correctly that the New
Yorker had not been informed fully and promptly on "surrender terms" that had already been received from another
candidate.

At this critical moment, in the judgment of the astute William Allen White of Kansas, it was the blunder of inaction
on the part of Al Smith that insured Roosevelt's nomination,
the very result he wanted to avoid. By this time it was apparent that Roosevelt was assured of a sizable number of
votes from the South and West as long as Smith was in the
race, because those two sections were voting against Smith
by casting their ballots for Roosevelt. In White's opinion, if
Smith had withdrawn after the third ballot, the Roosevelt
bloc would have been broken and Southern and Western
delegates would have led the parade to Baker. Because of
their knowledge of sentiment within State delegations Hayes
and journalist Roy Howard were also certain that this would
have been the result if Smith had withdrawn. Because he did
not do so White concluded that Smith "displayed the talents
of a provincial politician, not much wiser than Charlie Murphy, or Coker, with a misunderstanding of the West and

South, indeed everybody west of Buffalo, that was abysmal and tragic in the end."

During these strategic hours several other men were extremely busy. One of them was Jim Farley who wanted Roosevelt nominated. Others were the Californians Hearst and McAdoo who realized that Garner could not be nominated and who now wanted to stop Baker. The isolationist Hearst and the internationalist Baker had nothing in common, and relations between McAdoo and the Clevelander had never been exactly cordial. Farley had warned Hearst time and again that a deadlock would probably nominate Baker—the candidate the newspaperman detested most. Joseph Kennedy, the Massachusetts millionaire who was then supporting Roosevelt, was so worried about the drift to Baker that he was "frightened stiff." While the first three indecisive ballots were being taken he thought the "Baker thing" had become so menacing that he decided something desperate had to be done. As a panic measure he called Hearst at five o'clock in the morning and said that unless the journalist was in a position to do something for Roosevelt, and quickly, "the fat was going to be in the fire." Kennedy was sure that the consequence of this early-morning talk was that Hearst, who had no particular enthusiasm for Roosevelt but had an undying hatred of Baker, got busy. Kennedy's assumption was corroborated by George Rothwell Brown, who was the political analyst in Washington for the Hearst papers. According to Brown he received orders from Hearst, within a few hours after the Kennedy telephone conversation with "the Boss," to ascertain from Garner (who had remained in Washington) whether he would throw his votes to Roosevelt to save the country from the "peril" of Baker or Smith. As Brown told the story Garner agreed at eleven o'clock in the morning but his decision was so well kept that not even his own Texas delegates were informed until six o'clock that evening—an hour after Roosevelt had placed his desperate call to Baker.

In any case Texas and California started the bandwagon, there was a general rush to clamber aboard, and Roosevelt was easily nominated on the fourth ballot.[9]

After the shouting was over Hayes returned to his hotel to find there a sympathetic telegram from Mr. Baker. It read: "I wish you could be as contented as I am." Along with other reasons for this statement, Baker was beginning to wonder whether the radio—with one hundred and twenty million people listening to a bawling and brawling mob—had not destroyed the presidential nominating convention as either a dignified or effective method of selecting the chief executive of the greatest republic in the world. Two months later, in reply to a query from the Senate Committee on Campaign Expenditures, Baker replied that the only personal expense incurred was for a negligible amount of postage spent on letters declining offers of support from friends who wanted to start an agitation in his favor. In spite of this indifference, many of his supporters believed his nomination had been a "near miss." Roy Howard thought Baker had come "a damned sight nearer being nominated than he suspected," although he admitted that discussing it was a good bit like telling about the fish one hooked but didn't land. The Indiana Democrat Paul McNutt claimed that if the battle had lasted twenty-four hours longer it would have been possible to bring up the "Lost Battalion" of delegates. Hayes joked that if the third ballot had ended at 10:00 P.M. rather than 9:00 A.M., the sudden Hearst-Garner deal would not have been possible because the evening hour was past Mr. Garner's bedtime. Joe Kennedy, the Roosevelt supporter, was very frank in admitting that few people knew what a close shave Roosevelt had or how near Baker came to winning the nomination. Even Baker admitted there might be something in all the speculation. He recalled that when somebody asked the old Duke of Wellington about the Battle of Waterloo, the Duke had contented himself with grunting, "It was a damn near thing."

After the Convention Hayes spent two days in Cleveland making up for the sleep he had lost and accounting at first hand for what had happened at Chicago. Baker had been wondering for some time whether he was acting conscientiously in permitting his friend to devote a year of incredible labor to a task which he was making almost impossible with his own "pre-Victorian ideals and reserves." There is little question that he would have accepted the nomination if Hayes had brought off his *coup*, but without this denouement Baker would never have been able to manufacture a personal sense of obligation about the Presidency and he had an "unbelievable sense of relief and freedom" that the duty had never become a reality. Because of Hayes's insistent enthusiasm he had permitted him to see the convention to its end in order to "complete his political education"; at the same time he agreed with Roy Howard that he could think of nothing more calculated to make life more worth living than to be able to inspire loyalty like that given by Hayes, and he was immeasurably grateful that in spite of Hayes's ambitions no unworthy compromise had ever been entertained. He was amazed that Hayes in a single and unselfish effort could have so much effect on the "vast and inchoate thing" known as a political convention, but in his own mind he was certain that he could accomplish more through speeches and patriotic service than as President.

Hayes could not agree. Having learned "847 things . . . in that mangling machine at Chicago" he was already laying plans for Baker's nomination in 1936! He advised his candidate not to break training, and warned him to avoid "the multitude of fly-by-night, catch-as-catch-can speeches on which you have spent yourself" along with "all the uplift committees and boards which have consumed so much of your time."[10]

From the beginning Baker maintained that he would vote for Roosevelt but he was not sure that he would make any speeches for him because of the liaison with Hearst. His feeling was much like that of many fellow citizens: he had a strong desire to see Hoover out, but only a moderate fancy to see Roosevelt in. He had long preached the duty of reforming the Party from the inside rather than throwing stones from the side lines, but he needed assurance that he would not "be put in bed with Mr. Hearst before he would take a reserved room in the Democratic hotel." He said he had used every brand of tooth paste without success in removing the bad taste of the Hearst-Garner-Roosevelt episode. In his judgment Hearst was the worst influence in the public and private life of the country; he was certain that they agreed on nothing and "if that makes him as proud as it makes me, it leaves two very contented people." At one time there was a rumor that Hearst had an obsession to be Secretary of the Navy and that Roosevelt intended to select him for the post. Baker agreed with James M. Cox that the appointment would be a grand one if Hearst was sent to sea permanently, without shore leave or radio contact with the mainland. Because of this mutual animosity he thought it probable that if he had been nominated, the journalist would have influenced California and other States to vote for Republican Herbert Hoover.

There were other reservations about Roosevelt. He appeared to be an intellectual isolationist about international affairs, and he had an impulsive, demagogic strain—a "fatal touch of the Boy Scout"—that was reminiscent of cousin Theodore. Much was made of Baker's failure to appear at the Cleveland airport on the morning of July 2 when Roosevelt's plane, carrying him to Chicago to accept the nomination, touched down briefly. Baker explained that with business appointments already scheduled he saw no reason to spend the morning at an airport twenty miles distant for a momentary glimpse of the candidate as he waved his hand from the aircraft. He was sure FDR did not misunderstand, and was surprised at the journalistic "color" given to the incident. A month later when he rode by train with Roosevelt from Cleveland to Columbus and had a pleasant chat with the Governor and Mrs. Roosevelt, the newspapers scarcely noted that he had done so.

Whatever the doubts may have been Baker donned campaign harness and made a number of speeches for Roosevelt —a half dozen in Cleveland and one each at Cincinnati, Brooklyn, Boston, Montclair (New Jersey), Harvard, and Princeton. He corresponded with Raymond Moley, who was writing speeches for Roosevelt, about international matters and he served as vice chairman of the Lawyer's Division of the Roosevelt Business and Professional League. He enjoyed most the addresses at Harvard and Princeton because for him there was no equivalent to a crowd of young men in the inspiring atmosphere of a great academic tradition. He brought laughter when he said that the price of wheat had gone to the lowest point since Shakespeare, and his conclusion was scholarly but undogmatic—"I venture to advise you to vote for Roosevelt and Garner."[11]

Throughout 1932 there were newspaper stories that Baker was about to be appointed to a variety of positions, so many that he remonstrated that it had become a habit of journalists to suggest his name for any vacancy beginning with that of town constable. In January it was rumored that he would succeed Justice Oliver Wendell Holmes on the Supreme Court. The offer never came, but Baker said that he would decline it because he could be more useful as a private citizen with freedom to express his opinions on all kinds of national and international questions, than would be the case "in the hermitage which membership in the Court entails."

Late in the year he was mentioned for the Cabinet of President-elect Roosevelt, usually as Secretary of State. This was manifestly improbable because it would have produced a frightful altercation between Roosevelt and Hearst, who had provided the strategic assistance at Chicago. In any case Baker was certain that either career diplomat Norman Davis or the lawyer-politician John W. Davis was better qualified for the post because of their fluency in French and their recent close relationships with Europe.

In July one public appointment had been offered and declined. It came from President Hoover who wanted Baker to become Chairman of the Reconstruction Finance Corporation. Baker's description of the meeting at the White House was that it was "all very gracious, dignified and kind, but quite impossible," because of his lack of experience as either financier or economist. Privately Baker gave Justice Clarke another reason for the declination. He wrote that he had "less than no sympathy" for the policy of lending government money at low rates of interest to industries for the purpose of making goods which no one could afford to buy.[12]

XIV. Unhappy Democrat

For the beginning of the New Deal—the famous Hundred Days—Baker had great admiration. In his judgment no one else could have shown such amazing courage and good cheer as President Roosevelt. Although some of the new policies appeared to be at variance with the lessons of history, he hoped they would be restrained within practical limits. In any case the Republicans were responsible for the Draconian measures of the New Deal because their high tariffs had brought on the lush but short-lived Babylonian prosperity of the 1920s with the result that the economic battle had been lost by the time Roosevelt became commander in chief of the national forces. Baker's relations with the new administration in its early days were infrequent but cordial. He was offered the ambassadorship in Berlin and turned it down. He heard Mrs. Roosevelt speak at a Community Fund Conference in Chicago and, while not enthusiastic about her voice and forensic technique, had never seen a more intelligent and gracious woman. When illness forced him to miss the 1933

Conference on Mobilization of Human Needs in Washington, during which he was to have been a guest at the White House, President Roosevelt not only expressed his personal regret but told Baker to watch his health because "we all need you."[1]

The honeymoon between Baker and the New Deal was a brief one. As a nineteenth-century liberal he believed in little government; he was greatly troubled by the tremendous growth of national authority which he feared had made the President as powerful as Mussolini and Hitler, and had given some of his aides delusions of grandeur that were almost pathological. He thought the National Recovery Administration, which was designed to stimulate business, was headed toward the establishment of a permanent control of industry from Washington; the Robinson-Patman Act (which attempted to define price discrimination by large corporations) was so complicated and hazy in its terminology that it reminded him of the ancient tyrant who had his laws written in fine print in incomprehensible language and then proceeded to penalize everybody who violated them.

In his judgment the Democratic Party had ceased to be liberal because it subordinated the individual to the state, and he echoed the philosophy of the conservative Democrat Grover Cleveland (for whom he had cast his first vote for President) when he said that the Party now believed that the citizen was created for the state—rather than that the state was created by and for the citizen. He wrote an article for the *Atlantic Monthly* entitled "The Decay of Self-Reliance," in which he expressed fear that the younger generation wanted only security in a state which did all the planning and thinking and providing for it. To an exceptional youth who wished to become a trapper in the Arctic Circle, Baker said mournfully: "I wonder whether you are not in fact the last young man I shall ever see who is not afraid of the dark and of hardship, and wants to stand on his own feet and force his own way by the vigor of his own spirit and the strength of his own hands." There was disagreement among conservatives on this point; Russell Leffingwell of J. P. Morgan & Company had given a Congressional committee another version of the current condition of self-reliance. "The growth of corporate enterprise," Leffingwell testified, "has been drying up individual independence and initiative. . . . We are becoming a nation of hired men, hired by great aggregates of capital." Baker could not agree, and when his friend William Mennen sent him a sample of a new lotion called "Skin Bracer," the letter of thanks included a suggestion for the development of a much-needed spinal invigorant to be known as "Backbone Bracer."

He was disturbed by the creation of a vast bureaucracy whose bright but cocky young men assumed that they held in their hands the sovereign power of the United States, appropriated the functions of the legislative branch, and sought to escape judicial review through the creation of administrative law. He was distressed by what he called contemptuous disregard of individual rights by Congressional committees, particularly the investigation of Senator Hugo Black into the public utility lobby which left Baker (who represented some of the companies) wondering whether he ran a law office or a criminal conspiracy. There was no doubt in his mind that some of the practices of utility concerns had been vicious and wicked but he did not believe that the existence of these evils justified an investigatory procedure that was scarcely "less ruthless than that of the Hottentots, who . . . execute the victim first and make their inquiry afterward."

He had felt the same way in 1933 when the Senate Banking and Currency Committee, with Ferdinand Pecora as counsel, revealed that he was on J. P. Morgan & Company's "preferred list" of friends who were given the privilege of purchasing certain stocks below the market price. The fact that Baker appeared to be in distinguished company did not soften the blow; among those also listed were William Gibbs McAdoo, General John J. Pershing, Charles A. Lindbergh, Owen D. Young, John W. Davis, Calvin Coolidge, and the current Democratic Secretary of the Treasury William H. Woodin. Baker denied that he had ever been obligated to Morgan in any way, and said he would have been happy to tell Mr. Pecora so if he had been asked to testify. (It appears that Baker's name was on the "preferred list" because the Van Sweringen brothers, whom he had represented in specific legal cases, had requested the Morgan Company to offer associates and friends stock in the Allegheny Corporation at a net price without dealer or underwriters' commissions.) Baker thought the basic investigation was a good idea because many bankers had been "drunk with power and maddened with greed," but in his judgment the method with which the inquiry had been conducted was characteristic of senatorial probes done "with a perfectly ruthless disregard of possible injury or annoyance to individuals."

His disagreement with the accretion of national authority was particularly noticeable on the question of electric power and the establishment of the Tennessee Valley Authority, among whose designs was the provision of a national "yardstick" to measure the rates of utility companies which were interstate in character and beyond the effective regulation of State or local commissions. Many had expected Baker to support the Roosevelt power policy because he had sponsored the municipal light plant in Cleveland, as Secretary of War had been the first Chairman of the Federal Power Commission, had been in charge of the construction of the dam at Muscle Shoals to produce nitrates in the First World War, and had opposed its sale to Henry Ford in 1923. In the 1930s, however, he not only represented utility companies but was opposed to regional planning in the Tennessee Valley—in spite of a personal letter from President Roosevelt asking for his aid in preventing the utility holding companies from committing "suicide" through their opposition. He thought that the Federal Government had the right to build dams to produce nitrogen for war purposes or to stimulate shipping on navigable streams, but he found nothing in the Constitution that authorized it to destroy local investments by entering into the business of producing electric power as a commercial undertaking. As a believer in "little government" he was certain that local was better than State regulation, and by the same token both were to be preferred to national control; in Cleveland he had always believed that a higher grade of talent and experience was available locally than the State of Ohio had been able to secure for service in the Public Utilities Commission. It might be that the Supreme Court would decide that Federal "yardsticks" were constitutional—just as it might "some day hold that the regulation of utility rates in an inland city is not a problem of local self-government and that whenever the Federal Government becomes dissatisfied with the way local authorities exercise their police power, that dissatisfaction creates a constitutional power in the Federal Government to overrule the local authorities and to impose the National Will in local concerns." If that happened, Baker observed sadly, the Constitution would have a meaning "which no lawyer and no judge has ever yet believed it to mean."[2]

It was again the old argument of little versus big government, of limited versus implied powers. Wise men, such as Jefferson and Hamilton, had differed drastically but sincerely on these issues. When Justice Harlan Stone read the manuscript of *The Challenge to Liberty* at the request of its author Herbert Hoover, he commented to the ex-President on the perpetual and perhaps irreconcilable conflict between the demands of individual liberty and the necessities of an increasingly complex civilization, in which individuals and

groups were becoming more interdependent with every passing day. Times had changed since Jefferson. Stone concluded:
"I like the Jeffersonian state better, but I have to recognize
that because I live in a highly industrialized modern state,
in order to make the system work, I have to suffer restrictions
on individual liberty which Jefferson would probably have
regarded as intolerable." As a son of the South, Baker was
content to stand resolutely with the Sage of Monticello for
philosophical reasons alone, but some of his critics interpreted his position on economic rather than ideological
grounds. One of them said that underneath Newton remained
the same sweet and lovable person but that he got interested
in making money and became a "safe" civic leader. Jack
Raper, the veteran single-taxer and caustic columnist of the
Cleveland Press, was less generous. When Baker joined forces
with the conservative Republican lawyer James M. Beck in
fighting TVA, Raper characterized Beck as "Pennsylvania's
great gift to paleontology" and said that Baker would be
known "by the company that keeps him." Raper paraphrased
Baker's famous anti-utility speech of 1911 with the statement
that Baker had put the principles of Tom Johnson in his
pocket and "turned his back upon the House that Has Not
and gone over to the House that Has and Wants More."
When Baker was proposed as a possible ambassador to Great
Britain the *Akron Beacon Journal* thought it a splendid idea
because the Clevelander had strayed so far from his early
ideals that he would feel at home in any monarchy, constitutional or otherwise. Baker did not seem to mind the conservative badge that had been pinned on him, for he wrote
Virginian Carter Glass that he was delighted to join him in
the Tory ranks.[3]

He was not Tory enough to join any of the coalitions of
conservative Republicans and Democrats which were planned
during the 1930s, although he received many "feelers" to

ascertain his interest. As Baker analyzed the situation, if the Republicans thought they could win they would not want any Democrat around; if they were likely to lose, no Democrat would want to be around. One of the fusion movements was the Liberty League, an organization of conservatives founded in 1934 to defend constitutional rights against the "statism" of the New Deal. Its financial assistance was bipartisan from the Du Ponts, Alfred P. Sloan and William S. Knudsen of General Motors, J. Howard Pew of Sun Oil, and Sewell Avery of Montgomery Ward; so was the shouting support from Republicans James M. Beck and James W. Wadsworth and Democrats Al Smith, John J. Raskob, and John W. Davis. Josephus Daniels thought that the brotherhood should be called the "livery league" because of the plutocratic trappings of its members, the Democratic publicist Charles Michelson spoke of its "dupontifical" propaganda, and President Roosevelt referred to the organization as the "I Can't Take It Club." Former President Hoover was contemptuous of the League's Democratic contingent which had previously directed the smear campaign against him, and concluded that he had "no more confidence in the Wall Street model of human liberty, which this group so well represents, than I have in the Pennsylvania Avenue model upon which the country now rides." Because of its identification with plutocracy the League proffered its services to all who felt their constitutional rights in jeopardy, but when the offer was accepted by the American Civil Liberties Union and the Hod Carriers Union of York, Pennsylvania (one of whose members had been arrested for speaking on the public common), nothing happened. Idaho's Senator William E. Borah was not surprised. He said: "They were deeply moved about the Constitution of the United States. They had just discovered it."

It was difficult for Baker to refuse the invitation from his old friend John W. Davis to join the League, but he did so diplomatically by claiming that "the other 3,561 organizations" to which he belonged had mortgaged all his time. To others the declination was more direct. He said that the Liberty League (despite its disguise) was really a political organization, and he preferred to devote his efforts to keeping the Democratic Party as vigorous and upright as he could. His reaction was the same in June 1936 when the *New York Herald-Tribune* suggested that the Republicans nominate a Democrat for Vice-President and proposed for consideration on the Republican national ticket such "disgruntled" Democrats as Baker, Senator Harry Byrd, or Lewis Douglas (who had resigned as Director of the Budget because of disagreements over New Deal fiscal policies). Baker claimed that he was not a disgruntled Democrat, and he certainly did not propose to be labeled one by the Republican National Convention. Privately he admitted to Walter Lippmann that he was finding it "difficult to be a Democrat and impossible to be a Republican"; his aversion for the Republican Old Deal was matched by his dissent from the doctrines of the Democratic New Deal.[4]

Within twenty-four hours after it suggested Baker or Douglas as candidates for Vice-President on the Republican ticket, the *Herald-Tribune* had good reason to be thankful that there had been no immediate acceptance of the proposal. On June 3, 1936, Baker and Douglas, joined by economist Leo Wolman, published a long letter in *The New York Times* in which both the Republican and Democratic parties were lambasted for following policies since World War I that marked a regrettable departure from the enduring principles of American society. The three correspondents were Democrats of the laissez-faire school of liberalism, dedicated in the tradition of Grover Cleveland to sound money, fiscal orthodoxy, tariff reduction, and small government. Wolman was a professor of economics at Columbia who had been Chairman of the Labor Advisory Board of the NRA, but had disapproved of the Wagner Labor Relations Act. A member of an Arizona copper-mining family, Douglas had served with distinction in the Argonne and Flanders during the First World War, had won national attention as a member of Congress in the late 1920s when he fought for government economy by daring to oppose the raids on the Treasury by the veteran's lobby, and as FDR's first Director of the Budget had regarded the inflationary policies of the New Deal as the "end of western civilization." In their open letter the three men stated that the so-called Republican "New Era" under Harding, Coolidge, and Hoover had used the protective tariff and other devices to foster private monopoly in the name of national prosperity. The Democratic New Deal, by contrast, had developed state-controlled monopolies in the name of national welfare. To the Baker-Douglas-Wolman trio this had resulted in a Democratic abuse of public power as an answer to the Republican abuse of private power; it was the danger-ous employment of fire to fight fire. In either case the people suffered the losses—from the disaster of private privilege under the Republicans *and* from the evils of bureaucracy, statism, and extravagant expenditures under the Democrats.

As a salvo for the classical laissez-faire system of the nine-teenth century, the Baker-Douglas-Wolman letter turned out to be a dud. There was a barely audible response from Demo-crats, while the Republicans shivered over the recollection that two of the signers had recently been proposed as their vice-presidential nominee. The original plan had been to have the letter signed by twenty-five to thirty "old-fashioned" Dem-ocrats—including Dean Acheson, Harry Byrd and Carter Glass of Virginia, and Governors Wilbur Cross and Joseph Ely of Connecticut and Massachusetts—but all had begged off for one reason or another. Perhaps it was just as well because the editorial reaction to the letter had been one of indifference or opposition. The *Cincinnati Enquirer* noted the political loneliness of the three distinguished signers who were as far from the Liberty League as they were from the New Deal, but added that they might as well recognize that big government was necessary to serve as arbiter among other big groups —industry, agriculture, and labor. The *Boston Herald* thought that the trio, in advocating a return to laissez faire, was really more reactionary than the two parties that were accused of reactionary policies. Indiana's Democratic Senator Sherman Minton went further; he preferred the repudiation of Newton Baker rather than the New Deal.[5]

Baker's ambivalent attitude toward the Democratic Party aroused speculation as to whether he would "take a walk" during the national presidential campaign of 1936, in which Roosevelt ran for the second time, against Kansan Alf Landon. For some time Baker had been unable to agree with his old friend Justice Clarke, who had retired to California and was convinced that the New Deal—through deficit financing and relief measures—had averted a revolution on the part of desperate and unemployed citizens. Clarke wrote Baker that both of them could pay several times their present taxes without bringing the wolf to the door, and that the sacrifice was much to be preferred over riot and common ruin. The Judge agreed fully with Edward A. Filene, the prominent department-store magnate from Boston who had introduced bargain basements, developed credit unions, and organized the Twentieth Century Fund—of which Baker was a director. Filene accepted New Deal taxes with equanimity. He said: "Why shouldn't the American people take half my money from me? I took it all from them." Baker could not concur. He did not share Clarke's opinion that an insurrection was imminent, and in any case he could not agree that the fear of revolution justified the demagogic "bread and circus" appeal and the financial extravagance of the New Deal. The administration's fiscal irresponsibility, he asserted, was such that he was afraid to put a half dollar in his pocket for fear it would be a quarter when he took it out. He could only conclude that Clarke's "Arcadian retreat" on the West Coast was so far removed from affairs that he did not know what was really going on in Washington. By June of 1936 Clarke was so disturbed by the unexpected sharpness of Baker's style that he suggested that they discuss books in place of politics, and added in conciliatory fashion that even if Baker supported Alf Landon for the Presidency "I shall still love you."

In spite of all the soul-searching Baker took no "walk" in 1936. In the last analysis he could have no part of a Republican Party which "for fifty years had darkened the councils with a pagan philosophy." Although the Democratic Party had left him in isolation, this situation did not mean that his own political boat was left stranded on Republican shores. When William Allen White asked him to vote for the Republican candidate Baker said that it was impossible because Landon's archaic views on the tariff made him sound like McKinley at his worst. Under the circumstances he was satisfied with Roosevelt's re-election and a year later wrote Clarke, "If I were put up to the same choice next time between him and Landon, I would use it again as I did last time in his favor." He would have preferred a smaller Democratic majority in Congress so that a "few sensible and courageous men" could hold the balance of power. He sympathized with some of Roosevelt's objectives but believed that precipitous action, which was accelerated by landslide majorities, had resulted in a great deal of intemperance and instability. He had learned the wisdom of contemplative action in the Tom Johnson days; in his judgment the street railroad experiment would have succeeded if the great Mayor had only "made haste slowly." This plea for deliberation, no matter how cogent it may have been, was anachronistic in the 1930s. In that decade, according to Arthur Krock of *The New York Times,* Washington was experiencing the sensation of a man

on a life-and-death errand—with thousands of miles yet to
go—who found himself switched suddenly from an ox cart
to an airplane.[6]

Within a very short time Baker had reason to worry about
national action at breakneck speed. During his first administration President Roosevelt had fretted about the "nine old
men" on the Supreme Court, which had invalidated a number
of New Deal laws. Emboldened by the smashing victory over
Landon (who carried only Maine and Vermont) he attacked
the judiciary, which had become a stronghold of Republican
principles, with his daring and unsuccessful court-packing
bill. In order to assure the appointment of sympathetic justices Roosevelt proposed an increase in the Court from nine
to fifteen—provided the six judges over 70 did not retire.

The reaction was immediate and unfavorable. Louis Brandeis, the eldest of the justices and one of the greatest liberals
who ever sat on the bench, was cut to the quick by the President's assault upon age. Justice Roberts, the youngest and
not a direct target of the President's attack, decided to resign
if the measure passed. Chief Justice Hughes said: "If they
want me to preside over a convention, I can do it." Baker
believed the measure to be impolitic, unwise, and destructive
of our constitutional system; in effect, he thought, the proposal was the same as a constitutional amendment which
might read: "Whenever the Congress of the United States, in
response to an order from the President, shall pass a law,
the said law shall be constitutional, anything in the Constitution to the contrary notwithstanding." He was certain that
such a measure would expose all minorities—including Catholics, Jews, and Negroes—to Congressional gusts of passion
without recourse to due process of law. On the question of
age he could not believe that democracy was imperiled by
seventy-year-old wisdom in a country where psychologists
stated that average intelligence was that of a twelve-year-old.

He amused a Court of Appeals, before which he was presenting an argument in 1937, by questioning the propriety of
introducing a constitutional issue in view of his advanced
age—which was sixty-five at the time. He was consoled by the
reflection that, in a life of more than six decades, he had
found that the worst never happens; for that reason he assumed correctly that the country would steer past the present
crisis without disaster.

Late in 1937, in spite of the "cynical and contemptuous"
Court proposal, Baker began to worry about the President's
health. He had heard that Roosevelt was beginning to look
incredibly old, and this caused him great concern because
"bad as he is, or perhaps I should say, naughty as he is, his
disappearance, if followed by Garner's taking office would
. . . lead to very bad results." Within two months of his
own death, in a letter to Justice Clarke, he again summarized
his feelings toward the President. He said that he had been
sympathetic with the objectives but extremely impatient with
the methods of the New Deal; he was sure that Roosevelt
was doing better than any Republican could do, but still a
very bad job as a Democrat![7]

XV. Sentimental Stoic

During the last ten years of his life Baker's health presented a continuing problem. In 1928 he had suffered his first heart attack on a train en route to St. Louis to make a speech for Al Smith. Two years later a siege of bronchial pneumonia brought on a heart lesion which required six weeks in bed. According to Baker's version of the difficulty his heart "resented having to take care of any troubles except its own and served a notice which the doctors thought indicated an intention to quit on the job." In 1933 he was ordered to bed for ten days because of "subtle evidences" which the doctors found in his physical condition. Vacation trips for the purpose of rest became more frequent—to Hawaii, Mexico, Banff, and the Mediterranean. In one way the enforced idleness was pleasant. He sat in a chair with his feet propped up, a table on either side, one filled with Virginia tobacco and briar pipes, and the other with books he had spent a lifetime looking for the leisure to read. At the end of the retreat he felt not only hale and hearty, but better educated than he had been since leaving college.

During the summer of 1937 he went to Saratoga Springs
in New York to take the baths with Mrs. Baker who was
suffering from arthritis. There he fell unconscious at the
lunch table; it was a slight cerebral thrombosis from which
he never recovered completely, although he was able to visit
the office from time to time. With great regret he resigned
from the numerous boards and committees on which he had
served for many years. In September he told his old Cabinet
colleague David Houston that it was necessary to leave the
Board of the Mutual Life Insurance Company because his
doctor had "laid down a system of rules by which I can continue to live a short time at the expense of most of the
pleasures life has for me." In November, when Baker had
a little more than a month to live, his departure from the
Board of the Carnegie Foundation was a most reluctant one
—but he noted that one got too old to do all the things one
liked to do and that "gradually I am getting used to folding
the corners of my tent."

On his sixty-sixth birthday, which was on December 3,
1937, he became ill at the office and had to go home for
two weeks of "necessary repairs." On the seventeenth he
wrote that his knowledge of immortality was limited but
that he was "very sure that God in His wisdom has some
plans which perfect our spirits for participation in a higher
kind of life." Six days later a personal message gave un-
mistakable indications to Ralph Hayes that Baker "was looking over Jordan when he wrote it and knew that the passing
was at hand." In this letter Baker had mused:

> This thing of being sixty-six years old turns out to have
> many disqualifications, but really I have every reason in the
> world to feel highly satisfied with what life has been to me
> most of my years. It was highly fortunate that I was as young
> as I was when I had to go to Washington and assume a burden
> that would have been difficult for a man of much greater age.
> When Washington was through with me, I was pretty well

worked out, but my partners had kept up the law office, so that all I needed to do was rest and recuperate to go from that episode to the active practice of law which has now lasted through sixteen years of fruitful, happy work.

Meanwhile, my children are all grown with youngsters of their own to look after and I really have not a care in the world except Mrs. Baker, who is much better than she was a year ago and able to carry on without me when the time comes. I hope the end will come suddenly when it does come and not leave me for any length of time a burden on Mrs. Baker's hands, to all of which she is entirely equal but the task would be a sad one if she had to stand for long the care of a sick old man. So you see, I am entirely content and have but one anxiety left, which seems fair to dispose of itself in a proper way.

On Christmas Eve he suffered another heart attack as he helped Mrs. Baker with the tree—but the next morning he opened presents, read cards, and enjoyed a merry visit with an old friend who dropped in. A short time later his tired heart ceased to beat.[1]

It had been a satisfying life—unusual because of the intelligence, graciousness, idealism, and serenity with which it was lived. He had a humble opinion about his own intellect, saying that it was like a draft horse that did not rear but followed its own little road back and forth. He was also certain that accidental acquaintance with four very great men (never identified but probably the two Wilsons, Tom Johnson, and Justice Clarke) had been instrumental in molding his own thinking. But President Wilson testified that Baker's mind was like chain lightning, and Justice Clarke experienced a dual feeling of admiration and despair because of the extraordinary rapidity with which it operated.

His affection for friends knew no limits; he remembered everything that concerned them and gave all alike—high or low, famous or unknown—the wealth of his understanding. Josephus Daniels spoke of him as a golden-hearted gentleman. Brand Whitlock supposed that he never said an unkind word about anyone, adding that the statement sounded extravagant "but . . . Newton Baker has been extravagant with kindness." Henry F. Pringle noted that he was the despair of many friends who thought it human, and even praiseworthy, to grow angry and strike back when groundless accusations were made. There is no record that he ever did so; on his own Baker admitted that his tongue avoided profanity, but his mind was sometimes given to it. He answered every communication even when he had to reply, "I acknowledge your letter and say that I do not agree with anything in it." There was quite a correspondence with a fellow who was certain that the world was flat. Baker's reply was polite and quaint:

> So many fantastically improbable things have turned out to be true that it seems within the realm of imaginative possibility that you may be right about the Earth's being flat. . . . Just at the time, however, when everybody in the world except you believes the earth to be a globe, I find it much more convenient to accept the majority view and devote my time to other things. . . .

No man was too humble for his notice, nor too great for his candid criticism when he thought it was deserved.

Everyone noted his serenity of attitude, a tranquil bearing which Raymond Fosdick believed to be his most distinguishing characteristic and which he thought was derived from some "unknown alchemy of the human spirit." Felix Frankfurter disagreed with Baker on occasion, but told him that he wanted to express his devotion "for the qualities of serenity and sweetness, if I may say so without offending your modesty, which make you so unique a personality." Baker said that he spent his life dodging excitement, but on occasion there was unanticipated involvement in some of it. According to Ralph Hayes, Baker once identified two arrested gunmen by the pistol they carried. He had been held up by them and had observed that the revolver pointing into his face had a triangular piece of enamel chipped off the end of the barrel. Hayes couldn't understand such imperturbability; under similar circumstances, he said, "I shouldn't have known whether I was gazing into the muzzle of a Colt or the keyhole of Hell."

In international affairs he favored the elimination of trade barriers and was a strong advocate of the League of Nations. On the domestic scene he believed with Jefferson that that government was best which governed least. He was liberal in local affairs, more conservative on State matters, and located on the right wing in his definition of national authority. The one exception was his own participation in a strong national regime during the international emergency of World War I, but Baker could not rationalize a similar accretion of national authority during the economic emergency of the 1930s.

Baker regarded Thomas Jefferson as the greatest of American statesmen because he was both progressive in political philosophy and an advocate of strong local government. Long after Jefferson was dead the New Deal provided a different combination of progressivism and strong national government. This new departure introduced the interesting speculation as to whether Jefferson would have been a New Dealer, and on this conundrum historians have drawn varying conclusions. The eminent Claude Bowers, who admired Jefferson, implied that the Sage of Monticello would have applauded the New Deal. The equally eminent James Truslow Adams, who admired Jefferson, stated that the Virginian would have disapproved of FDR. Baker knew both Bowers and Adams, and read their books—but on this issue he agreed with Adams. In Baker's phrase, the voracious centralist government of the New Deal was "eating us up!" This point of view appears old-fashioned to many, but is applauded by others who worry from time to time about the concentration of authority in

Washington, the evils of bureaucracy, the tendency to rely on Uncle Sam as the doctor who heals all wounds, and the steadily mounting Federal debt. On this puzzling issue one factor was certain: both Jefferson and Baker were gentle spirits who were willing to listen to all points of view. It was for this reason that Frank R. Kent once characterized Baker as a conservative with an open mind.

Austere in his ethical code and serene of spirit, he was a follower of the Greek Zeno and his Stoics. But Newton Baker's adaptation of the classical code went beyond Zeno. He was a sentimental Stoic, optimistic and compassionate to the point of occasionally avoiding unpleasant things. He would not read novels that were too somber or tragic; he told Whitlock that he would not read his novel about prisons (*The Turn of the Balance*) because he knew it was too terrible. Long training in politics and in the law had taught him the danger of permanent resentments, the necessity of suffering fools gladly, and the futility of regarding disagreement as a proof of original sin. If democracy was to succeed at all, he thought, it must be on these terms:

> that men shall cooperate to study and solve their problems, without envy or personal ambition, and find their reward in a handsome aggregate result in which their touch can be felt but from which their grasp is absent!

When Yale University conferred the honorary Doctor of Laws in 1932, it cited Baker as "an idealist with a disproportionate amount of common sense." There were those who argued about the meanings of "idealism" and "common sense," but all admired the catholicity of Baker's tastes and interests, the graciousness of his attitude, and the receptiveness of his mind. Here lies the explanation for the warm associations he enjoyed with those who agreed and disagreed with him, and the extraordinary weight given over the years to his judgments on law, politics, education, and social issues.[2]

Bibliography and Notes

NOTE ON MANUSCRIPT
COLLECTIONS

The basic manuscript collections, on which this biography is based, are the following:

1. Newton Diehl Baker Papers at the Library of Congress. This collection, which has more than 100,000 items, is contained in 254 boxes of correspondence, speeches, writings, and other papers. It covers the period from early 1916 through 1937.
2. Ralph Hayes-Newton D. Baker Papers at the Library of Congress. There are 11 boxes in this collection of correspondence, clippings, material on the funeral and memorial services, and the controversy over the biographical sketch in the *Encyclopaedia Britannica*.
3. Scattered papers on Baker as City Solicitor and Mayor of Cleveland, covering the period from 1903 to August 1913, found in the City Hall in Cleveland. There are both personal and official letters in this collection. Unfortunately the major portion of the papers for Baker as Mayor of Cleveland were inadvertently destroyed.
4. Munson Havens-Newton D. Baker correspondence made available to the author through the courtesy of Curtis Lee Smith, President of the Cleveland Chamber of Commerce. There are 60 letters in this collection.

5. Documents at the office of Baker, Hostetler and Patterson. These comprise 25 large volumes of newspaper clippings from 1901 to 1938, and varied memorabilia. In addition Baker, Hostetler and Patterson generously made available the files of law cases selected for discussion in this biography.
6. Documents made available through the courtesy of Mrs. Joseph C. Hostetler. These are in 18 large volumes which include newspaper clippings on Cleveland municipal affairs from 1911 to 1916, correspondence on the League of Nations speech in 1924, minutes of the Council of National Defense (and its Advisory Commission), and correspondence between Baker and Woodrow Wilson, Tasker H. Bliss, and John J. Pershing. Reference to this collection in the notes is made by the citation "Hostetler Papers."

Other manuscript collections consulted were those of:

John Hessin Clarke, Western Reserve University
Charles S. Hamlin, Library of Congress
Thomas W. Gregory, Library of Congress
Brand Whitlock, Library of Congress
Theodore Roosevelt, Library of Congress
Woodrow Wilson, Library of Congress
William G. McAdoo, Library of Congress
John J. Pershing, Library of Congress
Franklin D. Roosevelt, Hyde Park, New York

Unless otherwise identified, correspondence cited in the notes is found in the Baker or the Hayes-Baker Collections at the Library of Congress. The Baker Papers are arranged both alphabetically and chronologically; where the letter or document might be difficult to find a specific box number is cited in the Baker Collection at the Library of Congress; e.g., LOC 246.

NOTES BY CHAPTERS

In the following notes the John H. Clarke Papers at Western Reserve University have been referred to as WRU; the Baker Papers at Cleveland City Hall as CCH; the Munson Havens Papers made available by Curtis Lee Smith as CLS.

I. MARTINSBURG TO CLEVELAND

1. Newton D. Baker (NDB) to John H. Finley 10 Dec. 1928, Munson Havens 19 June 1922 (CLS), M. S. Billmeyer 1 Dec. 1931, George Fort Milton 30 April 1936, O. F. Bond 13 Jan. 1933, T. Kemp 13 Aug. 1931; Evans, Willis F., *History of Berkeley County, West Virginia* (Martinsburg, 1928), 176-7; Alexander, Herbert, *A Short History of the Late Honorable Newton D. Baker* (Martinsburg, n.d.); 175th Anniversary Celebration Committee, *Martinsburg and Her 175 Years in History* (Martinsburg, 1953); NDB's statement on the 40th Anniversary of The Cleveland Trust Company, 1935 (LOC 71); Hendrick, B. J., "Mayor Tom's Successor," *World's Work*, April 1914.
2. NDB to H. B. Wilson 5 Sept. 1936, M. Dukehart 5 Jan. 1933, D. L. Chambers 22 Oct. 1926, J. K. Baker 3 Jan. 1933, J. N. Baker 21 June 1928, Anna D. Gustin 10 Oct. 1932, Ralph Hayes

18 May 1926, G. F. Peabody 20 Oct. 1919. Baker's father fin-
ished one year at Wittenberg College in Ohio before the Civil
War and after his service as a Confederate soldier was gradu-
ated in medicine by the University of Maryland in 1867. In
Martinsburg the son's name is perpetuated in the Newton D.
Baker Veteran's Administration Center, a 1,000-bed Government
Hospital.

3. NDB to Louis Post 10 Feb. 1903 (CCH), K. J. Dennis 3 Jan.
1925, R. J. Jordan 8 Dec. 1933, F. M. Davis 25 Jan. 1917, M. E.
Raymond 25 Oct. 1935, T. M. Banks 12 June 1935, Josephus
Daniels 24 Aug. 1933, Rabbi R. Brickner 4 Dec. 1930, Walter
Lippmann 14 May 1929.

4. NDB to Hayes 10 Sept. 1924, 30 June 1930, and 12 June 1931,
W. J. Newlin 10 May 1933, C. M. Bainbridge 28 April 1910
(CCH), Mark Sullivan 24 Jan. 1927, W. E. Moore 20 Sept. 1929,
T. M. Floyd 5 April 1937, L. J. Glaser 27 Dec. 1931; Whitlock,
Brand, *Forty Years of It* (D. Appleton, 1914), 171; Palmer, Fred-
erick, *Newton D. Baker, America At War* (Dodd, Mead, 1931),
I, 158; Sullivan, Mark, *Our Times* (Scribner's, 1927), II, 31-2,
68; *Cleveland Press* 10 April 1936; *Cleveland Plain Dealer* 8
Jan. 1905.

5. NDB to H. O. Murfee 30 Aug. 1935, D. S. Freeman 2 Jan. 1935,
R. D. Lewis 19 Aug. 1909 (CCH), Elizabeth Chesnut 4 June
1936, Whitlock 26 July 1916, John H. Clarke 26 May 1937.
The influence of Burke on Baker began with birth. He was
born on East Burke Street in Martinsburg, and graduated from
the Burke Street Grammar School.

6. NDB to G. C. Babcock 19 Dec. 1935, F. C. Smith 5 Aug. 1925,
Evarts B. Greene 14 Nov. 1925, A. F. Kelley 10 May 1934,
R. T. Ely 28 July 1930, Clarke 14 March 1930, P. M. Evarts
15 March 1932, B. Avery 24 Oct. 1933, F. J. Hogan 23 April
1937, H. S. Ensminger 26 March 1934; Kelley, Fred C., "Newton
D. Baker, Practical Scholar," *Collier's*, 6 May 1916; Keppel,
Frederick P., "Newton D. Baker," *Foreign Affairs*, April 1938;
Howe, Frederick C., *Confessions of a Reformer* (Scribner's,
1925), 31-2.

7. NDB to W. Calvin Chesnut 24 Sept. 1893 and 29 Dec. 1895,
Hayes 13 Sept. 1926, W. W. Masters 26 March 1928; Summers,
Festus P., *William L. Wilson and Tariff Reform* (Rutgers, 1953),
257; Hervier, Paul L., "American Silhouettes," *Living Age*,
7 Sept. 1918.

8. NDB to Max Stuart 10 Nov. 1933, J. C. Long 20 Dec. 1927, Chesnut 29 Dec. 1895, 11 Dec. 1896, and 13 July 1933; Summers, *op. cit.*, 16, 93, 225-6; Summers, Festus P. (ed.), *The Cabinet Diary of William L. Wilson* (University of North Carolina, 1957), xv-xx.
9. NDB to F. Palmer 4 Aug. 1931, Chesnut 11 Feb. 1897; Evans, *op. cit.*, 176-7. Baker enjoyed the European tour so much that in 1907 he repeated the experience with Mrs. Baker. His third trip abroad was in 1914, when he was Mayor of Cleveland.
10. NDB to Frank Baker 8 May 1907 (CCH); Howe, *op. cit.*, 190; memorial address by Baker to the Cleveland Bar Association, 13 Dec. 1921 (LOC 245).
11. NDB to Ralph Leopold 23 Jan. 1911 (CCH), Mary Jamar 29 March 1910 (CCH), Clarke 10 May 1921 (WRU), Georgia S. Flick 3 Feb. 1903 (CCH), J. G. Harbord 10 April 1935; Hayes to NDB 18 May 1928; *Cleveland Plain Dealer* 16 Oct. 1919, 10 May 1928, 31 March 1932, 24 Aug. 1951; *Cleveland Press* 23 Jan. 1911. In Cleveland the Bakers lived successively at the Northampton Apartments on Prospect Avenue, and in houses at East 24th Street and Chester (until mid-1908), 1851 Crawford Road (until 1923), and 19200 South Woodland Avenue.

II. TOM JOHNSON

On the Johnson regime the following secondary sources have been most useful: Howe, Frederick C., *Confessions of a Reformer;* Warner, Hoyt L., *Ohio's Crusade for Reform, 1897–1917* (unpublished doctoral dissertation at Harvard University, 1950); Lorenz, Carl, *Tom L. Johnson, Mayor of Cleveland* (A. S. Barnes, 1911); and five articles by Eugene C. Murdock in the *Ohio Historical Quarterly,* Oct. 1953, Oct. 1954, Jan. 1956, Oct. 1957, and Jan. 1958.
1. NDB to E. L. Duncan 2 Dec. 1935; Nevins, Allen, *The Letters and Journals of Brand Whitlock* (Appleton-Century, 1936), xiii, xxxiv. The introductions in this volume are by Nevins and Baker.
2. NDB to *The Nation* 31 July 1911 (CCH), L. E. Holden 1 June 1907 (CCH); Butler, Margaret M., articles in *Cleveland Plain Dealer* 4 and 6 Aug. 1951; Johnson, Tom, *My Story* (B. W. Huebsch, 1915), 82; Warner, *op. cit.*, 76, 126ff., 204.
3. NDB to V. V. McNitt 19 March 1936, J. M. Dabney 25 Feb. 1907 (CCH), Ernest M. Hopkins 18 Sept. 1924, Fred Howe 23 June 1909 (CCH); Wittke, Carl, "Peter Witt, Tribune of the

People," *Ohio Archaeological and Historical Quarterly,* Oct. 1949. By 1919 Witt and Baker had parted company because of the former's pro-German position (NDB to Boyd Gurley 4 Dec. 1930).

4. NDB to Ben B. Hoover 10 June 1936, Henry Ware Allen 19 June 1931, Anna George de Mille 24 Aug. 1933; Johnson, *op. cit.,* 173. In his earlier and plush days, Johnson, because of high regard for his City Solicitor, had placed various securities in a safety deposit box for Baker. After Johnson's death, when the estate was being settled, Baker refused this generous gift and the securities reverted to the estate. Mrs. Johnson never understood the transaction and always thought Baker profited from it. Relations were so strained with Johnson's heirs that Baker was to write Fred Howe: "Poor dear old Tom conferred nothing but favors on any of us except when he presented us with his family." NDB to Howe 14 June 1911 (CCH), Mrs. T. L. Johnson 29 Aug. 1921 and Feb. (no specific date) 1912 (CCH).

5. NDB to V. V. Smith 14 Jan. 1903 (CCH), R. S. Childs 30 Aug. 1909 (CCH), Howe 8 Oct. 1909 (CCH), L. P. Lewis 26 Nov. 1909 (CCH), G. S. MacFarland 2 Oct. 1922; Whitlock, *op. cit.,* 172-4.

6. NDB to J. H. Hall 18 Nov. 1909 (CCH), Tom Johnson 27 Sept. 1910 (CCH), J. H. Perkins 19 Nov. 1910 (CCH), Atlee Pomerene 29 April 1910 (CCH), E. K. Bruce 19 Nov. 1910 (CCH), F. E. Dellenbaugh 3 Nov. 1909 (CCH); *Cleveland Plain Dealer* 5 Nov. 1911 and 5 Oct. 1912.

III. MAYOR

Unfortunately Mayor Baker's correspondence at the Cleveland City Hall, except for a few letters through 7 August 1913, was destroyed inadvertently. For the period from 1912 through 1916, therefore, chief reliance has been placed on reminiscent letters found in the voluminous Baker Collection at the Library of Congress, on the four major Cleveland newspapers, and on secondary accounts. Of the latter the most useful have been: Arbuthnot, C. C., "Mayor Baker's Administration in Cleveland," *National Municipal Review,* April 1916; Hopwood, E. D., "Newton D. Baker's Administration in Cleveland," *National Municipal Review,* July 1913; and Warner, H. L., *Ohio's Crusade for Reform, 1897–1917 (loc. cit.).*

1. *Cleveland Plain Dealer* 10 and 16 Oct., 1 Nov. 1911; *Cleveland Leader* 2, 6, and 7 Sept., 20 Oct., 1 and 6 Nov. 1911. Baker had the support of the *Plain Dealer,* the most influential morning

paper, and of the powerful *Cleveland Press* (at that time a member of the Scripps-McRae organization). The *Leader* and the *News,* controlled by the Hanna interests, were bitter in their attacks on him.

2. NDB to Jennie L. Baker 10 Sept. 1911 (CCH); *Leader* 5 Nov. 1911, 18 Dec. 1912; *Plain Dealer* 26 Dec. 1937; Hendrick, *loc. cit.*

3. NDB to the Editor, *Cleveland Plain Dealer* 6 Sept. 1907 (CCH); *Plain Dealer* 10 Oct. 1923; *Literary Digest* 20 June 1914; Nevins, *op. cit.,* xv.

4. NDB to James R. Garfield 18 Feb. 1903 (CCH), George Norris 21 and 27 Feb. 1925; testimony of David Lilienthal before the House Committee on Military Affairs on the McSwain Bill to amend the TVA Act, 28 March 1935 (LOC 157); *Plain Dealer* 4 and 9 June 1912, 24 Oct. and 2 Nov. 1913; *Cleveland Press* 27 Dec. 1937; Young, Dallas M., *Twentieth-Century Experience in Urban Transit—A Study of the Cleveland System,* (Western Reserve University, 1960), 9-11; Wittke, *loc. cit.* Paradoxically, in later life Witt became a consultant for private interests, and in the 1930s assisted the speculative Van Sweringen brothers in their successful effort to gain control of the Cleveland transit system. In 1941, just before the City of Cleveland finally purchased the street railways, Witt proposed the sale of stock at a price favorable to private interests; i.e., at $100 per share against an approximate market price of $45 (Young, *op. cit.,* 17); *Plain Dealer* 8 Nov. 1911.

5. NDB to Hayes 8 April 1932; *Plain Dealer* 11 and 29 Dec. 1914, 15 Dec. 1957; Bushea, Frances F., "Newton D. Baker Had Faith in Business Women," *Baltimore and Ohio Magazine,* May 1938.

6. NDB to J. M. Young 19 April 1929; *Plain Dealer* 18 March 1913; *Leader* 16 Feb., 10 and 18 March, 21 and 31 Oct. 1913; *Press* 8 April 1913 and 17 Jan. 1922; Rose, William Ganson, *Cleveland: The Making of a City* (World, 1950) 730.

7. NDB to J. F. Kilfoyle 20 May 1903 (CCH); *Plain Dealer* 8, 11, 23, 24, 25, 29 Oct. 1913 and 17 Jan. 1914; *Leader* 20 March, 7, 30, 31 Oct., and 5 Nov. 1913. In 1913 first-place ballots were cast as follows: Baker 41,296, Davis 36,119, and Robb (Socialist) 5,768. Baker was 329 votes short of the necessary majority, although he had a plurality in first-place ballots of 5,117. Under the preferential ballot the second-place votes gave Baker a majority of 3,258, in spite of the fact that he trailed his rivals in this category (Robb 9,247, Davis 3,928, Baker 3,554).

8. NDB to *Press* 21 Feb. 1930; *Press* 8 April 1936 and 12 Dec. 1950; *New York Times* 21 Nov. 1931; Raper, John W., *The Soviet Table or the Rise of Civilization in Cleveland* (Public Affairs Committee of Cuyahoga County, 1935), 19-20.

9. NDB to Carl Friebolin 26 Sept. 1923, A. A. Clark 26 Nov. 1928, H. E. Coffin 2 April 1928, E. R. Ailes 18 Feb. 1928, J. T. Kerr 17 Dec. 1931, Alfred A. Benesch 22 Sept. 1932, John W. Davis 7 March 1933.

10. NDB to Roy Howard 11 July 1931, E. Horowitz 19 Jan. 1932, Rabbi Stephen Wise 10 Nov. 1924; Howard to NDB 14 July 1931; NDB, "National Ideals," *Survey,* 25 Nov. 1916; Nevins, *op. cit.,* viii.

IV. ORATOR

The most detailed study of Baker as an orator is a doctoral dissertation by Eugene R. Moulton, *An Evaluation of the Speaking Effectiveness of Newton D. Baker* (Western Reserve University, 1953).

1. NDB to S. A. Hooker 15 April 1912 (CCH), Tom Johnson 27 Sept. 1910 (CCH), E. J. Parrish 16 Feb. 1912 (CCH), G. L. Coffinberry 29 April 1912 (CCH), Hayes 25 May 1932; *Plain Dealer* 23 and 28 May, 6 and 28 June, 4 July 1912; *Leader* 29 March 1912; *Illinois State Register* (no specific date) June 1931 (LOC 82); Daniels, Josephus, *The Wilson Era; Years of Peace— 1910–1917* (University of North Carolina, 1944), 54; Link, Arthur S., *Wilson—The Road to the White House* (Princeton, 1947), 418-9, 439-40.

2. *Plain Dealer* 27 June 1912; Woodson, Urey (ed.), *Official Report of the Proceedings of the Democratic National Convention, 1912* (Peterson Linotyping Co., 1912), 65ff.; Cox, James M., *Journey Through My Years* (Simon and Schuster, 1946), 132-4.

3. NDB to W. Hurt 18 July 1912 (CCH), H. D. Baker 30 July 1912 (CCH), C. D. Wilson 2 Oct. 1912 (CCH), Frank Baker 1 May 1912 (CCH), Louis Post 9 March 1912 (CCH), Woodrow Wilson 29 Nov. 1911 (CCH), Walter Lippmann 6 Feb. 1926; Lawrence, David, *The True Story of Woodrow Wilson* (George H. Doran, 1924), 87-8; McAdoo, W. G., *Crowded Years* (Houghton Mifflin, 1931), 182; Baker, Ray Stannard, *Woodrow Wilson, Life and Letters* (Doubleday Doran, 1927–39), III, 454.

4. NDB to L. G. Painter 30 April 1935, R. C. Ussery 29 Nov. 1930,

J. L. Hefferman 29 Feb. 1932, C. S. Williams 9 Nov. 1934, G. H. Blakeslee 13 Jan. 1937, H. A. Van Kirk 30 March 1928, J. P. Foster 4 Nov. 1931, Ethel Warner 2 April 1934; Altgeld, John P., *Oratory: Its Requirements and Its Rewards* (Charles H. Kerr, 1901); *Cleveland Leader* 7 Sept. 1913.

5. NDB to B. H. Darrow 30 March 1934, James M. Beck 17 July 1935, Arch Klumph 31 Jan. 1935, Charles F. Thwing 21 Dec. 1912 (CCH), Fred M. Davis 25 Jan. 1917; Hayes to NDB 25 July 1929 and 31 July 1931; *Leader* 18 Dec. 1912; speech by NDB at the Palestine Restoration Fund Banquet, New York, 8 Feb. 1920 (LOC 245); Raper, *op. cit.;* Kelley, Fred C., *loc. cit.*

V. SECRETARY OF WAR

1. McAdoo, *op. cit.*, 185-6, 339-42; Baker, R. S., *op. cit.*, VI, 12; Daniels, *op. cit.*, 447ff.; Lawrence, *op. cit.*, 149ff. Garrison also thought Wilson's policy in Mexico and the Philippines lacked aggressiveness, and as an advocate of moderate protection decried the low-tariff policies of the President.

2. NDB to Wilson, and Wilson to NDB 6 March 1916 (Wilson Papers); Wilson to NDB 5 June 1921 (Hostetler Papers); NDB to Clarke 13 March 1916; Peyton C. March to NDB 11 Aug. 1924; *New York Times* and *Washington Post* 7 March 1916; *North American Review* April 1916; address by NDB to the Army War College 11 May 1929 on "The Secretary of War During the World War" (LOC 247); Baker, R. S., *op. cit.*, VI, 38; Daniels, *op. cit.*, 19ff. Wilson offered Baker the Cabinet position on 4 March, he was confirmed by the Senate on 7 March, and assumed the office on 9 March.

3. NDB to W. D. Connor 6 July 1928, James Truslow Adams 20 Nov. 1933, Daniels 9 Sept. 1931, Roy Howard 3 Aug. 1933; *Dayton Daily News* 2 March 1924; *North American Review's War Weekly* 4 May and 24 Aug. 1918; *North American Review* March 1918; *Cleveland Leader* 7 March 1916; Bartlett, Ruel J., *The League to Enforce Peace* (University of North Carolina, 1944), 39; Daniels, Josephus, *Wilson Era: Years of War and After* (University of North Carolina, 1946), 183-4; Nevins, Allen, and Hill, Frank Ernest, "Henry Ford and His Peace Ship," *American Heritage*, Feb. 1958; *Cleveland Plain Dealer* 4 April 1915.

4. NDB to Clarke 13 March 1916, T. G. Frothingham 11 Feb. 1927, C. R. Lingley 26 July 1926, Hayes 12 June 1922; Tasker H. Bliss to Hayes 4 Aug. 1922 (LOC 42); NDB to the Army War College 11 May 1929, *loc. cit.* As Secretary of War Baker circumvented the issue that had caused Garrison's resignation. He helped secure the passage of the National Defense Act of 1916, placing chief emphasis on the National Guard rather than the large Regular Army favored by Garrison. Under the new act the Regular Army was to be expanded from 175,000 to 223,000 over a five-year period, and the National Guard was to have a strength of 450,000 men.

5. NDB to R. S. Baker 6 Aug. 1928 and 30 April 1932, B. T. Cable 17 Nov. 1916; *New York Tribune* 20 Oct. 1916; *New York American* 26 Oct. 1916; *Literary Digest* 4 Nov. 1916; Baker, R. S., *op. cit.,* VI, 255, 263-4. Historian William E. Dodd said that the original quotation from Baker's speech was not far from the truth. Dodd wrote Baker that the American Revolution was "a war of the most brutal savagery and Americans as well as English burned, robbed and raped in a manner that was even then regarded as outrageous." (Dodd to NDB 11 Nov. 1916.)

6. NDB to Wilson 16 Nov. 1916, W. Hurt 27 Oct. 1916, J. S. Bryan 5 Nov. 1917; Whitlock to NDB 24 Nov. 1916; Wilson to NDB 18 Nov. 1916; Col. E. M. House to NDB 28 Oct. 1916.

7. NDB to P. Molyneaux 19 Oct. 1936, J. Daniels 23 April 1937, Hayes 14 Oct. 1936; Daniels to NDB 28 April 1937; Baker, R. S., *op. cit.,* VI, 257; Arnett, Alex M., *Claude Kitchin and the Wilson War Policies* (Little, Brown, 1937), 183-92.

8. NDB to H. M. Ayers 7 Feb. 1930, Hayes 28 Nov. 1934, R. S. Baker 23 Dec. 1933, Dean Bates 23 June 1931, C. T. Kilbourne 26 July 1934, to *New York Times* 11 Nov. 1935; Daniels to NDB 19 Nov. 1935; NDB, "Why We Went to War," *Foreign Affairs,* Oct. 1936; *New Republic* 26 Sept. 1936; Seldes, George, *Freedom of the Press* (Bobbs-Merrill, 1935), 117-19.

VI. SECRETARY OF A WAR—MEN

1. NDB to E. M. Hopkins 22 May 1926; Whitlock to NDB 13 Oct. 1918; *Plain Dealer* 16 Oct. 1919; Frothingham, Thomas G., *The*

American Reinforcement in the World War (Doubleday, Page, 1927), 51.

2. NDB to T. G. Frothingham 27 Feb. and 22 Sept. 1935, D. C. Westenhaver 9 June 1917 and 12 June 1928; T. H. Bliss to Hayes 4 Aug. 1922 (LOC 42); NDB, address to the Army War College 11 May 1929, *loc. cit.;* Sullivan, *op. cit.,* V, 286ff., 302 ff.; Palmer, *op. cit.,* I, 180; Scott, Hugh L., *Some Memories of a Soldier* (Century, 1928), 559.

3. Fosdick, Raymond, *Chronicle of a Generation* (Harper, 1958), 135ff., 144, 171; Ayres, Leonard P., *The War With Germany, A Statistical Summary* (Government Printing Office, 1919), 123-4; Frothingham, *op. cit.,* 148; Sullivan, *op. cit.,* V, 309ff.; Daniels, J., *Years of War,* 187ff.; Rutstein, David, "The Influenza Epidemic," *Harper's,* Aug. 1957.

4. NDB to Mrs. Sam Gompers 30 June 1932, E. M. Hopkins 22 May 1926, Wilson 2 May 1920, James M. Cox 23 Jan. 1924, Roosevelt 23 May 1935, J. W. Fawcett 22 Dec. 1921, F. Palmer 2 April 1930, G. S. Yorke 1 June 1926, Laurence Stallings 26 Mar. 1925; L. P. Ayers to NDB 15 Sept. 1921.

5. NDB to Irita Van Doren 9 May 1924, Wilson 1 July 1919 (Wilson Papers), Julian Mack 25 June 1923, R. H. Seibert 12 Dec. 1935; Benedict Crowell to Wilson 19 March 1918 (Wilson Papers); Peterson, H. C. and Fite, G. C., *Opponents of War, 1917–1918* (University of Wisconsin, 1957), 121-5, 131, 135-6, 274; Kellogg, Walter G., *The Conscientious Objector* (Boni and Liveright, 1919), 121, 127; NDB, "Some Legal Phases of the War," *American Bar Association Journal,* July 1921; Thomas, Norman, *The Conscientious Objector in America* (B. W. Huebsch, 1923), 252; Sullivan, *op. cit.,* V, 363-4; Baker, R. S., *op. cit.,* VII, 275; Daniels, J., *Years of War,* 161.

6. NDB to Wilson 4 May and 26 June 1918, 1 May, 11 July, and 19 Aug. 1919, F. A. Scott 22 Jan. 1924, T. C. Williams 6 Aug. 1927; Wilson to NDB 13 May 1918; NDB, address to the Cleveland Bar Association 29 March 1929 (LOC 245); *Christian Science Monitor* 4 April 1919 (LOC 9).

7. TR to NDB 19 and 23 March 1917; NDB to TR 20 and 26 March 1917; TR to Arthur Woods 27 June 1916 (Roosevelt Papers, Letter Book 395), to Julian Baker 1 May 1917 and W. E. Borah 1 May 1917 (Roosevelt Papers, No. 113), James A. Garfield 7 March 1917 (Roosevelt Papers, No. 106); Creel, George,

The War, the World, and Wilson (Harper, 1920), 76ff.; Pringle, Henry F., *Theodore Roosevelt* (Harcourt Brace, 1931), II, 904; Sullivan, *op. cit.*, V, 492ff.

8. TR to NDB 12 and 22 April, 8 May 1917; NDB to TR 13 April, 5 and 11 May 1917, J. G. Harbord 29 Dec. 1933, Frank Baker 3 June 1912 (CCH), Hayes 4 Feb. 1925 and 30 April 1934, Daniel Willard 5 Dec. 1931; TR to Owen Wister 10 May 1917 (Roosevelt Papers, No. 114), Gov. A. E. Willson 10 May 1917 (Roosevelt Papers, No. 113); Baker, R. S., *op. cit.*, VII, 20, 48; Daniels, J., *Years of Peace*, 172, 286.

9. NDB to Daniels 7 Feb. 1936, H. Hagedorn 2 Nov. 1929; Wilson to NDB 13 Jan. 1917. Baker had considered the possibility that Pershing might be injured or disabled, and in that event had decided to appoint General James G. Harbord as his successor (NDB to H. J. Reilly 31 Oct. 1928). Harboard was Pershing's Chief of Staff, and later was a prominent executive in the Radio Corporation of America.

10. NDB to E. M. Hopkins 22 May 1926, Hayes 18 Sept. 1924, P. C. March 7 March 1928, Pershing 6 June 1918, Wood 5 June 1918, T. G. Frothingham 15 Nov. 1927, C. R. Lingley 7 Dec. 1931; Pershing to NDB 24 Feb. and 10 June 1918 (Pershing Papers); March to NDB 4 March 1928; Wood to NDB 2 and 22 June 1918; Fulton, John F., *Harvey Cushing, A Biography* (Charles C. Thomas, 1946), 308ff.; Daniels, J., *Years of War*, 183, 291.

11. NDB to Daniels 29 Feb. 1924, Little, Brown & Co., 30 Nov. 1936, P. C. March 16 June 1932, L. C. Griscom 24 June 1932; Bliss to Hayes 4 Aug. 1922 (LOC 192); Daniels, J., *Years of War*, 163-4.

12. NDB to Hayes 24 Dec. 1929, P. C. March 7 Sept. 1927, Wilson 27 Nov. 1918; Bliss to NDB 5 Oct. 1919; Halliday, E. M., "Where Ignorant Armies Clashed at Night," *American Heritage*, Dec. 1958; Kennan, George F., "American Troops in Russia: The True Record," *Atlantic*, Jan. 1959; Palmer, Frederick, *Bliss, Peacemaker* (Dodd, Mead, 1934), 302; Baker, R. S., *op. cit.*, VIII, 219, 319.

VII. SECRETARY OF A WAR—ADMINISTRATION

1. NDB to F. Palmer 24 Dec. 1930; speech by NDB before the Ohio Electric Light Association, *The Ohio Electric Light Association Monthly*, Dec. 1923; Lawrence, *op. cit.*, 223-4; Daniels, J., *Years of Peace*, 450-1.

2. NDB to Nicholas M. Butler 13 Feb. 1937, H. White 3 May 1925, Harry M. Daugherty 14 Sept. 1922; Hayes to NDB 14 Jan. 1931; Harbord, Gen. J. G., "A Chief of Staff in the Theatre of Operations," address to the Army War College 6 April 1939; Nelson, Otto Lauren, *National Security and the General Staff* (Infantry Journal Press, 1946), 3ff., 198ff.

3. NDB to Pershing 10 Sept. 1917 (Hostetler Papers), D. C. Westenhaver 12 June 1928, Cyrus McCormick and Ralph Budd 8 May 1936; March, P. C., address to the Army War College 3 Feb. 1931 (LOC 154); Scott, *op. cit.*, 519; Lovett, Robert M., "Candide of Candidates," *New Republic*, 18 May 1932; Palmer, F., *Newton D. Baker*, I, 14-15. During the Depression Baker also assisted the widow of General Bliss (NDB to F. P. Keppel 28 March 1934).

4. NDB to R. J. Bulkley 1 Dec. 1930; Palmer, F., *Bliss* 184, 247; address by NDB on the presentation of the Bliss portrait to the Council on Foreign Relations, New York, 18 Jan. 1933.

5. NDB to T. G. Frothingham 21 Feb. 1927, D. C. Westenhaver 12 June 1928, P. C. March 12 March 1936; P. C. March to NDB 5 Oct. 1932; Hugh Johnson to NDB 27 Jan. 1920; Nelson, *op. cit.*, 279; Keppel, F. P., "Newton D. Baker," *Foreign Affairs*, April 1938.

6. NDB to Wilson 24 Aug. 1918, Hayes 15 Aug. 1930, E. L. Holliday 30 April 1934, P. C. March 21 Jan. 1933; Wilson to NDB 27 Aug. 1918; NDB, *War in the Modern World* (Houghton Mifflin, 1935), 13-14.

7. NDB to J. T. Winterich 28 Oct. 1925, Thomas Nelson Page 22 June 1918, F. Palmer 24 Dec. 1930, Mrs. M. Andrews 23 Dec. 1927, S. N. Griffin 29 Nov. 1922, A. Cox 3 Dec. 1931, J. Hostetler 2 March 1919, T. G. Frothingham 9 Nov. 1925; Hayes to NDB 15 Jan. 1918, Joe Tumulty 12 July 1919; Nock to NDB 28 May 1918; Keppel, David, *FPK: An Intimate Biography of Frederick Paul Keppel* (privately printed in Washington, D.C., 1950), 108-9; NDB, address to Army Ordnance Association, New York, 21 Dec. 1932 (LOC 248); Hayes, Ralph A., *Secretary Baker at the Front* (Century, 1918), 13ff.; Hendrick, Burton J., *Life and Letters of Walter H. Page* (Doubleday, Page, 1922), II, 366-7; *Canadian Official Record* 14 Jan. 1919, address by NDB before the Canadian Club of Ottawa 11 Jan. 1919 (LOC 245); *North American Review* Sept. 1918; *North American Review's War Weekly* 20 April 1920; Daniels, J., *Years of War*, 170.

8. Bliss to Hayes 4 Aug. 1922 (LOC 42); NDB, address before the Army War College 11 May 1929 (LOC 247); Creel's release to morning newspapers 7 July 1918 (Cleveland Public Library);

North American Review's War Weekly 20 July 1918; *Washington Post* 27 June 1919; Houston, David F., *Eight Years with Wilson's Cabinet* (Doubleday, Page, 1926), I, 280-1; McAdoo, *op. cit.,* 342; Keppel, David, *op. cit.,* 32, 108. Harvey was quoting Senator Lawrence Y. Sherman of Illinois.

9. NDB to Hayes 28 July 1934, Daniel Willard 5 Dec. 1931; "Baker as Administrator," unsigned manuscript probably by Fred Keppel, found in Hayes-Baker Papers 1; Fosdick, *op. cit.,* 159.

VIII. SECRETARY OF A WAR—SUPPLIES

1. NDB to G. F. Peabody 23 May 1919, R. E. Vinson 19 April 1924, Grosvenor Clarkson 22 Oct. 1923, D. C. Westenhaver 23 Dec. 1917, Wilson 25 April 1920; NDB, speech to the City Club of Cleveland 12 March 1921 (LOC 245); NDB's introduction to Frothingham, T. G., *op. cit.,* vii; NDB, *Frontiers of Freedom* (George H. Doran, 1918), 33; Tumulty, Joseph, *Woodrow Wilson as I Know Him* (Doubleday, Page, 1921), 268-9; Clarkson, Grosvenor B., *Industrial America in the World War* (Houghton Mifflin, 1923), 38-9.

2. NDB to Hayes 24 Dec. 1932, D. C. Westenhaver 23 Dec. 1917 and 6 April 1919, C. J. Love 16 Feb. 1937, M. P. Andrews 19 Oct. 1927, W. G. McAdoo 12 June 1922; *Metropolitan Magazine* Feb. and Sept. 1918; Daniels, J., *Years of War,* 285ff.; Baker, R. S., *op. cit..* VIII, 332; *Time* 23 May 1932.

3. NDB to T. G. Frothingham 10 June 1927, J. T. Adams 20 Nov. 1933, J. H. Clarke 12 March 1931; Bassett, John S., *Our War with Germany* (Knopf, 1919), 164ff.; NDB, "Some Legal Phases of the War," *American Bar Association Journal,* July 1921; NDB, "Some Constitutional Problems," *American Bar Association Journal,* August 1925.

4. NDB to D. C. Westenhaver 22 July 1920, F. Palmer 5 March 1931, T. G. Frothingham 10 June 1927; Chamberlain to Wilson 14 Feb. 1916 (Wilson Papers); NDB, *Progress and the Constitution* (Scribner's, 1925), 28; Baker, R. S., *op. cit.,* VII, 484-6; Bassett, *op. cit.,* 171-2; Daniels, J., *Years of War,* 166-7.

5. F. A. Scott to NDB 13 Aug. 1926; Hayes to the *New York World* 6 April 1927.

6. NDB to Wilson 21 Jan. and 3 Feb. 1918, Stanley King 3 Jan. 1922, D. H. McClugage 2 Sept. 1924, M. P. Andrews 24 Sept. 1928; G. S. McFarland to NDB 5 Jan. 1918; Bassett, John S.,

op. cit., 183ff.; Cox, James M., *op. cit.*, 174; Frothingham, T. G., *op. cit.*, 336-7; Blum, John, *Joe Tumulty and the Wilson Era* (Houghton Mifflin, 1951), 143-4; Phillips, Harlan B., *Felix Frankfurter Reminisces* (Reynal, 1960), 53; Wilhelm, Donald, "If He Were President," *Independent*, 13 Sept. 1919. When the Secretary learned that his brother, H. D. Baker, was connected with a company (the Engel Aircraft Company) which had a contract with the Aircraft Production Board he directed that the following telegram be sent:

> By direction Secretary of War your contract for aircraft is hereby cancelled.
>
> Squier
> Major General
> Chief Signal Officer Army

This message was dispatched in spite of the evidence that H. D. Baker's interest in aviation antedated our entrance into World War I, and that the Engel concern was a reputable one. Newton Baker stated the case in simple terms: "H. D. Baker is my brother. I . . . realized the embarrassment of such a situation, and by telegraph cancelled the contract." (NDB to H. F. Goff 21 Jan. 1918; Squier to Engel Aircraft Company 21 Jan. 1918 (LOC 7); statement dated 31 Jan. 1918 in LOC 5.)

7. NDB to C. J. Lane 16 Feb. 1937; memorial address by Ralph Hayes to the Council on World Affairs 3 Dec. 1943 (Hayes-Baker LOC 7).

IX. SECRETARY OF WAR—DEMOBILIZATION

1. G. F. O'Shaunessy to NDB 31 Dec. 1918; memorandum from the Adjutant General to NDB 2 Sept. 1920 (Wilson Papers File VI, 42, Box 79); Palmer, F., *Newton D. Baker*, II, 384.
2. NDB to Wilson 23 and 25 Nov. 1918, McAdoo 2 July 1923, T. Sidlo 25 Nov. 1918; McAdoo to NDB 27 June and 10 July 1923; Palmer, F., *Newton D. Baker*, II, 379; Palmer, F., *Bliss*, 363. On the issue of prolongation of universal military training, which was being debated in 1919, Baker appears to have been inconsistent. In principle he was opposed to a continuation of selective service because such a system was contrary to the expectation that Wilson's League of Nations would make permanent militarization unnecessary. In actual practice, however, Representative

Fiorello La Guardia of New York was to be shocked when the Secretary of War presented to the House Military Affairs Committee a War Department plan asking for the draft of half a million men in peacetime. Baker's justification was that the United States would find it necessary to police mandates for the League, and that this responsibility would require several hundred thousand American troops abroad. (La Guardia to Hayes 13 Dec. 1943; Baker, R. S., *op. cit.*, VIII, 305-6.)

3. NDB to D. C. Westenhaver 26 Dec. 1919, Daniel Willard 30 Sept. 1932; Nock to NDB 9 June 1918; Bliss to NDB 18 Dec. 1918, 4 and 11 Jan. 1919; Hayes to NDB 18 Dec. 1918; Lippmann to NDB 12 Nov. 1918; Fosdick to NDB 26 March 1920; Hoover, Herbert, "The Ordeal of Woodrow Wilson," *American Heritage,* June 1958; Howe, F., *op. cit.*, 290.

4. NDB to Julius Pratt 5 July 1928; D. C. Westenhaver 5 Oct. 1919, Mary Black 14 Oct. 1926; Lawrence, D., *op. cit.*, 78-9; Daniels, J., *Years of War,* 519ff.; Walworth, Arthur, *Woodrow Wilson* (Longmans Green, 1958), II, 377.

5. NDB to Clarke 14 March 1921 (WRU), F. W. Brabson 27 Oct. 1928, G. Van H. Mosely 20 March 1929, F. H. Goff 16 March 1917, J. Hostetler 2 March 1919; J. H. Finley to NDB 18 May 1928; MacArthur to NDB 11 Sept. 1930; P. C. March to NDB 9 March 1921; John W. Weeks to NDB 12 March 1921; Pershing in NBC broadcast 2 Jan. 1938 (LOC 19); Clarke to NDB 26 and 29 March 1917; *Harvey's Weekly* 26 Feb. 1921; *Boston Herald* 4 Aug. 1918 (LOC 8); *New York World Telegram* 21 July 1936; Robert Sherwood, article in *Scribner's,* Dec. 1931; Baker, R. S., *op. cit.,* VIII, 586; Pringle, Henry F., "Dark Horse of Democracy," *Outlook and Independent,* 13 Jan. 1932.

6. NDB to H. A. Gibbons 9 Dec. 1925, Mark Watson 14 March 1936, F. A. Scott 29 Aug. 1932, Hayes 20 June 1925, 22 May 1926, and 13 Sept. 1932, F. Palmer 16 Dec. 1930, Daniels 12 March 1926, J. Durban 6 Feb. 1926, Frank L. Polk 1 April 1925.

7. NDB to Hayes 9 Sept. 1922, Clarke 13 Sept. 1922, G. A. Chapin 25 Feb. 1924, A. P. Vioslawsky 5 Dec. 1922, H. M. Bates 18 Oct. 1923; Hayes to T. Blegen 3 Feb. 1923, Guy S. Ford 18 Nov. 1922 and 25 Jan. 1923; Bliss to Hayes 4 Aug. 1922; press release by Hayes 24 Dec. 1924; Hayes in speech to the American Legion, Cleveland, 11 Nov. 1930; Fred Kelley to Hayes 2 Feb. 1923; Clarke to NDB 3 Aug. 1922; Daniels, J., *Years of War,* 178ff. Most of the correspondence on the *Britannica* controversy is found in the Hayes-Baker Collection at the Library of Congress.

X. LAWYER

1. *Cleveland Plain Dealer* 28 May 1955, 13 Nov. 1954, and 3 Dec. 1958; *Cleveland Press* 3 Dec. 1958. In 1931 the name of the partnership was changed to Baker, Hostetler, Sidlo and Patterson, becoming Baker, Hostetler and Patterson after Sidlo's retirement in 1938. Paul Patterson was a graduate of Yale, took his law degree at Harvard, served as a captain in the Rainbow Division in World War I, and became a partner in the Baker firm in 1924.
2. NDB to E. A. Filene 12 March 1926, Munson Havens 26 Aug. 1915 (CLS); Hayes to NDB 4 Jan. 1935; Will and Estate of NDB, Document 296, No. 259888, Probate Court of Cuyahoga County.
3. On the *Cleveland Press* case, Seltzer, Louis B., *The Years Were Good* (World, 1956), 194ff.; 31 Ohio Reporter 394; *New York Times* 17 July 1929; A. F. Vandenberg to NDB 24 July 1929. On the Bostwick case, 29 O.N.P. (N.S.) 22; 125 O.S. 182; *Columbus Citizen* 19 Sept. 1931; *Columbus Dispatch* 27 Aug. 1931. On Factor's extradition, NDB to Hudson 13 and 16 March 1934; Hudson to NDB 14 March 1934; 290 U.S. 191; *New York Times* 16 and 17 May 1931, 23 Feb. 1934; Hudson, Manley O., "The Factor Case and Double Indemnity in Extradition," *American Journal of International Law,* April 1934. On the Scripps case, NDB to F. A. Scott 31 July 1928; 40 F 2d 176; 282 U.S. 866; *New York Times* 18 April 1930. On the McCormick suit, 260 Ill. App. 36; 345 Ill. Rep. 461; *Cleveland Plain Dealer* 26 April 1930 and 20 Jan. 1947. On the Battle of Youngstown, NDB to Edmund Platt 17 April 1930; 31 O.N.P. (N.S.) 289; 46 Ohio App. 253; 127 O.S. 379; *New York Times* 20 and 28 June, 18 July, 21 Sept., 16 Oct., and 7 Nov. 1930; Fall, Frank A., "The Battle of Youngstown," *Outlook and Independent,* 21 Jan. 1931.
4. NDB to Nathan Loeser 28 April 1934, B. B. Bingham 27 April 1933, Hayes 11 Sept. 1925, G. F. Peabody 24 Dec. 1934, Rabbi Stephen Wise 10 Nov. 1924, Lippmann 13 March 1926, D. C. Westenhaver 31 May 1919, Munson Havens 6 Aug. 1925 (CLS); Clarke to W. G. Leutner 27 March 1936 (WRU); W. Calvin Chesnut to NDB 24 March 1936; B. B. Bingham to NDB 24 April 1933; address of W. H. Bemis at dinner for staff of Baker, Hostetler and Patterson 20 Feb. 1960; Pusey, Merlo J., *Charles Evans Hughes* (Macmillan, 1951), II, 638ff.; Warner, H. L., *Ohio's Crusade for Reform,* 61.

XI. PRO BONO PUBLICO

1. NDB to L. Tyson 8 Dec. 1932, Carlton Matson 1 Feb. and 6 July 1926; Hayes to NDB 6 Aug. 1932; *Newsweek* 28 July 1934; *Final Report of the War Department Special Committee on the Army Air Corps* 17 April 1934.

2. NDB to R. F. Nelson 11 March 1932, Lippmann 17 Sept. 1931, Ellen G. Hood 12 March 1936, Everett R. Clinchy 20 Jan. 1935; R. F. Nelson to NDB 10 March 1932; *New York Times* 29 July 1957.

3. NDB to G. H. Armstead 16 Feb. 1937, John A. Ryan 7 March 1934, Hayes 11 April 1932, Emily S. Marconnier 6 Jan. 1937, Florence Kelley 6 Oct. 1923; Kelley to NDB 29 Aug. 1923; Goldmark, Josephine, "50 Years—National Consumers' League," *Survey*, Dec. 1949; Linn, James W., *Jane Addams* (D. Appleton-Century, 1935), 329-30; Kelley, Florence, "25 Years of the Consumers' League Movement," *Survey*, 17 Nov. 1915; Goldmark, Josephine, *Impatient Crusader* (University of Illinois, 1953), viii, 128-31, 207; NDB, *Frontiers of Freedom*, 61.

4. NDB to George White 8 June 1933, Felix Frankfurter 17 Jan. 1923, G. N. Brown 13 March 1923, Lippmann 27 Jan. 1936, G. S. MacFarland 17 April 1922; McAdoo to NDB 29 April 1922; *Cleveland Plain Dealer* 19 Aug. 1932; *Cleveland Federationist* 24 Aug. 1922 (LOC 102); speech by NDB "A Labor Policy for Cleveland" before the Chamber of Commerce, 17 April 1923 (LOC 246); Baker-Gompers correspondence in *American Federationist* Nov. 1922; Palmer, F., *Newton D. Baker*, I, 266.

5. NDB to C. W. Kern 31 Dec. 1928, James B. Scott 4 Feb. 1929, Fred W. Scott 29 Aug. 1932, Harry F. Byrd 30 March 1929, Daniel Willard 28 April 1934, W. R. Vickery 10 April 1909 (CCH); Clarke to NDB 27 Jan. and 8 Feb. 1922; M. A. McRae to NDB 2 July 1929.

6. NDB to Munson Havens 7 Sept. 1933, R. M. Lester 4 Dec. 1931, Hayes 10 June 1920, M. S. Kaufmann 3 May 1934, V. V. McNitt 19 March 1936, Brooks Emeny 9 Jan. 1934; minutes of the Cleveland College Board of Trustees 1 Sept. 1933 (LOC 67); A. Caswell Ellis, "Cleveland College: An Adventure in Adult Education," *Journal of Adult Education*, April 1931; Edgar Lee Masters to NDB 9 Nov. 1931; Fosdick, R., *op. cit.*, 180; NDB, "As a Bystander Sees It," *Journal of Adult Education Association* Oct.

1929; NDB, "From Bayonets to Books," *Independent*, 16 Aug. 1919.

7. NDB to W. E. Dodd 13 Sept. 1932, Caswell Ellis 14 Sept. 1926 and 29 Dec. 1932, Mrs. Chester C. Bolton 1 Dec. 1932, L. P. Lewis 14 July 1908 (CCH), Munson Havens 16 Feb. 1927 (CLS); NDB, "Men and Manners," *The Ohio Stater*, Nov. 1934; NDB, "Community Responsibility for Human Welfare," address before Association of Community Chests and Councils, Washington, D.C. 20 Feb. 1928 (LOC 247).

8. NDB to H. S. Atkinson 26 Oct. 1934, James N. Veeck 29 March 1935, E. A. Ross 9 Jan. 1933, Henry M. Bates 18 Oct. 1923; W. G. Leutner to NDB 7 Jan. 1933; NDB in *The Reserve Weekly* 11 April 1933 (LOC 232).

9. NDB to W. Calvin Chesnut 4 March 1912 (CCH), Charles S. Weaver 18 Jan. 1913 (CCH), John W. Blough 15 Jan. 1937, Philip S. Morgan 20 Dec. 1933, E. B. Hulley 10 April 1912 (CCH), Robert Reinow 25 Jan. 1926; *Minneapolis Journal* 3 May 1928 (LOC 188); articles by Frederick C. Howe and Cecil J. Wilkinson in *The Phi Gamma Delta* March 1932 and February 1938.

XII. TREATY OF VERSAILLES AND THE LEAGUE OF NATIONS

1. NDB to Democratic National Convention 23 June 1924 (LOC 246), Lawyer's Association of Kansas City 26 Feb. 1937 (LOC 250), H. B. McGraw 19 Jan. 1932, R. H. Chesley 17 May 1937; *The Torch* Oct. 1931 (LOC 248); *New York Times* 17 Feb. 1924; *Cleveland News* 1 May 1932; *The Cleveland Clipper* Feb. 1935.

2. NDB to D. F. Pugh 8 April 1925, Fosdick 11 July 1922, Leon Dessez 6 Nov. 1920, Clarke 1 April 1932; Fosdick to NDB 13 July 1922; Daniels, J., *Years of War*, 458.

3. NDB to Hayes 15 March 1920, Richard Hooper 26 Sept. 1919, Whitlock 4 April and 17 July 1920, J. M. Woodward 5 Nov. 1920, D. C. Westenhaver 26 Dec. 1919, 11 Aug. and 6 Nov. 1920; Whitlock to NDB 17 Jan. 1917 and 23 June 1920; Clarke to NDB 13 Jan. 1920.

4. NDB to Clarke 8 Nov. 1922, R. E. Tulloss 12 Jan. 1924; Wilson to NDB 18 June 1922 (Hostetler Papers); Willkie to NDB 13 Sept. 1924; Fosdick to NDB 4 Dec. 1924; Krock to NDB 2 Jan. 1923; Clarke to NDB 31 March 1923; *Baltimore Sun* 5 Sept. 1922; *New York Times* 11 Jan. 1923; Warner, H., *op. cit.*, 194ff.

5. NDB to W. P. Simms 12 June 1924, F. W. Kelsey 6 Dec. 1923,

J. Durban 22 Aug. 1924, James F. Byrnes 18 May 1926, D. L. Chambers 22 Oct. 1922; White to NDB 28 March 1929; *New York Times* 25, 26, and 29 June 1924; *Cleveland Plain Dealer* 30 June 1924.

6. NDB to Wise 1 April 1924, Hayes 13 July 1923, McAdoo 3 July 1923, Lippmann 25 and 27 Oct. 1923, J. McF. Howie 5 Aug. 1924, E. Cockrell 13 June 1924, Fosdick 15 July 1924, C. J. Lane 27 May 1924, Cox 12 July 1924, E. J. Chapman 21 Oct. 1924, Whitlock 25 Aug. 1925, J. W. Kern 19 Nov. 1924; Cox, James, *op. cit.*, 327 ff.; *Cleveland Plain Dealer* 5 and 6 July 1924. Harold Ross contended that in a Baker administration he wanted to be Secretary of the Treasury, but for a brief period only—"just long enough to straighten up my income tax and . . . release a few bottles of bourbon whisky." (Ross to NDB 31 Dec. 1927.)

7. NDB to Louis Wiley 22 June 1928, Ellen G. Hood 6 July 1928, Hayes 2 July and 7 Nov. 1928, F. D. Roosevelt 6 July 1928, H. G. Barclay 17 Jan. 1928, Frank Baker 11 July 1928, Citizen's League of Cleveland 11 July 1928; NDB, address to the Democratic Women's Luncheon Club of Philadelphia 11 April 1927 (LOC 247).

8. NDB to J. Hostetler 3 July 1928, Jack Bethea 21 Dec. 1927, Hayes 26 Sept. 1926, 8 April and 2 July 1928; Hayes to NDB 27 March and 4 Sept. 1926; Hayes to Clarke 28 June 1928; Lippmann to NDB 3 July 1928; W. Atkinson to NDB 20 June 1928.

9. NDB to Frank Baker 1 Feb. 1930, Stanley Mullen 6 Oct. 1928, Ellen G. Hood 23 March 1921 and 6 July 1928, Phillip S. Morgan 20 Dec. 1933, W. E. Chilton 17 Aug. 1928, James M. Beck 28 June 1933, J. H. Simmons 6 July 1928, John S. Bryan 3 May 1928, Meredith Nicholson 29 Aug. 1928, Lippmann 31 Oct. 1928, Bliss 6 Nov. 1928, W. Coates 25 Jan. 1924, Harbord 30 Oct. 1928, F. L. Siddons 10 Nov. 1928, Munson Havens 24 Jan. 1929.

10. NDB to G. G. Battle 4 May 1925, Manley Hudson 9 June 1925, M. T. Manton 1 Nov. 1934, Arthur Sweetzer 15 Feb. 1935, James G. McDonald 25 Sept. and 7 June 1926, Henry Dennison 2 June 1932, Ellery Sedgwick 2 Aug. 1920; *Trade Winds* 30 Aug. 1926 (LOC 246); *Cleveland Plain Dealer* 29 Jan. 1935 and 26 Dec. 1937; *New York Times* 25 Sept. 1932; *New York American* 30 June 1932; NDB, *Progress and the Constitution*, 91.

11. NDB to Arthur Sweetzer 13 Feb. 1935, E. M. Baker 22 Jan. 1937,

Lippmann 26 May 1932, Frank Kingdon 21 Oct. 1935, James T. Shotwell 1 April 1936, Philip Kerr 20 March 1929, Arthur Vandenberg 19 and 25 Nov. 1935, Cordell Hull 23 Nov. 1935, W. W. Brown 12 March 1934; *Cleveland Press* 12 April 1935; NDB, "Education and the State," *School and Society,* 19 Nov. 1927.

XIII. RELUCTANT CANDIDATE

1. NDB to Clarke 21 March and 9 Dec. 1931, Hayes 12 April 1932; Hayes to NDB 8 and 12 April, 10 and 18 May, 9 June 1932, 24 Dec. 1935, Mark Sullivan 2 June 1931, Roy Howard 6 April 1932; J. M. Mothershead to NDB 30 June 1936; P. Arden to NDB 22 June 1932; J. S. Bryan to NDB 4 May 1931; Roy Howard to NDB 12 Feb. 1932; Lippmann to NDB 18 Sept. 1931; Sherwood to Hayes 22 Dec. 1931; Mark Sullivan to NDB 14 April 1932; *New York Sun* 29 June 1931 (LOC 150); *Richmond News-Leader* 14 Sept. 1931 (LOC 100); *Portsmouth Star* 20 Sept. 1931 (LOC 105); *New York Herald Tribune* 12 Feb. 1932. In June 1932 the Scripps-Howard papers came out for the nomination of Al Smith whom they had supported in 1928 (Hayes to J. S. Bryan 10 June 1932, LOC 116).
2. NDB to J. McF. Howie 27 Feb. 1926, Clarke 23 May 1923, W. I. Behr 14 Nov. 1930, F. Palmer 30 Nov. 1931, B. R. Newton 3 and 6 March 1931; Hayes to NDB 20 Oct. 1930 and 21 May 1932, C. L. Jones 27 May 1932; Howard to NDB 27 April 1932; W. I. Behr to NDB 12 Nov. 1930; *Cleveland Plain Dealer* 26 and 28 Dec. 1937.
3. NDB to Norman Hapgood 18 Jan. 1932, Clarke 3 March 1932, G. S. Brown 18 Feb. 1932; *New York Evening Sun* 18 Jan. 1932; *Wichita Falls* (Texas) *Times* 6 Jan. 1932; *Coshocton* (Ohio) *Tribune* 8 Feb. 1932; *Pittsburgh Press* 30 Jan. 1932; *Literary Digest* 6 Feb. 1932. The newspaper clippings are from the Hayes-Baker Collection, Boxes 10 and 11.
4. NDB to Hayes 29 July 1930 and 11 April 1932, Frank Baker 31 July 1931, Norman Hapgood 29 Feb. 1932; Clarke to Hayes 12 April 1932; F. C. Leubuscher to Frank Baker 29 July 1931 (LOC 36); *Cleveland Plain Dealer* 9 April 1932; *Nation* 13 April 1932; Kilpatrick, Carroll, *Roosevelt and Daniels—A Friendship in Politics* (University of North Carolina, 1952), 116.
5. NDB to W. S. Crandall 30 Sept. 1930, Hayes 27 April 1931,

Clarke 9 April 1931; Hayes to NDB 11 April 1932; *Literary Digest* 9 Jan. 1932.

6. NDB to Clarke 22 Feb. and 3 March 1932; Clarke to NDB 25 Oct. and 17 Dec. 1931; Hayes to NDB 18 Feb. and 1 April 1932, Ayers 7 April 1932; *Literary Digest* 15 Aug. 1931.

7. NDB to G. S. Brown 6 Oct. 1928, Hayes 24 Dec. 1931; Clarke to NDB 19 Dec. 1931; Dr. Scott to Hayes 20 Jan. 1932; Hayes to NDB 9 April 1932.

8. NDB to Clarke 23 May 1932, Willkie 23 July 1932, W. E. Dodd 25 July 1932; Hayes to NDB 8 June and 15 July 1932, Clarke 6 July 1932; James M. Cox to NDB 15 July 1932; *Cleveland Plain Dealer* 29 June 1932; *Cleveland Press,* 28 June and 2 July 1932; *New York American* 30 June 1932.

9. NDB to John S. Bryan 6 Aug. 1932; Hayes to NDB 8 July 1932, Clarke 6 July 1932; W. A. White to Hayes 18 July 1932; Howard to NDB 12 July 1932; Schlesinger, A. M., Jr., *Roosevelt Era: The Crisis of the Old Order* (Houghton Mifflin, 1957), 304; Coblentz, Edmond D. (ed.), *William Randolph Hearst: A Portrait in His Own Words* (Simon and Schuster, 1952), 126ff.

10. NDB to J. M. Proskauer 11 July 1932, R. B. Powell 17 Sept. 1932, Carter Glass 6 Sept. 1932, James M. Durban 7 July 1932, Clarke 9 July 1932, J. S. Bryan 4 July 1932, Willkie 23 July 1932; Howard to NDB 12 July 1932; Hayes to NDB 8 July 1932 and 2 Sept. 1936, Clarke 6 July 1932.

11. NDB to J. S. Bryan 6 Aug. 1932, G. F. Peabody 12 July 1932, W. E. Dodd 23 July 1932, Clarke 10 Sept. and 16 Nov. 1932, Raymond Moley 15 July and 10 Sept. 1932, W. A. Wolff 9 July 1932, Hayes 27 Aug. 1932; Hayes to NDB 2 Sept. 1932; James M. Cox to NDB 20 Sept. 1932; F. D. Roosevelt to NDB 25 Aug. 1932; *Boston Evening Transcript* 3 Nov. 1935 (LOC 45).

12. NDB to Clarke 16 Jan., 12 Aug., and 16 Nov. 1932, Hayes 21 July 1932, U. C. Delford 14 Jan. 1932, K. M. Sills 19 Dec. 1932.

XIV. UNHAPPY DEMOCRAT

1. NDB to H. M. Ayers 29 Aug. 1933, Ogden Mills 21 Jan. 1935, Clarke 31 Oct. 1933; F. D. Roosevelt to NDB 6 Oct. 1933, Cordell Hull 20 April 1933 (Hyde Park); NDB to F. D. Roosevelt 21 April and 6 Sept. 1933 (Hyde Park).

2. NDB to Lippmann 5 Feb. 1936, Eugene Meyer 17 Nov. 1936, Louis Alber 5 Oct. 1933, S. B. Jacoby 23 July 1936, L. P. Ayers 17 Nov. 1934, W. G. Mennen 20 May 1935, Clarke 3 Nov. 1934, Hayes 7 June 1933, 18 Nov. 1935, 2 and 10 June 1936, A. J. Roulhac 17 April 1924, Carter Glass 25 March 1924, J. J. McSwain 3 April 1935, Henry Stimson 23 Jan. 1925, Frank R. McNinch 12 and 24 Dec. 1934; F. D. Roosevelt to NDB 8 Nov. 1934; *Cleveland Plain Dealer* 25 May 1933; NDB, "The Decay of Self-Reliance," *Atlantic*, Dec. 1934; Schlesinger, A. M., Jr., *Age of Roosevelt—The Coming of the New Deal* (Houghton Mifflin, 1958), 436, 476.

3. NDB to Carter Glass 23 Dec. 1933; Raper, John W., *op. cit.*, 23-4; *Akron Beacon-Journal* 1 Feb. 1933; Schlesinger, A. M., Jr., *Coming of the New Deal*, 494.

4. NDB to Bainbridge Colby 1 June 1935, John W. Davis 18 Jan. 1935, H. B. McGraw 6 April 1935, Hayes 2 June 1936, Lippmann 27 Jan. 1936; J. Daniels to NDB 3 Feb. 1936; Keller, Morton, *In Defense of Yesterday* (Coward-McCann, 1958) 260; Schlesinger, A. M., Jr., *Coming of the New Deal*, 486-9.

5. NDB to Hayes 10 June 1936, *Cincinnati Enquirer* 7 June 1936 (LOC 87); *New York Times* 5 June 1936; *Boston Herald* 5 June 1936 (LOC 87); Schlesinger, A. M., Jr., *Coming of the New Deal*, 8-9, 18, 201.

6. NDB to Clarke 15 May and 20 Nov. 1936, 26 Nov. 1937, W. E. Dodd 10 Sept. 1936, Hayes 13 July and 14 Sept. 1934, R. W. Aigler 31 July 1936, W. A. White 19 Oct. 1936; Clarke to NDB 7 Aug. 1934, 16 and 22 June 1936; Schlesinger, A. M., Jr., *Coming of the New Deal*, 22, 494.

7. NDB to Frank Baker 9 March 1937, N. R. Rowell 10 March 1937, Hayes 9 and 27 Nov. 1937, Clarke 20 Oct. 1937; *Cleveland Plain Dealer* 26 Dec. 1937; Pusey, Merlo J., "F.D.R. vs. the Supreme Court," *American Heritage*, April 1958.

XV. SENTIMENTAL STOIC

1. NDB to A. S. Burleson 8 May 1930, Clarke 31 Oct. 1933 (WRU), Carter Glass 6 Sept. 1932, Hayes 17 and 23 Dec. 1937, Houston 9 Sept. 1937, Henry James 23 Nov. 1937, W. H. Sizer 18 Dec. 1937; Hayes to Clarke 3 Jan. 1938; Dorothy Cook to Clarke 25

Jan. 1938 (WRU); Mrs. N. D. Baker to Clarke 1 Aug. 1937
(WRU); *Cleveland Plain Dealer* 30 April 1930.

2. NDB to S. N. Schwartz 4 June 1926, Munson Havens 18 Aug.
1922 (CLS), Gustave F. Ebding 28 July 1930, Elton Hoyt II 6
Jan. 1931; Clarke to NDB 27 Jan. 1922, W. G. Leutner 27 Jan.
1938 (WRU); Frankfurter to NDB 13 Nov. 1924; Daniels to
Hayes 11 March 1938; Hayes, Ralph, article on NDB dated 11
Feb. 1935 (LOC 117); Kent, Frank R., in *Forum* 1 Nov. 1931;
Whitlock, Brand, "A Sketch of Newton D. Baker," *Public*, 15
Sept. 1911; Whitlock, Brand, *Forty Years of It*, 358; Fosdick, R.,
op. cit., 243; Pringle, H. F., "Dark-Horse of Democracy," *Out-
look*, 13 Jan. 1932; *Time* 23 May 1932.

INDEX

Adams, Herbert Baxter, 23
Adams, James Truslow, 21, 276
Addams, Jane, 81, 192, 233
Allen, Florence E., 54
Altgeld, John Peter, 71-2, 192
American Expeditionary Force, University of, 199-200
Ayres, Leonard, 250

Baehr, Herman C., 45, 46, 52
Baker, Elizabeth (daughter of NDB), 32
Baker, Elizabeth Leopold (wife of NDB), 31, 32, 33, 132, 173, 174, 227, 229, 240, 248, 273, 274
Baker, Harry D. (brother of NDB), 295
Baker, Julian (brother of NDB), 110

Baker, Margaret (daughter of NDB), 32, 33
Baker, Newton D., I (father of NDB), 14, 15, 22, 26, 32, 95
Baker, Mrs. Newton D., I (Dukehart, Mary Ann, mother of NDB), 14, 16
Baker, Newton D., II
Life—
birth, 13; ancestry, 14-18; youth, 13-22; appearance, 18, 19, 79, 132-3; education, 19-25; marriage and family, 31-3; health, 229-30, 247, 272-4; death, 274
Public activities—
Post Office Department, 27-9; City Solicitor of Cleveland, 21, 34, 40-5, 172; Mayor of Cleveland, 34-5, 46-63, 70-1, 172;

305

Baker, Newton D., II (continued)
    Secretary of War, 22-3, 54, 64,
    76-170; in Presidential cam-
    paigns: (1896) 28, (1912) 64-
    70, (1916) 84-9, (1920) 156, 212-
    15, (1924) 217-23, (1928) 223-
    30, (1932) 235-58, (1936) 268-
    9; law practice, 26-31, 34, 40,
    76, 171-86, 188-9
    Commentary on—
    conscientious objectors, 104-7;
    education, 201-7; *Encylopae-
    dia Britannica*, 167-70; fra-
    ternity, 25, 207-8; labor, 193-7;
    as orator, 64-75, 84-7, 146-7,
    185, 209, 219-20; charge of
    pacifism, 79-82, 167, 168; po-
    litical philosophy, 41, 60-3,
    244-5, 259-64, 276-7; prohibi-
    tion, 214, 227-8, 245; religion,
    16-18; reasons for entry into
    World War I, 88-92; volun-
    tary organizations, 187-208; on
    war debts, 230-1
Baker, Newton D., III (son of
    NDB), 32
Baker, Ray Stannard, 146
Barnes, Harry Elmer, 91
Baruch, Bernard, 140
Beck, James M., 264, 265
Bemis, Edward W., 38, 39
Benesch, Alfred A., 39
Bethlehem Steel Corporation, 90,
    181, 182, 183
Black, Hugo, 261
Bliss, Tasker H., 119, 121, 125, 126,
    127, 135, 158, 159, 164, 166,
    168, 229
Bolton, Mrs. Chester C., 201
Borah, William Edgar, 110, 186,
    230, 231, 232, 265

Borglum, Gutzon, 151, 152
Bostwick, Homer Z., 175, 177, 178,
    179
Bowers, Claude, 21, 276
Brandeis, Louis, 141, 180, 191, 270
Brown, George Rothwell, 253
Bryan, John Stewart, 236, 250, 251
Bryan, William Jennings, 28, 65,
    66, 68, 77, 214
Bulkley, Robert J., 39, 50, 236, 239
Burton, Harold, 224-5
Burton, Theodore, 38, 48, 229
Bushea, Frances, 54
Bustard, William W., 47, 55
Byrd, Harry F., 236, 266, 267

Cadman, S. Parkes, 189
Chadsey, Mildred, 54
Chamberlain, George E., 109, 145,
    146, 148, 149
Chesnut, W. Calvin, 207
Clark, Champ, 65, 68, 88, 89, 97
Clarke, John Hessin, 73, 78, 133,
    165, 169, 185, 213, 216, 217,
    225, 235, 243, 245, 246, 247,
    258, 268, 269, 271, 274
Clarkson, Grosvenor, 140
Clemenceau, Georges, 101, 113,
    116, 117, 132, 158, 161, 166
Cleveland Chamber of Commerce,
    47, 189, 192, 194, 196, 202
Cleveland College, 72, 197, 198,
    199
Cleveland Electric Illuminating
    Co., 46, 48, 51, 57
Cleveland, Grover, 28, 260, 266
Cleveland Plain Dealer, 45, 59,
    66, 236, 237
Cleveland Press, 32, 59, 60-1, 74,
    175, 176, 177, 264
Coffin, Howard E., 151

Colby, Bainbridge, 162
Columbus Citizen, 175, 177, 178
Commission on Training Camp Activities (C.T.C.A.), 99-101, 104, 136
Conscientious objectors, 104-7
Cooley, Harris R., 38, 39, 41, 47, 58
Coolidge, Calvin, 188, 223, 231, 232, 262, 267
Coughlin, Father (Charles Edward), 190, 231, 232
Council of National Defense, 135, 139, 140
Cox, James M., 68, 215, 222, 256
Creel, George, 134
Crosser, Robert, 39
Crowder, Enoch, 96, 97, 129
Crowell, Benedict, 141

Daniels, Josephus, on NDB as speaker, 64, 147; in Navy Department, 77, 88, 90, 98, 99, 122, 142, 145, 148, 162; on Encyclopaedia Britannica, 169; as editor, 215; on League of Nations, 224; on NDB as Presidential candidate, 242; on Liberty League, 265; on NDB's personality, 274
Davis, Harry L., 57, 58, 59
Davis, John W., 71, 172, 186, 221, 222, 249, 250, 258, 262, 265
Dawes, Charles Gates, 150
Debs, Eugene V., 70
Deeds, Edward A., 151, 152
Dodd, William E., 21, 290
Douglas, Lewis, 266, 267

Eaton, Cyrus, 182, 183
Ely, Richard T., 23

Encyclopaedia Britannica, 19, 167-70
Evans, Evan A., 180

Factor, John (Jake the Barber), 179, 180, 183
Farley, James, 242, 253
Filene, Edward A., 268
Flick, W. H. H., 29
Flood, Harry, 88, 89
Foch, Ferdinand, 164, 166
Folk, Joseph, 35
Foran, Martin, 29, 30, 31
Ford, Guy Stanton, 168
Ford, Henry, 17, 18, 221, 262
Fosdick, Raymond, 99, 100, 101, 104, 160, 211, 216, 275
Frankfurter, Felix, 63, 133, 151, 185, 186, 191, 243, 275
Freeman, Douglas Southall, 21
Friebolin, Carl, 39

Garner, John Nance, 248, 249, 251, 253, 254, 256, 257, 271
Garrison, Lindley M., 76, 77, 79, 122, 125, 146, 289
George, Henry, 36, 41
Gilman, Daniel Coit, 23, 24
Glass, Carter, 221, 222, 224, 236, 264, 267
Gompers, Samuel, 102, 103, 168, 194, 196, 197
Gongwer, W. Burr, 59, 60, 250
Grace, Eugene, 181, 182
Grayson, Cary T., 161

Hamlin, Charles Sumner, 220
Hand, Learned, 186, 216
Hanna, Marcus A., 38, 42, 70

Harbord, James G., 292
Harding, Warren G., 79, 163, 164, 212, 213, 215, 223, 229, 267
Harmon, Judson, 65, 66, 68
Harvey, George B. Mc., 79, 80, 132, 134, 163, 167, 169, 211, 212
Havens, Munson, 202
Hayes, Carlton, 189
Hayes, Ralph, 33, 73; in War Department, 90, 130, 133, 147, 154; in Paris, 158; on *Encyclopaedia Britannica*, 170; on NDB as lawyer, 174; on activities of NDB, 187; on NDB as Presidential candidate, 225-7, 235-58; on last illness of NDB, 273; on personality of NDB, 275-6
Hearst, William Randolph, 68, 130, 175, 215, 231, 248, 251, 253, 254, 256, 258
Herrick, Myron T., 38
Hogen, Frank B., 46
Holmes, Oliver Wendell, 184, 186, 257
Hoover, Herbert, 159, 188, 213, 223, 229, 231, 246, 256, 258, 263, 265, 267
Hopkins, Ernest M., 168, 207
Hostetler, Joseph C., 76, 133, 171, 249
House, Edward M., 70, 90, 159, 166, 167, 225
Houston, David, 78, 134, 188, 221, 273
Howard, Nathaniel, 59
Howard Roy, 82, 238, 239, 252, 254, 255
Howe, Frederick C., 30, 39, 207, 243
Hudson, Manley O., 180

Hughes, Charles Evans, 85, 151, 152, 172, 181, 189, 232, 270
Hunt, Henry T., 45

James, Ollie, 146, 147
Jefferson, Thomas, 21, 36, 193, 197, 263, 264, 276, 277
Joffre, Joseph J. C., 94
Johns Hopkins University, 23, 24, 39, 184, 197, 198, 207
Johnson, Hiram, 212
Johnson, Homer H., 38
Johnson, Hugh S., 96, 164
Johnson, Tom L., 29, 30, 34-45, 46, 47, 48, 49, 52, 54, 59, 199, 215, 216, 243, 264, 274, 286
Jones, Samuel ("Golden Rule"), 35, 43

Kahn, Julius, 97
Kelley, Florence, 190, 191, 192
Kellogg, Walter G., 107
Kennedy, Joseph P., 253, 254
Kent, Frank R., 277
Keppel, Frederick, 133, 135, 136, 141
King, Stanley, 133, 141
Kitchin, Claude, 88, 89, 97
Kohler, Fred, 55
Krock, Arthur, 216, 269

LaFollette, Robert M., 35, 60, 222
Landon, Alfred M., 268, 269, 270
Lansing, Robert, 89, 90, 157, 161, 162
League of Nations, 209-34, 240, 241
Liberty League, 265-6, 268
Lippmann, Walter, 17, 63, 133, 159, 222, 226, 238, 249, 266

Lloyd George, David, 116, 117, 158
Lodge, Henry Cabot, 114, 130, 169, 210, 211, 212, 219, 224
Lowden, Frank, 212, 213
Lowell, A. Lawrence, 81, 216, 233

MacArthur, Douglas, 129, 163
Mack, Julian W., 102, 107
March, Peyton C., 115, 125, 126, 128, 138, 164, 165, 166, 167, 168
Martinsburg, W. Va., 14, 15, 20, 22, 23, 26, 27, 29, 30, 31, 34
Masters, Edgar Lee, 200
Mather, Samuel, 217
Matson, Carlton, 175, 176, 177
McAdoo, William Gibbs, 77, 102, 156, 157, 194, 214, 217, 218, 221, 222, 248, 253, 262
McCormick, Stanley, 181
McDonough, Tim, 47, 58
McNutt, Paul V., 254
Mellon, Andrew, 211, 231
Meyer, Eugene, 133
Miller, Ray T., 236
Millis, Walter, 91-2
Milton, George Fort, 21
Moley, Raymond C., 257
Moore, John Bassett, 232
Morrow, Dwight W., 168
Moskowitz, Belle, 226, 227

National Conference of Christians and Jews, 189, 190
National Consumers' League, 190-3
Nock, Alfred Jay, 21, 132, 158
Norris, George, 35, 244
Nye, Gerald P., 87

O'Neill, Ralph T., 250

Otis, Charles, 182

Paderewski, Ignace, 156, 163
Page, Walter Hines, 87, 89, 90
Palmer, A. Mitchell, 76, 214
Patterson, Paul, 297
Peck, John Weld, 181
Pecora, Ferdinand, 261, 262
Pepper, George Wharton, 223
Pershing, John J., 83, 94, 95, 101, 108, 109, 114-17, 131, 135, 136, 138, 144, 145, 163, 164, 165, 166, 167, 168, 262
Pétain, Henri Philippe, 94, 131
Phi Beta Kappa, 24
Phi Gamma Delta, 25, 207, 208
Pingree, Hazen, 35
Polk, Frank L., 162
Pound, Roscoe, 168, 185, 186
Proskauer, Joseph, 226, 227
Pyke, Bernice S., 54, 250

Raper, Jack, 59, 60, 74, 264
Raskob, John J., 225, 265
Ritchie, Albert C., 239
Roberts, Owen J., 180, 270
Rockefeller, John D., 47
Roosevelt, Franklin D., 103, 137, 186, 188, 225, 233; nomination (1932), 239, 242, 243, 244, 248, 249, 251, 252, 253, 254; NDB supports in campaign (1932), 256, 257; NDB differs with, 259, 260, 265, 267, 269, 270, 271, 276
Root, Elihu, 110, 123, 124, 142, 210, 232
Rosenwald, Julius, 141, 168

Salen, Charles P., 38, 41

Scott, Emmet J., 141
Scott, Frank A., 140, 150
Scott, Hugh L., 96, 97, 125, 126
Scott, R. W., 174, 247, 248
Scripps, E. W., 63, 181
Seabury, Samuel, 250
Sedgwick, Ellery, 250
Seltzer, Louis, 175, 176, 177
Sherwood, Robert, 163, 238
Shotwell, James T., 238
Sidlo, Thomas L., 76, 171, 249
Smith, Alfred E., 217, 218, 221,
    223, 225, 226, 227, 228, 229,
    230, 248, 249, 251, 252, 253,
    265, 272
Stage, Charles W. ("Billy"), 38, 39
Stettinius, E. R., 140
Stone, Harlan F., 107, 180, 263, 264
Straus, Roger W., 189
Sullivan, Mark, 238
Sunrise Conference, 88-9
Swanson, Claude, 146, 147

Taft, William Howard, 38, 69, 81,
    112, 133, 184, 210
Tayler, Robert W., 52
Tennessee Valley Authority, 262,
    263, 264
Timmner, Christian, 53
Tumulty, Joseph P., 70, 76

Vandenberg, Arthur H., 175, 233
Van Sweringen brothers, 60, 174,
    242, 243, 262
Villard, Oswald Garrison, 234, 242,
    243

Wadsworth, James, 168, 265
Walther, Frederick, 175, 176, 177
Washington and Lee University,
    24, 25, 197, 198

Weeks, John W., 164
Westenhaver, David C., 29
Western Reserve University, 39,
    197, 234, 235, 247
White, George S., 239, 251
White, William Allen, 215, 219,
    252, 269
Whitlock, Brand, 18, 21, 22, 35, 43,
    44, 45, 49-50, 63, 86, 94, 156,
    212, 275, 277
Wickersham, George W., 216
Wickersham Commission on Law
    Enforcement, 188, 245
Willard, Daniel, 140, 141
Willkie, Wendell, 216, 250
Wilson, William L., 26, 27, 28,
    34, 274
Wilson, Woodrow, 21, 23, 35; in-
    fluence on NDB, 42, 274; cam-
    paign of 1912, 64-8; offers
    NDB Cabinet post (1913), 70;
    relations with NDB as Sec-
    retary of War, 77-9, 82, 84,
    86-90, 96, 101, 105, 106, 108-14,
    116-20, 122, 123, 129, 133, 140,
    146, 151, 161, 162, 164-6, 233;
    at Peace Conference, 156, 158-
    60; League of Nations, 210-16;
    NDB tribute to, 219, 220
Wise, Stephen S., 168, 221
Witt, Peter, 38, 39, 40, 41, 47, 52,
    53, 56, 58, 59, 60, 185, 287
Wolman, Leo, 266, 267
Wood, Leonard, 77, 96, 106, 114,
    115, 116, 136, 212, 213

Young, Owen D., 236, 239, 243,
    249, 262
Youngstown Sheet & Tube Co.,
    181, 182, 183, 242

ILLUSTRATION CREDITS

Cleveland News: NDB as a boy; NDB as a young lawyer; Wilson and the Cabinet; the fight against the unit rule (cartoon).

Cleveland Plain Dealer: Here Is the Man (cartoon); Bakerized Streets (cartoon from the *Cleveland Leader*).

The Cleveland Press: Mayor Baker; NDB on way to take oath as Secretary of War; NDB nominating Cox; the photograph on the dust jacket.

The Denver Post: The Show-Down (cartoon); When Uncle Sam Laughs (cartoon).

The National Archives: Wilson and NDB reviewing National Guard; Wilson and NDB at Fort Myer; NDB with King Albert and Generals March and Pershing.

Underwood and Underwood: NDB drawing numbers in second draft; NDB and Pershing somewhere in France.

United Press International: NDB with Franklin Roosevelt.

The Washington Star: Baker beats the drum (cartoon).

The Western Reserve Historical Society: NDB with Witt and Johnson.

ABOUT THE AUTHOR

C. H. Cramer was born in Eureka, Kansas, in 1905. A graduate of Ohio State University, he received his Ph.D. from that institution in 1931, specializing in the field of American history. World War II interrupted his career as a professor of history at Southern Illinois University and in 1942 Dr. Cramer joined the Board of Economic Warfare as Director of Foreign Personnel. Between 1944 and 1948 he served with UNRRA's Displaced Persons' Operation in Germany and with the International Refugee Organization in Geneva.

Returning to America in 1949, Dr. Cramer became Professor of History at Western Reserve University and in 1954 assumed additional duties as Dean of Adelbert College. The author of articles in historical journals, Dr. Cramer has written one previous book, *Royal Bob: The Life of Robert G. Ingersoll,* which was published in 1952.

Dean Cramer and his wife make their home in Cleveland Heights. As a resident of the Cleveland area, the author has had ample opportunity to discuss the career and personality of Newton D. Baker with those who knew him well. The present biography is the product of more than three years' original research into the extensive papers that Baker left to the nation.